DEVELOPING THE GIFTS & TALENTS

OF ALL STUDENTS

IN THE REGULAR CLASSROOM

DEVELOPING THE GIFTS & TALENTS
OF ALL STUDENTS
IN THE REGULAR CLASSROOM

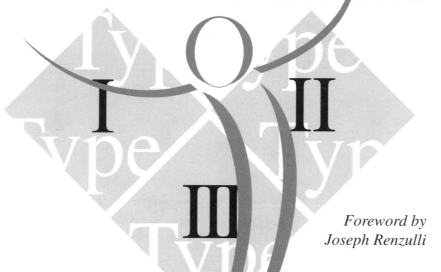

Foreword by
Joseph Renzulli

AN INNOVATIVE CURRICULAR DESIGN

BASED ON THE ENRICHMENT TRIAD MODEL

By Margaret Beecher

Creative Learning Press, Inc.
P.O. Box 320, Mansfield Center, Connecticut 06250

Consulting Editor:
Debra L. Briatico

Cover Design & Graphics:
Amy R. Soward

Book Layout & Design:
Siamak Vahidi

ISBN: 0-936386-68-1

© 1995 Creative Learning Press, Inc.
Second Printing, 1996

Creative Learning Press, Inc.
P.O. Box 320
Mansfield Center, CT 06250
(860) 429-8118

Dedication

To my........

Dad & Mom
Donald & Isabella Beecher
for sharing their gifts;

Husband, Jim Hlavacek, who
enthusiastically supports
my endless endeavors;

Children, Michael and Maria Cellerino;
my most treasured teachers.

Acknowledgments

The author is grateful to Dr. Carol Story for her contributions to the development of this model. Without her collaboration, this book wouldn't have become a reality. Special appreciation to Dr. Joseph Renzulli and Dr. Sally Reis for their work on the *Enrichment Triad Model* and *Schoolwide Enrichment Model*. Both models provide the foundation for this book and have transformed education for the gifted and talented by making enrichment opportunities available to *all* students. A special thanks to Bob Gioscia for being an "enabler" and allowing me the freedom to take risks, to Dr. Alex Nardone for his continued advocacy for enrichment programs, to Paul Berkel for supporting the differentiation of curriculum, to Nancy Harrington and Ethyl Ault for bringing this model to so many teachers and assisting them in its implementation, and to Dr. E. Jean Gubbins for her valuable counsel.

The author sincerely thanks and appreciates all of the teachers whose studies are found in this book: kindergarten teachers Hannah Shapiro and Michelle Griffith; third grade teacher Nancy Thurmond; the middle school teacher team—Don Stone, Nancy Horton, Monique Petty, Bob Evenski, and Lucy Read; and high school social studies teacher Mimi McKenna-Hostetter. They embraced the concepts in the model and enthusiastically implemented them in their classrooms. Special accolades to Beverly Favreau, the teacher who took her students *a giant step beyond* the curriculum. Thanks to Phil Freemer, Tina Merz, and Arlene Grandbois for helping a middle school review their curriculum through mapping, thus, setting the stage for integrated learning. Additional thanks to John Konefal, Anne Keegan, Bill Atkins, and Mary Fulton for sharing their curriculum maps. The Mentors, Dr. Mario D'Angelo, Robert Kenney, and Raymond Bentley, are to be commended for the time and energy they have devoted to so many students. The work of these individuals and hundreds of others who are using this model should be applauded. They have enriched the lives of hundreds of youngsters. They are our *teachers of tomorrow*!

About the Author

Margaret Beecher has spent the past twelve years developing and implementing differentiated curriculum designed to meet the needs of all children in the regular classroom. She has taught at all grade levels as a classroom teacher and has been a teacher and program director in the areas of reading and gifted/talented. Her work with curriculum has been extensive. She has written curricular models for the Connecticut State Department of Education, has served as a curriculum specialist at the elementary and middle school levels, and has been an instructional development coordinator for a Connecticut Regional Education Center which provided training in curriculum development and innovative instructional methods to administrators and teachers in thirty-three school districts. She has developed Schoolwide Enrichment programs in twenty-five schools and has also coordinated the Young Scholars' Saturday Program for students throughout Connecticut. At the present time, Margaret is the curriculum specialist for West Hartford Public Schools and director of their Saturday Enrichment Program which serves students from West Hartford and many neighboring communities.

She has been active at the state level and served on the Content Validation Committee for Connecticut's Competency Examination for Prospective Teachers, been a facilitator for the state's Program Improvement Institute, served as an assessor for the state's BEST Program for Beginning Teachers, chaired the Connecticut Educator's Network for Talented and Gifted, and served on the state's Task Force for Gifted and Talented.

The author has published articles in national journals and been a keynote speaker and workshop presented for state departments and school districts in thirty-five states, Canada and Japan. Her areas of expertise include: developing differentiated curriculum, integrated studies, curriculum compacting, flexible grouping practices, performance-based assessment, mentor/volunteer programs, clinical supervision, instructional theory into practice, the Talents Unlimited thinking skills program, and education of the gifted and talented.

Foreword

I am delighted that Peg Beecher has taken the time to write this book. I first met Peg almost twenty years ago when she was an enrichment teacher using the *Enrichment Triad Model* in a program for high ability students in a small district in northwestern Connecticut. Each year the Type III products that her students completed and the various innovations that Peg developed as a part of her work in the development of the *Triad Model* was exceptional. In fact, it was seeing the many innovations of Peg and other creative resource teachers that led my colleagues and me to develop the *Schoolwide Enrichment Model*. Peg is and continues to be a superlative teacher. She is interested and committed to quality and always insisted on the highest level of work from all of her students. The program she developed became a model program. Visitors often came from all over the country to see her resource room and talk with administrators and the classroom teachers with whom she worked. What most impressed me about Peg's work was the way in which she interacted with classroom teachers who were interested in extending some of the ideas they saw being used in the resource room with high potential youth into the classroom where they could be used with all other youngsters.

When the original *Enrichment Triad Model* was developed, I indicated that Types I and II Enrichment were good and appropriate for all students. However, in reality, in many districts that used the *Triad Model*, these types of enrichment were not provided for any students except those who were identified as gifted. Peg developed a model in which teachers could extend the ideas presented in the resource room into their own classroom instruction.

The model that Peg has developed takes the best aspects of Triad and enrichment teaching and learning and incorporates them into classrooms. This approach enables all students to be challenged and to develop their interests, learning styles, and achievement levels. When reading this book, the following points should be considered:

1. STUDENTS' INTERESTS—This model is developed to take into account students' interests and choices. The use of Triad in the classroom enables students to pursue topics of interest and to develop a product that they select from the general theme being presented and studied.

2. CURRICULUM DIFFERENTIATION—This model incorporates various strategies of curriculum differentiation as defined by Sandra Kaplan, including big ideas, overarching themes, and other strategies for differentiation.

3. AUTHENTIC CURRICULUM DIFFERENTIATION—The model presents methods for using interdisciplinary curriculum and for mapping the curriculum across multiple content areas to ensure interdisciplinary integration.

4. EXTENDING REGULAR CURRICULUM—Students have the opportunity to go beyond the regular curriculum to explore topics, problems, issues, and themes that have a special interest to them.

5. GOING BEYOND TEXTBOOK LEARNING—By extending the regular curriculum, students are able to learn content that is not in their textbooks and take control of various types of learning by exploring various resources such as speakers, films, videos, interest centers, and computer programs. The teacher stops being the only giver of information.

6. TYPE II TRAINING—Students are able to learn thinking skills which can be applied to other content areas. Using the lesson planning guide that Peg developed, teachers can decide which Type II skills to offer within the theme they select.

7. TYPE III PRODUCTS—In this model, students decide on the topic they will study, the products they will create, and the audience with whom they will share their work. Students will be able to choose a product that is of interest to them and which fits into the themes of classroom study. Because students choose their own study, they are motivated and committed to complete their work.

8. TEACHER AS FACILITATOR—Teachers enable children to direct their own learning and to contribute to what happens in their classroom, rather than being the sole decision-maker for all curriculum and instruction.

I have had the pleasure of talking to and watching teachers who have used this model in their classrooms. **It works!!** They feel energized and proud of what they are able to achieve. The integration

of constructivist learning, authentic assessment, integrated thematic studies, whole language, flexible grouping, curriculum compacting, use of learning styles, and development of interest-based products is consistent with what is advocated by the reform movement in education. It is my sincere hope that those of you who read this book will try the many exciting ideas that Peg has proposed.

Joseph S. Renzulli, September 1995

Table of Contents

List of Figures

List of Charts

Appendix A Listing

Interdisciplinary Studies Lesson Planning Guides
Native Americans of the Plains Study

Lesson 1: Tower Simulation (Cooperative Group Lesson)
Lesson 2: Introduction to Brainstorming*
Lesson 3: Introduction to SCAMPER*
Lesson 4: SCAMPER/Brainstorming
Lesson 5: Introduction to Webbing*
Lesson 6: Webbing
Lesson 7: Outlining
Lesson 8: Introduction to Decision Making*
Lesson 9: Decision Making
Lesson 10: Introduction to Creative Problem Solving*
Lesson 11: Creative Problem Solving
Lesson 12: Type I Debriefing or Follow-up Discussion
Lesson 13: Sequencing/Task Analysis
Lesson 14: Compare and Contrast
Lesson 15: Cause and Effect
Lesson 16: Expository Writing: Descriptive Essay
Lesson 17: Information Gathering
Lesson 18: Analysis of Dwellings
Lesson 19: Oral Presentation Skills
Lesson 20: Topic/Problem Focusing
Lesson 21: Modified Management Plan

*General introductory lessons not related to the theme.

INTRODUCTION

Introduction

Frameworks and Models

*We must...provide a richer curriculum for all students, realize
each student's potential, and develop outstanding talent.*
-United States Department of Education, 1993

This book has been written for general education and its primary
goal is to improve teaching and learning in the regular
classroom. During the past decade, it has become evident that
enrichment teaching and learning has played a critical role in the
education of *all* children. Although most people agree that students
differ in ability, there is a growing concern that educators may not be
challenging today's students. Public confidence in schools continues
to deteriorate and there is a general feeling that educators have failed
to provide an adequate education for many students. Districts across
the country have been feverishly involved in school reform, national
standards have been or are being established in major curricular areas,
and assessment of student performance is becoming more authentic.
Through these collective efforts, the educational community is
attempting to elevate student expectations, improve student
performance, and change the way curriculum is delivered.

Roland Barth (1990) states, "Rarely do outside of school remedies
work their way into the fabric of the school or into educators' lives,
and more rarely into classrooms. Therefore, they offer only modest
hope of influencing the basic culture of the schools." This book presents
a model which improves schools from within the classroom. It is based
on several enrichment models and frameworks whose origins stem from
special programs for high ability students. The concepts presented in
these models are based on sound research and have been widely used
in both regular and special education programs.

The Enrichment Models

The Enrichment Triad Model (Renzulli, 1977) provides a method and means of serving high ability youngsters by offering three different types of enrichment. This book is based primarily on this model and two sequels to the Triad, The *Revolving Door Identification Model* (Renzulli, Reis & Smith, 1981) and The *Schoolwide Enrichment Model* (Renzulli & Reis, 1985). Figure 1 provides a visual representation of the three types of enrichment presented in the *Enrichment Triad Model*.

Type I Enrichment includes experiences and activities that are purposefully designed to expose students to a wide variety of disciplines topics, issues, occupations, hobbies, persons, places, and events that are not ordinarily covered in the regular curriculum.

The target audience for this type of enrichment includes talent pool students, students identified as being gifted and talented, and all students in the school population. The three objectives of Type I Enrichment include the following:

1. To enrich the lives of all students by expanding the scope of experiences provided by the school.
2. To stimulate new interests that might lead to more intensive follow-up activities (Type III Investigations of Real Problems) on the parts of individuals or small groups of students.
3. To give teachers direction in making meaningful decisions about the kind of Type II Enrichment activities that should be selected for particular groups of students.

Type I's are designed to be dynamic activities that stimulate new interests in certain students and take on many shapes and forms. A Type I may involve presentations or performances by resource persons and can be presented as mini-courses, demonstrations, artistic performances, panel discussions, and debates. They may involve the media and include films, slides, videotapes, computer programs, television programs, newspapers, and magazine articles. Interest centers, displays, field trips, and museum programs are also examples of Type I experiences (Renzulli & Reis, 1985).

Type II Enrichment includes instructional methods and materials that are purposefully designed to promote the development of thinking and feeling processes. The basic training in these experiences is designed for all students and focuses on more advanced level experiences based on individual abilities and interests. The four primary objectives of Type II training are:

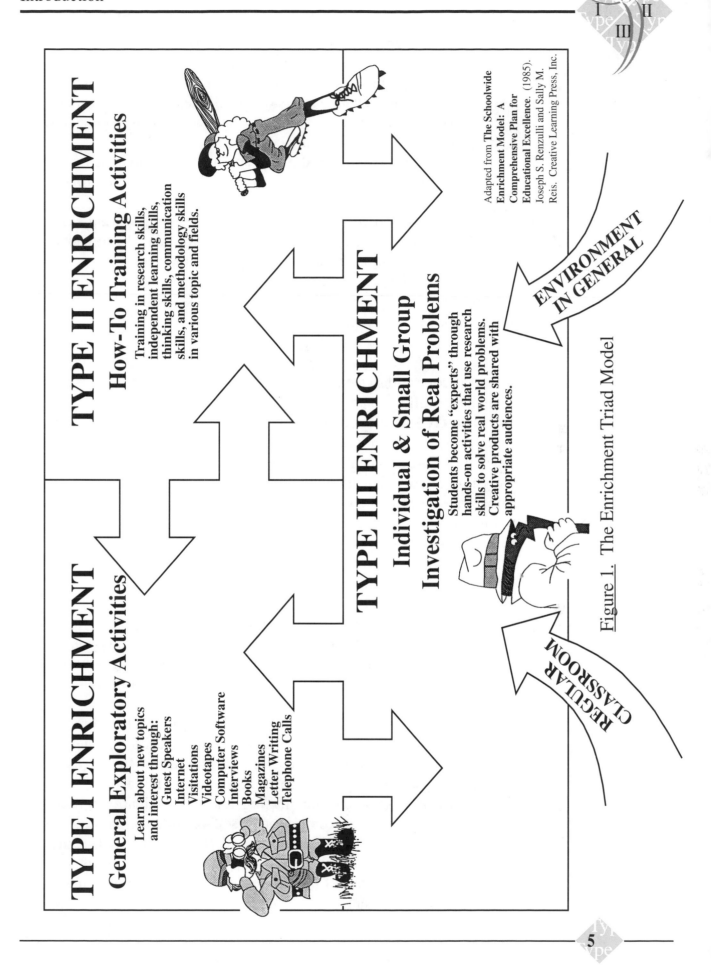

TYPE I ENRICHMENT
General Exploratory Activities

Learn about new topics and interest through:

Guest Speakers
Internet
Visitations
Videotapes
Computer Software
Interviews
Books
Magazines
Letter Writing
Telephone Calls

TYPE II ENRICHMENT
How-To Training Activities

Training in research skills, independent learning skills, thinking skills, communication skills, and methodology skills in various topic and fields.

TYPE III ENRICHMENT
Individual & Small Group
Investigation of Real Problems

Students become "experts" through hands-on activities that use research skills to solve real world problems. Creative products are shared with appropriate audiences.

ENVIRONMENT IN GENERAL

REGULAR CLASSROOM

Adapted from *The Schoolwide Enrichment Model: A Comprehensive Plan for Educational Excellence.* (1985). Joseph S. Renzulli and Sally M. Reis. Creative Learning Press, Inc.

Figure 1. The Enrichment Triad Model

1. To develop general skills in creative thinking, problem solving, critical thinking, and affective processes such as sensing, appreciating, and valuing.
2. To develop a wide variety of specific learning how-to-learn skills such as notetaking, interviewing, classifying and analyzing data, drawing conclusions, etc.
3. To develop skills in the appropriate use of advanced level reference materials such as readers guides, directories, abstracts, etc.
4. To develop written, oral, and visual communication skills that are primarily directed toward maximizing the impact of students' products upon appropriate audiences.

A Taxonomy of Type II Enrichment Processes (Renzulli & Reis, 1985) provides a comprehensive list of the specific skills in each of these four areas. (For a complete listing of the Type II Taxonomy, please see Appendix C.) Curriculum and/or enrichment specialists develop a scope and sequence of Type II training for their students and infuse these skills, as appropriate, into the content of the curriculum.

Type III Enrichment is defined as investigative activities and artistic productions in which the learner assumes the role of a first-hand inquirer—the student thinking, feeling, and acting like a practicing professional. Participants include individuals and small groups who demonstrate sincere interest in particular topics or problems and show a willingness to pursue these topics at advanced levels of involvement. The objectives include the following:

1. To provide opportunities in which students can apply their interests, knowledge, creative ideas, and task commitment to a self-selected problem or area of study.
2. To acquire advanced level understanding of the knowledge (content) and methodology (process) that are used within particular disciplines, artistic areas of expression and interdisciplinary studies.
3. To develop authentic products that are primarily directed toward having a desired impact upon a specified audience.
4. To develop self-directed learning skills in the areas of planning, organization, resource utilization, time management, decision making, and self-evaluation.
5. To develop task commitment, self-confidence, feelings of creative accomplishment, and the ability to interact effectively with other students, teachers, and persons with advanced levels of interest and expertise in a common area of involvement.

The learner is transformed during a Type III study from a lesson learner to a first-hand inquirer who learns by doing and produces real and original products for real audiences. The growth students experience as learners, as individuals, and as contributing members of a group, school, or community is truly immeasurable. Students from kindergarten to grade twelve have pursued Type III studies by exploring topics of interest to them and have written, directed and produced their own plays; changed laws; created and marketed new inventions; designed and built robots; conducted original scientific experiments; written and published poems, short stories, and books; and created walking tours of their communities. The students are "highly" motivated and acquire an in-depth understanding of their topic. As a result of these studies, students often make original contributions to a field of study or discipline. They become experts in their areas of study and learn how to take charge of their own learning.

The students' teachers also become experts, but not in the content that their students are studying. They become expert facilitators and learn how to guide students through the entire process of a Type III study. It is a challenging and complex role to play and requires a transition from being "sage on the stage" to "guide on the side" (Renzulli, 1982).

Revolving Door Identification Model

The Revolving Door Identification Model (RDIM) provides the vehicle for students to come into and out of advanced levels of task-specific enrichment as the need arises. It is an approach designed to increase substantially the number of students involved in special services, minimize the concerns about elitism by doing away with the you have-it or you don't-have-it concept, and most importantly, provide supplementary services at the time and in the performance area where such services have the high potential for doing the most good for a particular youngster.

-Renzulli, Reis & Smith, 1981

This model allows flexibility within an enrichment program by providing the opportunities for any child to participate in different types and levels of enrichment and to pursue an in-depth or Type III investigation. The scope of this model is too extensive to discuss at this time, but can be found in **The Revolving Door Identification Model** (Renzulli, Reis & Smith, 1981). However, the following four general goals of the *Triad/Revolving Door Identification Model* will

help the reader better understand the connections being made between the regular classroom and the enrichment or gifted program:

1. To provide various types and levels of enrichment to a broader spectrum of the school population.
2. To integrate the special program with the regular classroom and to develop a cooperative, rather than competitive, relationship between classroom teachers and personnel who have been assigned to the gifted program.
3. To minimize concerns about elitism and the negative attitudes that are often expressed toward students participating in special programs for the gifted.
4. To improve the extent and quality of enrichment for all students and to promote a "radiation of excellence" (Ward, 1961) throughout all aspects of the school environment.

The Schoolwide Enrichment Model

The Schoolwide Enrichment Model (SEM) offers a systematic set of specific strategies for increasing student effort, enjoyment, and performance, and for integrating a broad range of advanced level learning experiences and higher order thinking skills into any curricular area, course of study, or pattern of school organization.

-Renzulli & Reis, 1985

The concepts and information included in the *Schoolwide Enrichment Model* elaborate upon the ideas introduced in the *TRIAD/ RDIM*. The goals of this model include promoting the radiation of excellence throughout the entire school, integrating with the regular curriculum, and expanding services to a larger proportion of the school population. This model for change offers suggestions for improving the teaching and learning that goes on in the entire school.

The Schoolwide Enrichment Model: A Comprehensive Plan for Educational Excellence (Renzulli & Reis, 1985) outlines procedures for planning and implementing a comprehensive Type I and Type II Enrichment program and offers recommendations for evaluating this type of enrichment. The methodologies used during the Type III investigation, such as problem focusing, methodological resources, outlets and audiences for student products, and the techniques used in planning studies are explained. Teacher training activities are presented for all types of enrichment.

An overview of curriculum compacting, a procedure for modifying the regular curriculum for high ability students, is also introduced. The

authors present ideas for creating a more challenging learning environment, finding ways to guarantee proficiency of the regular curriculum, and organizing enrichment and acceleration activities. Community resources and procedures for recruiting resource people are also discussed. All of this information supports the Triad philosophy and provides an excellent resource for teachers implementing the model.

Schools for Talent Development: A Practical Plan for Total School Improvement

Dr. Renzulli's latest book provides a comprehensive plan for school improvement. One of the ideas introduced in this text—**Enrichment Learning and Teaching**—supports the model introduced in this book. This concept is defined in terms of the following four principles:

1. Each learner is unique, and, therefore, all learning experiences must be examined in ways that take into account the abilities, interests, and learning styles of the individual.
2. Learning is more effective when students enjoy what they are doing, and, therefore, learning experiences should be constructed and assessed with as much concern for enjoyment as for other goals.
3. Learning is more meaningful and enjoyable when content (i.e., knowledge) and process (i.e., thinking skills, methods of inquiry) are learned within the context of a real and present problem. Therefore, attention should be given to opportunities to personalize student choice in problem selection, the relevance of the problem for individual students at the time the problem is being addressed, and strategies for assisting students in personalizing problems they might choose to study.
4. Some formal instruction may be used in enrichment learning and teaching, but a major goal of this approach to learning is to enhance knowledge and thinking skill acquisition gained through teacher instruction with applications of knowledge and skills that result from students' construction of meaningfulness.

-Renzulli, 1994

Differentiated Curriculum

Another model which has been widely used in the field of gifted and talented education for curriculum development was developed by Sandra Kaplan. *The Grid: A Model to Construct Differentiated Curriculum for the Gifted* (Kaplan, 1986) provides a means of creating studies that are differentiated for gifted learners. Kaplan states the following rationale for the differentiation of studies:

> *They are differentiated because they are considered to be an appropriate match between the recognized needs, abilities, and interests of gifted students and the educational purposes and expectations held by these learners.*

The Principles of Differentiated Curriculum for the Gifted and Talented developed by the National/State Leadership Training Institute on the Gifted and Talented's Curriculum Council provide a framework for curriculum developers to determine the elements that differentiate curriculum for the gifted. The following list includes the elements proposed for inclusion in a differentiated curriculum which are founded upon and modified from this set of principles:

- Present content that is related to broad-based issues, themes, or problems.
- Integrate multiple disciplines into the area of study.
- Present comprehensive, related, and mutually reinforcing experiences within an area of study.
- Allow for the in-depth learning of a self-selected topic within the area of study.
- Develop independent or self-directed study skills.
- Develop productive, complex, abstract, and/or higher level thinking skills.
- Focus on open-ended tasks.
- Develop research skills and methods.
- Integrate basic skills and higher level thinking skills into the curriculum.
- Encourage the development of products that use techniques, materials, and forms.
- Encourage the development of self-understanding, i.e., recognizing and using one's abilities, becoming self-directed, and appreciating likenesses and differences between oneself and others.
- Evaluate student outcomes by using appropriate and specific criteria through self-appraisal, criterion referenced instruments, and/or standardized instruments.

The *Principles of Differentiated Curriculum* have been used as a framework for designing the model of curriculum developed in this book. The rationale for its use is the belief that **all** children can benefit from the principles listed above and can learn this way. For example, the first and second principles propose that content be presented as broad-based issues, themes, or problems that can be integrated into the multiple disciplines. In today's information age, there is a rapid proliferation of knowledge and, as a result, educators find themselves seeking ways to help students make sense out of the multitude of life's experiences and pieces of knowledge that are introduced in the typical period by period day that now exists in most schools.

Since 1942 more than eighty normative or comparative studies have been carried out on the effectiveness of integrative programs. In nearly every instance, students in various types of integrative/ interdisciplinary programs have performed as well or better on standardized achievement tests than students enrolled in the usual separate subjects (Vars, 1991). All children must possess the skills necessary to deal with the rapid changes taking place in our society. We can use the knowledge and expertise of educators in the field of gifted and talented education and share these ideas with the general population.

Teaching Models, Methodologies, and Strategies

This book discusses several models, methodologies, and strategies which may be new to the reader. These ideas relate primarily to Type II process training skills and include brainstorming, SCAMPER, webbing, decision making, creative problem solving, sequencing and task analysis, and the use of graphic organizers to teach students how to compare and contrast, determine cause and effect relationships, write descriptively, and take notes. The reader will find a lesson written for each of these processes in Appendix A.

Chapter 3 includes information about curriculum mapping (Jacobs, 1991) and provides a clear, concise method for mapping and editing an existing curricula. This is a prerequisite for developing integrated/ interdisciplinary studies that are based on the content of several disciplines. Chapter 3 also describes how to create and use an interest development center, match instructional styles to students learning styles, and teach all children to plan effectively and work independently.

How to Use This Book

This book has been written for teachers and curriculum specialists who are interested in developing differentiated, integrated curriculum. **Chapter 2** provides an overview of the model and presents the reader with a visual image of a completed study and the effect it had on participating students and teachers.

Chapter 3 outlines twelve steps to follow when creating this type of study. This how-to section specifically describes each phase of the study in a clear, concise manner. The rationale for the inclusion of these steps and the role each one plays in creating the final study are also discussed. The curriculum planner will only need the luxury of "time" in order develop this innovative study.

The following descriptions briefly describe the concepts and ideas included in each step.

Step 1: Selection of the Topic or Theme
> This step shows the reader how to select a topic or theme for an interdisciplinary study based on the content of their curriculum. The concept of curriculum mapping, a method of creating a "birds-eye" or panoramic view of the curriculum is included with a graphic organizer and specific examples of curriculum maps. This process is an essential precursor to determining a theme for a study.

Step 2: Preliminary Planning
> Content webbing is introduced in this step and used as a means of creating a visual representation of all the possible dimensions of a given topic or theme. This process has numerous applications in the classroom and is particularly helpful in demonstrating content connections and extensions.

Step 3: Student Outcomes
> When educators are planning studies, activities, and lessons, they often only write content outcomes for what students should know. This step describes how to write content, process, and attitudinal outcomes and discusses the role they play in a study. The need for establishing these outcomes is also highlighted.

Step 4: Getting Started
> A model of a student survey and its use prior to the implementation of a study is demonstrated. The majority of this step is devoted to describing Interest Development Centers and ways to incorporate them into the classroom. Unlike a learning center, the primary

goal of this type of center is to create interest, enthusiasm, and intellectual curiosity about the study.

Step 5: Disciplines or Subject Areas

Integrated and interdisciplinary approaches to learning and their historical value are highlighted in this step. The need for making authentic connections for students as they relate to the existing curriculum is also discussed.

Step 6: Content and Introductory Activities

One of the most challenging aspects of any study is to generate student interest. This step gives the reader some concrete ways to get all students engaged in a study. It also provides suggestions for locating and getting assistance from other educators, parents, and community resources.

Step 7: Process Training Lessons

This step discusses the inclusion of creative and critical thinking skills into the study and the use of questioning as a means of individualizing learning. Learning styles (Renzulli & Smith, 1978), their definitions, and suggestions for addressing different styles in the classroom are also highlighted. A Lesson Planning Guide, which is designed to help educators develop effective lessons that monitor instructional styles, is also described and included in this section.

Step 8: Interest-Based Independent Study

This step shows teachers how to guide their students through Type III training activities. The reader learns how to help students select topics, focus their problems, locate multiple resources, establish a timeline, and determine a unique product and audience based on a topic of their own choosing.

Step 9: Resources

Locating information and resources has taken on new meaning in our information age. This step includes tips on how to locate information and find individuals who can be of assistance to teachers and students as they stretch beyond the walls of their classrooms to make learning more relevant.

Step 10: Student Assessment

Several methods of authentic assessment are discussed in this step. Rubrics, classroom checklists, and scales are presented as they relate to this model.

Step 11: Timeline for Implementation
>   This step highlights a timeline that can be used for various topics, studies, and other purposes. The reader may wish to review it to see if it will meet his/her curricular needs.

Step 12: Evaluation of the Study
>   This section contains a brief discussion about evaluation and presents useful student and teacher forms.

Chapter 4 provides the reader with examples of studies completed at the primary, elementary, middle, and high school levels. This model is appropriate for all grade levels and this chapter highlights some of the unique differences at each level. Readers should review these samples before they begin planning their own study.

"A Giant Step Beyond" is the title of **Chapter 5**, which describes one teacher's experience with independent learning. This experience is outlined in detail and presents a challenge that educators might like to accept at some point in their career.

Finally, the most commonly asked questions about developing and implementing Triad in the Classroom studies are included in **Chapter 6.**

CHAPTER 1

THE RATIONALE FOR DEVELOPING THE MODEL

The Rationale for Developing the Model

It is the supreme art of the teacher to awaken joy in creative expression and knowledge.

-Albert Einstein

Only rarely do we have an opportunity to make a contribution that responds to the needs of teachers and students and significantly impacts the learning of both. This book represents this opportunity for me and also fulfills my own need to share an idea, which has evolved into a model designed to change the way many teachers teach and children learn. This model emerged from the field of gifted and talented education, reached into the classroom, and transformed the way in which curriculum was developed and implemented. The rationale for this transformation and my personal growth as an educator provides the foundation on which this model has been built. Join me as I share the many, unique facets of my learning as a teacher of the gifted and talented.

Although I had been a regular classroom teacher and a reading teacher, my most significant growth as an educator occurred when I began developing programs and curriculum for gifted children. My goal was clear and concise: to set the stage that would allow children to demonstrate their gifted behaviors. There was so much to learn and so many dimensions related to my new position. For the first time in my career as an educator, I did not have to use specified curriculum guides or textbooks. I needed to develop differentiated curriculum based on a scope and sequence of process training skills. During this process, I learned a variety of new teaching methodologies and instructional styles and quickly incorporated them into my planning. Creative problem solving, decision making, higher level thinking skills, simulations, open-ended activities and lessons, and logical reasoning

became infused into the program.

Student interest was a primary focus and all activities and curricular studies were developed based on an increased awareness of the things students like to learn, know, and do. The methodologies of independent, self-directed student learning and student choice was also a critical component of the program.

My work extended beyond the walls of the resource room. My weekly schedule included teaching model lessons in various classrooms in order to train teachers how to use new methodologies and strategies. I found myself traveling from class to class and grade to grade throughout the entire school year. My time was limited in the classrooms and it was difficult to significantly impact the students or teachers in such brief classes and isolated contexts.

In addition to model lessons, I also provided regular classroom training in curriculum compacting. Teachers were taught how to modify the curriculum and assure that all students were challenged and not asked to complete previously mastered work. Since so many of my students knew much of the curriculum or could master it quickly and easily, I provided the initial training in curriculum compacting and also offered continued support for teachers during small group or individual meetings before and after school.

The parent community became true partners in education as we surveyed their professions, interests, and hobbies and found links to the curriculum and students' interests. Parents came into the schools to share their knowledge and expertise with entire grade levels, whole classes, and individual students. Sometimes they were asked to be mentors for students who were involved in in-depth studies. They explored topics with individuals or small groups of students a few hours a week until the study was completed. The amount of time varied, but generally lasted between four to six months.

As a result of the enrichment program and these efforts, many children demonstrated gifted behaviors. Their above average ability, task commitment, and creativity were brought to bear upon special areas of interest (Renzulli, 1978). My own knowledge and expertise dramatically increased when, like my students, my energy and enthusiasm as a teacher and educator escalated. As I recalled my prior experiences as an educator, I regretted not having been introduced to these dynamic teaching methods much earlier in my career. However, it also became increasingly clear that many of the methodologies that were being employed so successfully in the gifted program would benefit **all** children and **all** teachers. The following question began to echo in my mind and as a result provided the framework for this book.

How can I share what I have learned with other teachers in order to benefit the gifted children and all children in the regular classroom?

A colleague, Dr. Carol Story, and I attempted to answer this question. Carol, who had been a regular classroom teacher and was working on her doctoral program, ended up doing an internship with me. After hours and months of brainstorming, a model emerged which successfully integrated the concepts of our gifted program into the regular classroom by means of an innovative approach to the regular curriculum. We strongly believed that it would energize the learning of all students and, therefore, initially called the model The *Energetic Evolution: Meeting the Needs of the Gifted in the Regular Classroom* in an article published in **Roeper Review** in 1983. However, it soon became apparent that the model met the needs of **all** children in the regular classroom.

Since its inception, the model has been implemented by hundreds of teachers both nationally and internationally with great success. Although there have been many changes and additions since our first brainstorming sessions, the core concepts remain the same. These concepts are particularly relevant and meaningful today, as we strive to restructure and reform our schools. If you believe that schools must improve from within and that the classroom is the place where true change occurs, then you will want to explore the contents of this book.

C H A P T E R 2

OVERVIEW OF THE MODEL

Overview of the Model

The video camera pans across the classroom and the scene records a Native American powwow. The viewer glimpses a display of Indian crafts, pottery with symbols adorning the sides. Each child's neck is bedecked with clay pendants. Tomahawks and bows and arrows decorate another corner. A story unfolds in sign language nearby. At the center of all this sits a youthful chief in front of a rather strange looking teepee. The cast of characters appears pale-faced and the setting is an elementary classroom. The photographer, a proud father of an "Indian," witnesses with many other parents this reenactment of a western Plains powwow. The fourth grade actors overflow with newly gleaned knowledge of the life and culture of the Native Americans of the Plains.

T he celebration highlighted above was the culminating activity of an integrated study of the Native Americans of the Plains which took place in a fourth grade classroom in a school of 500 students in northwestern Connecticut. The most dynamic processes employed in the enrichment program and the successful methodologies of the regular curriculum had been combined to create a new model.

The Enrichment Triad in the Regular Classroom

The *Enrichment Triad Model* was integrated into all classroom Triad studies and provided the rationale for implementing innovative teaching strategies. This new model integrated Type I activities and Type II training into the existing curriculum and Type III investigations were modified and defined as Type III training activities. All students

learned the independent study process and became more self-directed learners. *The Principles of Differentiated Curriculum for Gifted and Talented* (Kaplan, 1986) were incorporated into the studies and provided additional dimensions and challenges.

The goals of the new model were:

1. To differentiate and enrich the curriculum in the classroom for ALL students.
2. To integrate the curriculum through interdisciplinary studies.
3. To encourage the use of a wide variety of instructional strategies and styles.
4. To allow all students to experience self-directed learning.
5. To encourage gifted behavior to emerge in the classroom.
6. To allow classroom teachers and enrichment specialists to share methods and materials.

The following synthesis of the Triad study of the Native Americans of the Plains will help the reader understand the breadth and depth of these studies and the level of student interest and involvement. The regular classroom teacher and the enrichment specialist worked cooperatively in the development of this study.

The study of the Native Americans was part of the existing fourth grade social studies curriculum. The required objectives were clearly defined in the school's curriculum guide. These objectives and those in other curricular areas were reviewed and incorporated into this interdisciplinary study. Additional content, process, and attitudinal objectives were included as necessary and appropriate.

The Type I general exploratory experiences began with the teacher's creation of an Interest Development Center that focused on ideas and questions related to the Native Americans of the Plains, new terminology, and local, state, and national Native American resources. Maps, filmstrips, videos, books, photographs, and other Indian memorabilia were also included in the center. Students were encouraged to add materials and resources to the center throughout the study.

In addition to the Interest Development Center, the teacher planned a presentation by a Native American about the life-style and culture of the Indians. The presenter made the social studies textbook "come to life" for the students as he sat in the classroom surrounded by Indian memorabilia and dressed in authentic costume. During his visit, this animated storyteller wove a tale of Indian life that made learning fun and exciting. Indian art, songs, and games, which were enthusiastically presented by the school's art, music and physical education teachers,

added to the Indian pottery exhibit created by a skilled craftswoman from a nearby town. A parent provided an introduction to the silent world of sign language. A local historian discussed historical research methods. The classroom teacher enjoyed unfolding the mysteries of Indian myths and legends.

The enthusiasm of everyone involved in these learning experiences was contagious! Excited and eager, children wanted to explore further! The Type I experiences, provided by resource people within the school and from the local community, stimulated student interests and increased awareness of this culture. All students now had a strong knowledge base from which they could continue learning.

The Type II group training activities accompanied the Type I experiences and provided students with the necessary skills for further explorations. Children were enthusiastic because they wanted to know how to proceed. Research skills involved locating information and resources in libraries, the community, state, and country. Students wrote to Indian organizations throughout the United States requesting information. Creativity training included brainstorming, creative writing of myths, creative problem solving, and creative dramatics as students assumed the roles of the Native Americans. Webbing, a technique used to explain a topic (Baldwin, 1980), helped children explore the numerous aspects of the Indian way of life and determine the direction of their own investigations. They analyzed, synthesized, and evaluated a survey conducted earlier with the assistance of a parent volunteer. Once the children decided to have an Indian powwow at the conclusion of the study, organizational skills, decision making, and public speaking became the focus of classroom instruction. Students also continued to receive training in Indian songs, dance, and art with assistance from the music and art teachers.

However, the best was yet to come! Type I experiences and Type II training had opened the doors and shown the children the way. They now had an opportunity to become involved in Type III training activities. Students chose an aspect of the Indian culture that they wanted to further explore. Students selected their own topic, determined how they would explore it, and decided what form their final product would take. Introduction to a modified version of the Management Plan (Renzulli, 1981) provided students with the necessary organizational guidelines for their Type III investigations. The children worked industriously on their self-selected topics. The academically gifted and the artistically talented pursued their subject to whatever extent they desired. This was true of all children in the class. Whatever their abilities, they could "stretch their minds to their fullest capacity" (National Commission on Excellence, 1983). All children felt good about themselves and what they were doing. A feeling of sharing

permeated the classroom as they all helped and learned from each other. The classroom teacher became the facilitator of this process and guided students as they recreated an Indian culture.

During this study, one student decided to explore her family genealogy. Sparked by a Type I presentation about historical research and a Type II training activity involving the tracing of roots, she shared her idea for an authentic Type III with her classroom teacher, who referred her to the school's enrichment teacher. Following several discussions, the student decided to combine her interest in genealogy with her love of drama in order to create a "Living Genealogy." She wrote, produced, directed, and starred in a play depicting a day in the life of several generations of her female ancestors. Through a dialogue with a friend, this student played the role of herself, then she became her mother, her grandmother, and her great grandmother. Having created her own costumes and sets, she brought her own history to life. This was ultimately videotaped and aired on a local educational television station. The production was also awarded first place in children's programming by the National Federation of Cable Programmers.

For one brief morning these nine-year-olds became the Native Americans they studied. Authenticity was one of their primary goals and many of the parents who visited that day felt transported into the past as they viewed this fourth-grade Indian powwow. The Native American's love and respect for their natural environment; their unique customs; their original designs; their fine crafts, tools, and weaponry; their resourcefulness in finding food; their manufacture of clothing and building of homes; and their rhythmic songs, dances, and games came to life. The children captured the essence of this culture and conveyed it to their audience.

Student involvement in the study is a key factor to the its ultimate success and maximization of student learning. Students love to be give a choice! In fact, most people love to be given a choice. One of the primary reasons for the success of The *Enrichment Triad Model* is that many of the activities, projects, and lessons are based on students' interest and learning styles. Students will become enthusiastically engaged in learning when they are given "ownership" of the study.

At the conclusion of the Triad Native American study, there was little question that the experience was a memorable one for both the teacher and the students. The teacher said, "I learned new ways to teach my curriculum and look forward to doing this again!" Her students echoed her enthusiasm with these comments: "It was fun!" " We learned more than we usually do!" " I like to learn this way!"

CHAPTER 3

PLANNING AND IMPLEMENTING
A TRIAD STUDY

Planning and Implementing
a Triad Study

The Enrichment Triad Interdisciplinary Planning Matrix (Figure 2) is the primary vehicle for developing and organizing the study. It enables the curriculum developer, teacher, teacher team, and/or curriculum or enrichment specialist to outline the entire topic or theme and provide a blueprint for the study. As discussed in Chapter 1, many of the concepts presented in the *Enrichment Triad Model* will be transferred to the regular classroom setting while the studies are planned and developed. This encourages the utilization of a wide variety of teaching strategies, the development of student interests, and multiple opportunities for student choice. It also demonstrates the methodology of independent student work, assists teachers in making meaningful connections among all disciplines, and differentiates the curriculum for all children.

The major components of the Planning Matrix include:

- **Student Outcomes**
- **Getting Started**
- **Disciplines**
- **Type I - Content and Introductory Activities**
- **Type II - Process Training Lessons**
- **Type III Training Activities - Interest-Based Independent Projects/Studies**
- **Resources Needed**
- **Student Assessment**

When completed, the Matrix includes a concise listing of all activities and tasks necessary for the development of the study.

The **Student Outcomes** are based on content, thinking processes,

attitudes, and attributes. Tasks which need to be completed during the planning portion of the study are listed sequentially in the section entitled **Getting Started**. The first column of the matrix is entitled **Disciplines** and includes only those disciplines appropriate for the study being planned. The second column, **Type I - Content and Introductory Activities**, lists by discipline the specific student experiences that will introduce them to the content of the study. The third column, **Type II - Process Training Lessons** outlines the specific skills introduced to students during the study. The fourth column, **Type III - Training Activities: Interest-Based Independent Projects/ Studies**, includes a teacher generated list of possible student studies. Library, community, and human resources are listed under **Resources Needed** and a comprehensive list of all assessment procedures, which will be utilized during the study, appears in the box entitled **Student Assessment**. The teacher-created content or topical web appears on the reverse side of the Matrix and provides a panoramic view of the topic under consideration. The Matrix has been used successfully in planning and implementing studies at all grade levels and disciplines, in self-contained classrooms, and in team teaching situations.

All of the ideas and activities included in the Matrix are designed to be implemented or taught and the scope of the study should not be limited to those listed. Just as architects often modify their plans in order to meet the needs of consumers, teachers must monitor and adjust their teaching based on the varying needs, abilities, and interests of their students. The students become the barometer for determining the breadth and depth of the study and the manner in which it is ultimately developed and implemented.

This chapter will provide the reader with a detailed, step-by-step guide to planning and implementing a study. A completed Planning Matrix (Figure 3) used during the previously discussed study of the Native Americans of the Plains will become the model and basis for this discussion. In the next chapter, examples from other grade levels and disciplines will be shared and discussed. It should be noted here that the same planning procedure is followed regardless of the topic, theme, unit of study, or grade level.

Step One: Selection of the Topic or Theme

Educators are beginning to discover again the idea of integration...

-James A. Beane

The primary goal in the selection and development of the topic or theme is to make natural connections among the related disciplines in

Interdisciplinary Unit of Study
Planning Matrix

Teacher: _____ School: _____ Grade Level: _____ Topic/Theme/Unit of Study: _____ Duration of Study: _____

Student Outcomes

Content:
    The student will:

Process:
    The student will:

Attitudes and Attributes:
    The student will:

Getting Started

Disciplines	Type I Content and Introductory Activities	Type II Process Training Lessons	Type III Interest - Based Independent Projects/Studies	Resources Needed:
Language Arts				
Math				
Science				
Social Studies				
Art/Music				
				Student Assessment:

Matrix Developed by Margaret Beecher

Figure 2. The Enrichment Triad Interdisciplinary Planning Matrix—(FORM 1)

Interdisciplinary Unit of Study
Planning Matrix

Teacher: _____ School: _____ Grade Level: _____ Topic/Theme/Unit of Study: _____ Duration of Study: _____

Essential Questions	Disciplines	Type I Content and Introductory Activities	Type II Process Training Lessons	Type III Interest - Based Independent Projects/Studies	
	Language Arts				**Getting Started:**
	Math				**Resources Needed:**
	Social Studies				
Student Outcomes	Science				
					Student Assessment:

Figure 2. The Enrichment Triad Interdisciplinary Planning Matrix—(FORM 2)

Matrix Developed by Margaret Beecher

Interdisciplinary Unit of Study Planning Matrix

Teacher: Margaret Beecher   School: Smith School   Grade Level: 4   Topic/Theme/Unit of Study: Survival: Native Americans of the Plains   Duration of Study: Eight Weeks

Student Outcomes

Content:

The student will:

describe the culture of the Native American Indians of the Plains...
- way of life
- use of resources
- beliefs and customs
- art and artifacts
- adaptation to the environment;

list the factors that changed the Native Americans way of life.

Process:

The student will:

compare and contrast Plains, Desert, and Northwestern Costal tribes.

analyze the causes and effects of the Native American's conflict with the Europeans.

learn and apply the ten steps of the independent study process.

learn and utilize oral presentation skills.

Attitudes and Attributes:

The student will:

develop a sensitivity to and an understanding of the customs of the Native Americans.

demonstrate a questioning attitude, curiosity, and independent thinking.

Getting Started

Survey Students
Create a Topic Web
Establish Student Outcomes
Create an Interest Development Center
Plan Introductory or Type I Lessons and Activities
Contact Resource People and Schedule Presentations
Begin Writing Process Training Lessons and Activities
Determine Study Timeline

Disciplines	Type I Content and Introductory Activities	Type II Process Training Lessons	Type III Interest-Based Independent Projects/Studies
Language Arts	Book Talks: School Librarian Myths and Legends: The Gift of the Sacred Dog-- P. Goble Brother Eagle, Sister Sky A Message from Chief Seattle Student Survey Sign Language Mini-Course Instructor: Mark Smith	Read several myths and legends and write your own myth. Practice Oral Presentation Skills.* Learn Indian sign language and communicate with each other. Write a description of some aspect of the Native Americans way of life.* Brainstorming/SCAMPER Activity.*	Design an ABC Coloring Book about the Native Americans. Using a storyboard, plan a slide presentation entitled, "The Bountiful Buffalo." Become an Indian storyteller and share myths with others. Write and illustrate a poem(s).
Math/Science	Guessing and Dice Games Chance and Probability Science Text: The Ecosystems of the Plains Video Tape #1: "American Indian Death of the Bison" Indian Pottery: The Art Speaker: Maria Jones	Play Indian Guessing and Dice Game. Use Decision Making Strategy.* Simulate the plains ecosystem in a terrarium. Estimation - Buffalo Past/Present. Conduct Creative Problem Solving Simulation.*	Invent a probability game for children. Design your own winter count or calendar of events for the years 1800-1850. Construct a model of an Indian medicine wheel.
Social Studies	The Native American Culture Speaker: Tamunk Interest Development Center "The Hunt" Text: Houghton Mifflin, Unit 2 Chapter 5, From Sea to Shining Sea. Totem Poles Speaker: James Smith	Debriefing the Presentations: Class discussion following all presentations* Notetaking* Compare and contrast Indian dwellings* Letters to Reservations Compare and Contrast Plains, Desert, and Northwestern* Learn Research Skills as needed/appropriate	Become an Indian Tour Guide and develop a walking tour of a Plains village. Plan and create a "living diorama" of an aspect of Indian life. Make a clay sculpture of a horse, buffalo, or other Indian item.
Social Studies	Student Created Topic Web Indian Art and Artifacts: Plains, Desert, and Northwestern Coast Speaker: Edie Brown Video Tape #2: "American Indians Before European Settlement" Video Tape #3: "Indian Family of Long Ago"	Review strategies for reading in the content area. Determine causes and effects of conflict with Europeans.* Decision Making (Topic/Project).* Create Topic Webs and Outlines* Write Individual Modified Management Plan.*	Imagine you are an Indian child and write a daily diary about your life. Draw a mural from the point of view of an Indian brave after a battle using picture writing. Choreograph an original Native American dance.
Art/Music	Picture Writing and Painting Instructor: Jane Smith Quillwork and Beadwork Ceremonial Dress/Clothing Design Resource Books, Plains Clothing Mini-Course: Songs, Dances, Instruments Instructor: Francine Green	Plan and Construct a Teepee in the classroom.* (Write Group Sequence Chart) Use Indian picture writing to record an event you read about. Design a personal shield. Sing Indian songs and play instruments.	Design and make your own pottery. Compose your own song with musical accompaniment. Create a pictorial timeline from 1700 - 1850 and record important dates/events.
Religion	Ceremonies and Rituals: Sweat Lodge Ceremony Sun Dance (Simulation by Students)	Role Play: Sweat Lodge Ceremony Pantomine the Sun Dance	Compare and contrast one or more present day religious ceremonies with those of the Plains Indians.
Physical Education	Origin of Lacrosse Speaker: Tom Smith	Play a game of Lacrosse	Create an outdoor field game that Native American children might enjoy.

Resources Needed:

Human Resources:
Francine Green - Instrumental Music and Song
Mark Smith - Sign Language
James Smith - Totem Poles
Maria Jones - Indian Pottery
Tamunk - Native American
Edie Brown - Indian Art and Artifacts

Social Studies Text:
From Sea To Shining Sea, Unit 2, Chapter 5

Video Tapes:
American Indians Before the European Settlement
American Indian: Death of the Bison

Magazine:
Brandenburg, Jim. "The Land They Knew", National Geographic. © 1991

Teacher Reference Books:
Lowii, Robert H., Indians of the Plains, Museum of Natural History, © 1954.
Sheppard, Sally, Indians of the Plains, New York, Franklin Watts, © 1976.
Racklis, Eugene, Indians of the Plains, New York, American Heritage Publishing Company, © 1960.

Student Resource Books:
Obtain from school and public libraries and inter-library loan.

Student Assessment:

Writing - Descriptive and Fictional Holistic/Analytical Scoring

Chapter Test

Journal Entries

Independent Projects
Modified Student Project Assessment Form (Teacher/Self Assessment)

Student Development Rubric and Checklist for Assessment of Oral Presentations

Matrix Developed by Margaret Beecher

* See Interdisciplinary Studies Lesson Planning Guides.

Figure 3. A Completed Enrichment Triad Interdisciplinary Planning Matrix of the Native Americans of the Plains

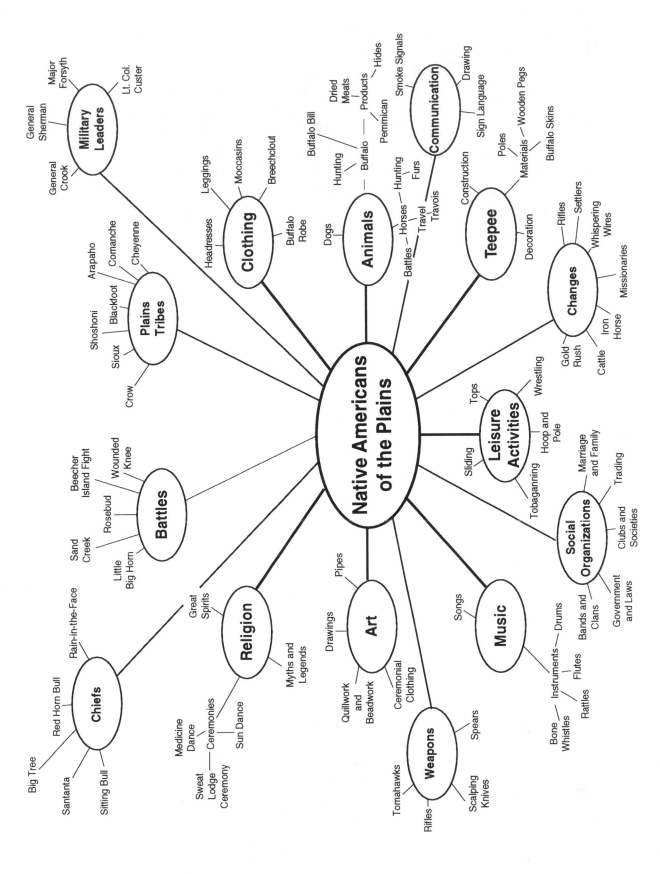

Native Americans of the Plains Content Web

order to make the study more meaningful to the students. As the reader knows, the "real world" is not divided into predetermined segments. It is the teacher's job to help students make connections among the disciplines.

The development and analysis of curriculum maps is one way to review the curriculum of a given grade level. The curriculum map shown in Figure 4 was designed by several middle school teachers and used by the district's two large middle schools to record the content and skills of the "taught" curriculum in all of the disciplines. The purpose of the maps is to review curriculum, foster communication among and across disciplines, and see possible curriculum connections. When completed, the information is reviewed and critiqued by a teacher or teacher team, who then make adjustments if curricular repetition or learning gaps are found. During this review, possible areas for integration are determined. A completed sixth grade team map is shown in Figure 5.

Some themes that are commonly used during interdisciplinary Triad studies include: survival, energy, transportation, the future, endangered species, human rights, cultural diversity, social responsibility, space exploration, communities, inventions, justice, and pollution. There is obviously no end to the themes that can become the basis for a study. Although they often emanate from the school's curriculum, it is not essential that they do so. James Beane, who has written extensively about middle school curriculum and its development, believes that we should select themes based on the interests of the students (Beane, 1990). Some of his recommended themes include: identities, wellness, social structure, commercialism, institutions, transitions, interdependence, and conflict resolution.

The study discussed in this chapter was based on the theme survival which had been selected by the teachers as the fourth grade theme for the school year. The Native Americans of the Plains was part of the curriculum and a topic within the grade level theme. Teachers believed that several disciplines, student outcomes, and meaningful activities could be integrated into this topic.

Step Two: Preliminary Planning

Once the topic or theme is chosen, the preliminary planning begins with a brainstorming session. The purpose of this session is to think of as many aspects of the theme as possible and to generate a list of words, ideas, possible activities, and general thoughts about the topic. This can be done by discipline, but that is not necessary.

The four basic rules for brainstorming (Osborne, 1963) include:

1. **The more ideas the better.** The key to a successful brainstorming session is to allow plenty of time for ideas to emerge. The first few dozen ideas are those that are fairly typical. It is not until the list becomes quite lengthy that the more unique and interesting ideas surface. Make the list as long as possible. Plan for a couple of brainstorming sessions and jot down some ideas as they come.

2. **No put-downs!** Every idea is considered acceptable in the first stage of brainstorming and should be recorded without commentary. Making any negative remark may repress a source of ideas. Too many positive comments can also inhibit responses. If one participant receives too much positive feedback, others may feel their ideas unworthy.

3. **Even silly ideas count.** Sometimes offerings seem strange, different, or even silly. These thoughts should be recorded along with all the rest. A group of architects designing a skyscraper decided to put mirrors beside elevator bays. Apparently they recognized some people would pause momentarily to glance at themselves and not rush or crowd onto already overworked equipment. The result was much more orderly evacuation of a busy building. In the brainstorming session the idea seemed silly and was one that emerged after many others. Eventually, it was adopted as the best idea to solve the original problem.

4. **Elaborate ideas and piggyback.** Many times one idea will give birth to another or be the seed of an even better idea. Use other ideas developed in the brainstorming session and add a new twist to them.

In the preliminary planning of the Native American study, two brainstorming sessions were held. During the first session, the study planners thought of all the words and phrases that were related to the Native Americans. This gave them an opportunity to review and list the content that was normally covered in the curriculum and add new thoughts and ideas to the study.

Textbooks and other reference books were used to provide additional information. Although many studies are done by teachers in self-contained classrooms, it can also be valuable for grade level teachers or teacher teams to plan together. This may add new and exciting dimensions to the study and offer more rewarding experiences for everyone involved.

Once the list is finished, the content should be organized on a "web." Webbing is an organized form of brainstorming; a way to develop a topical outline of the central theme (Baldwin, 1989). It is sometimes

Curriculum Mapping

TEAM MEMBERS: _____ GRADE LEVEL: _____ DATE COMPLETED: _____

Discipline	September	October	November	December	January
	Content: Skills:		Content: Skills:	Content: Skills:	Content: Skills:
	Content: Skills:		Content: Skills:	Content: Skills:	Content: Skills:
	Content: Skills:		Content: Skills:	Content: Skills:	Content: Skills:

Figure 4. Curriculum Mapping

Adapted from *The Curriculum Mapping Model* by Heidi Hayes Jacobs. (1991).

Curriculum Mapping

TEAM MEMBERS: _____   GRADE LEVEL: _____   DATE COMPLETED: _____

Discipline	February	March	April	May	June
	Content: Skills:	Content: Skills:	Content: Skills:	Content: Skills:	Content: Skills:
	Content: Skills:	Content: Skills:	Content: Skills:	Content: Skills:	Content: Skills:
	Content: Skills:	Content: Skills:	Content: Skills:	Content: Skills:	Content: Skills:

Adapted from *The Curriculum Mapping Model* by Heidi Hayes Jacobs. (1991).

Figure 4. Curriculum Mapping (continued)

Curriculum Mapping

TEAM MEMBERS: _Konefal, Keegan, Atkins, Fulton_ GRADE LEVEL: __6__ DATE COMPLETED: __1-22-93__

Discipline	September	October	November	December	January
Language Arts	Content: _Review for C.M.T.*_ _Novel and Basal (skills)_ _Vocabulary Level A_ _Units 1 and 2_ _Summer Book Reaction_ _English grammer-p. 20 Book_ _Daily Oral Language._ Skills: _Punctuation, Writing, Capitalizing, Reading, Spelling, Vocabulary, Sentence Structure, Paragraphing._	Content: _Novels and basal_ _Vocab. Level B Units 3 and 4_ _Short stories, Poems, Prose_ _English Grammar to pg. 42_ _Daily Oral Language_ _Writing: Explanatory, Poetry_ Skills: _Writing skills to express personal ideas, revising, clarifying. Interpreting the Text_	Content: _Novels, Textbook (S. Studies)_ _Vocabulary Level A - Units 5&6_ _English grammar unit 1-complete_ _Daily Oral Language_ _Writing: Explanatory, Research._ Skills: _Reading skills: meaning from text, strategies to learn facts from text, Main idea, note-taking, bibliography_	Content: _Novels, Textbooks (S. Studies)_ _Vocab. Units 7 & 8_ _Daily Oral Language_ _Writing: explanatory research, writing_ _Unit 2 Grammar-started_ Skills: _Reading skills & inferential Comprehension, critical and creative thinking._ _Compare & Contrast._	Content: _Novels, Mythology_ _Vocab. Units 9 & 10_ _Daily Oral Language_ _Writing: Creative, research, explanatory_ _Continue Unit 2-grammar_ Skills: _Inferential thinking - Creative & Critical Thinking._
Math	Content: _Review of fifth level Math concepts_ _Whole number concept_ _Exponents_ _Estimation_ Skills: _Problem Solving ----->_ _Computing, estimating, comparing, problem solving, reasoning, relating, reinforcing_	Content: _Decimals, + · x÷_ _Scientific notation_ _Simple graphing (1 quadrant)_ _Equations; number theory_ _Estimating_ Skills: _Problem Solving ----->_	Content: _Fractions: + · x÷_ _Primes & Composites_ _LCM, GCF_ _Comparing_ _Estimating_ Skills: _Problem Solving ----->_	Content: _Geometric Ideas -----> Angles, Lines, Polygons, Congruency, triangles, quadrilaterals, construction of figures, bisecting lines and angles_ _Decimal x÷_ Skills: _Problem Solving ----->_ _To identify geometric elements: angles, lines, figures._ _To classify angles, triangles, quadrilaterals._ _To identify congruent figures; corresponding parts of figures._	Content: _Angles, Lines Polygons, Congruency, triangles, quadrilaterals, construction of figures, bisecting lines and angles_ _Changing fractions to decimal_ _Number Theory and Equations_ Skills: _Problem Solving_

C.M.T. = Connecticut Mastery Test

Figure 5. A Completed Curriculum Map

Curriculum Mapping

TEAM MEMBERS: _Konefal, Keegan, Atkins, Fulton_   GRADE LEVEL: _6_   DATE COMPLETED: _1-22-93_

Discipline	February	March	April	May	June
Language Arts	Content: Novels, Mythology, Independent reading Vocab. Units 11 & 12 Daily Oral Language Writing: creative, research Grammar Unit 3 Skills: Punctuation, Writing, Capitalizing, Reading, Spelling, Vocabulary, Sentence Structure, Paragraphing.	Content: -----> Vocab. Units 13 and 14 Daily Oral Language Writing: creative, research Grammar Unit 3 Skills: -----> ----->	Content: Novels Vocabulary Units 15 & 16 Daily Oral Language Writing: Biographical, Creative Grammar Unit 4 Skills: Reading skills, main idea, inferential comprehension, critical and creative thinking. Compare & Contrast.	Content: Novels, Short Stories Vocab. Review Units Daily Oral Language Writing: Biographies, creative Grammar Unit 4 Skills: Writing skills, revising, clarifying. ----->	Content: Novels, Short Stories Daily Oral Language Writing: Business Letters, creative Grammar Unit 4 Skills: -----> Skills -----> Continue
Math	Content: Changing Fraction to decimal Ratio & Proportion Solving Proportions Common Fractions Skills: Problem Solving -----> Computing, estimating, comparing, problem solving, reasoning, relating, reinforcing	Content: Using percents: Finding: percent of a number; the number when % is known, understanding percents, discount, simple interest. Common Fractions x÷ Skills: Problem Solving -----> ----->	Content: _Geometry_ Integer and graphing Fractions: + - x÷ Equations using integers Inequalities Coordinate Plane, graphing Decimal Division Review Skills: Problem Solving -----> ----->	Content: _Geometric_ Review earlier teaching circles: area, circumference, volume, surface, area of polyhedrons and cylinders Geometry All Concepts. Skills: Problem Solving ----->	Content: Probability, Statistics Range and Mode Median & mean Relative frequencies Percent. Skills: Problem Solving ----->

Figure 5. A Completed Curriculum Map (continued)

Curriculum Mapping

TEAM MEMBERS: _Konefal, Keegan, Atkins, Fulton_   GRADE LEVEL: __6__   DATE COMPLETED: ___1-22-93___

Discipline	September	October	November	December	January
Science	Content: _Climate & Life_ _Study of Biomes and characteristics of plants and animals. Chapter 4_ Skills: _Observing, listing, identifying, reading a table, drawing conclusions, describing, classifying, comparing, reading a graph, graphing, hypothesizing, concluding, reading a diagram._	Content: -----> Skills: ----->	Content: _Conservation/Earth's Resources_ _Science Book Ch. 10 - S. Studies Book Ch. 7 Study renewable, non-renewable natural resources & understand how natural cycles replenish non-living renewable resources - concentration of U.S. and Canada_ Skills: -----> _Skills Continue_ -----> _Collecting Specimens_	Content: -----> -----> Skills: -----> ----->	Content: _Forecasting the Weather_ _Science Book - Ch. 12 Use weather instruments to measure and forecast weather._ Skills: -----> _Observe & predict_ -----> _Read & understand weather maps._
Social Studies	Content: _Geo-Themes_ _Learning To Use Maps Ch. 1_ Skills: _Identifying types of maps, Analyze for specific needs, Locating places through use of latitude and longitude, orienting._	Content: _Geo-Themes_ _Hands on Geography - Nystrom Time, Seasons, Weather and Climate Ch. 2 Connect with science: Biomes_ Skills: _"Its About Time" Exhibit. Developing ideas, Analyzing data, Research skills, Outline important details, Reading for information._	Content: _Geo-Themes_ -----> _Chapters 4 and 5 in S. Studies Book. Canadian Beginning Colony to nation Resources, land forms, tourist sites of Canada_ Skills:_"Its About Time" Exhibit. Describing the text, Identifying main ideas, Summarizing, Evaluate text structure, KWL strategy to learn comprehension._	Content: _Geo-Themes_ -----> _Hands on Geography_ -----> _S. Studies resources, land forms, tourist sites, etc. of Canada Chapter 6 Time Line, Project: Canada_ Skills: _Content reading skills, Identifying main idea, Evaluate text structure, Comprehension, Construct a Climograph._	Content: _Geo-Themes_ -----> _Hands on Geography Introducing The Americas Chapter 3_ Skills: -----> _mapping regions of Americas, Classifying economic, cultural, political activities. Recognizing the uses of 3 kinds of graphs._

Figure 5. A Completed Curriculum Map (continued)

Curriculum Mapping

TEAM MEMBERS: _Koneful, Keegan, Atkins, Fulton_   GRADE LEVEL: __6__   DATE COMPLETED: __1-22-93__

Discipline	February	March	April	May	June
Science	Content: _Forecasting the Weather (Cont.)_ Skills: _Observing, listing, identifying, reading a table, drawing conclusions, describing, classifying, comparing, reading a graph, inferring, hypothesizing, causes & effect._	Content: _Change in The Earth's Crust: Ch. 11-Science. Plate tectonics, study continental drift, sea floor spreading, volcanic activity and mountains building._ Skills: _Skills Cont. ----> Communicating information to each other_	_(content continues)_ Skills: _Skills Cont. ----->_	Content: _Exploring Space: Chapter 13. Use telescope to study planets and Sun, study Rocketry, build rockets, future implications of space exploration_ Skills: _Skills Cont. ----->_	_Skills Cont. ----->_
Social Studies	Content: _Geo-Themes -----> Hands on Geography-Nystrom -----> Ch. 11 Mexico: Independence to the Present. History of Mexico_ Skills: _Identifying physical and cultural features of Western Hemisphere, Reading a Map, Analyzing Photographs._	Content: _Geo-Themes -----> -----> Ch. 12 Mexico's Land and People today. Economics and physical features_ Skills: _Reading a Map-location of places, Analyzing a Graph, Classifying information, Compare & Contrast information on Climographs._	Content: _Geo-Themes -----> Hands on Geography -----> Ch. 18 Brazil ----->_ Skills: _Use latitude & Longitude for absolute location. Analyzing graphs. Compare & Contrast information on a map_	Content: _Geo-Themes -----> Hands on Geography -----> Caravans ----->_ Skills: _Identifying major physical and cultural features of Brazil and the West Indies. Reading the text for main ideas. Understanding distance on a map. Research skills._	Content: _Geo-Themes, Hands on Geography, Caravans_ Skills:

Figure 5. A Completed Curriculum Map (continued)

done after brainstorming in order to organize or provide clarity to the ideas. When creating a web, the word or phrase that represents the topic, theme, or unit should be written in the center of a piece of paper. The major related subtopics should then be scattered around the central topic. Radiating from these subtopics should be the specific details.

Webs are designed to help the planner see the topic from numerous dimensions and give insight into the depth and breadth of the topic. Webbing is a continuous process that should continue throughout the study as long as new ideas are discovered. The list of words/ideas and the web created for the Native American study are shown in Chart 1 and Chart 2. The web can be written on the reverse side of the Planning Matrix as presented in the foldout on pages 33 and 34.

During the second brainstorming session, the teachers of the Native American of the Plains study brainstormed a list of possible activity and project ideas. This list, which was organized by disciplines, included the following ideas.

Language Arts
Write Letters to Reservations
Read Myths and Legends
   The Gift of the Sacred Dog
   Brother Eagle, Sister Sky
Find a Resource Person to Teach Sign Language
Survey Student Interests
Use Graphic Organizers
Concept Map, KWL Chart, Semantic Analysis, Cause/Effect
   Chart, Venn Diagram
Develop a List of New Vocabulary

Social Studies
Read Text, **From Sea to Shining Sea**
Create and Interest Development Center
   Write Problem Questions and Product Ideas Cards
   Collect, with students, Native American Memorabilia
   Current List of Reservations
Locate a Variety of Resources Books at several Grade Levels
Possible Speakers:
   A Native American
   Potter
Review Videotape Catalog and Locate Videos

Science
Study Ecosystems of the Plains
Incorporate the Student Outcomes from Science Curriculum
Make a Terrarium which Simulates the Plains Ecosystem

Chart 1
Native Americans of the Plains
Content Brainstorming

Plains	smoke signals	barter
Navajo	council	scalps
Woodland	Sun Dance	wars
teepees	Sweat Lodge Ceremony	reservations
caves	Gods	peace pipes
wigwams	adobe	moccasins
religion	hides	maize
ceremonies	wampum	painting
games	trading	war paint
dances	braves	shields
rituals	Native Americans	snowshoes
chiefs	designs	masks
Sitting Bull	circular stories	warriors
Santanta	myths and legends	villages
Big Tree	travois	lodges
squaws	sled	marriage
medicine men	canoes	family
powwows	longhouses	fire-walking
bows and arrows	campfire	feasts
clay pots	crafts	Ghost Dance
maple syrup	children	herbs
corn	Comanche	weapons
popcorn	Blackfoot	rifles
cornmeal	Black Hills	spears
hunting	Grass Dance	furs
fishing	Custer	government
buffalo	Sioux	bands
cattle	Cheyenne	settlers
Pemmican	Gold Rush	covered wagons
Hides	tomahawks	missionaries
cattle	scalping knives	iron horse
farming	dolls	whispering wires
sign language	beaver	barbed wire

Chart 2
Native Americans of the Plains
Content Web

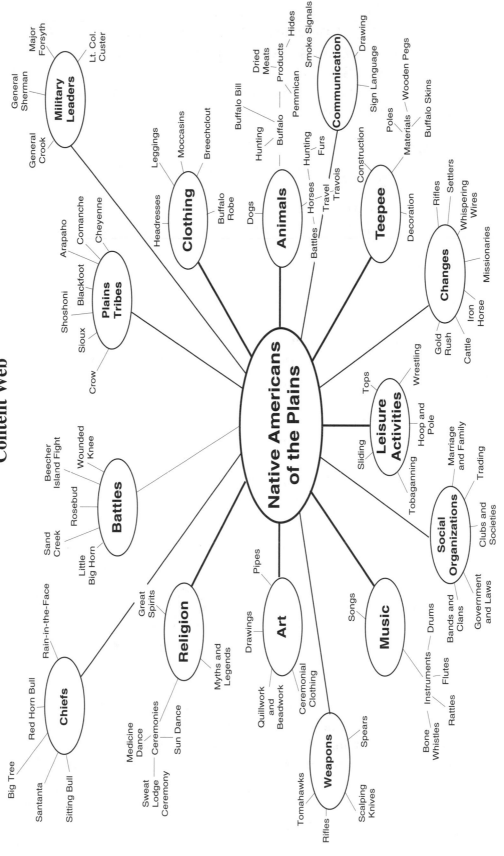

Math

> Study Chance and Probability
> Learn about Native American Guessing and Dice Games
> Create Games of Chance and Probability
> Learn Basic Statistics
> Make Predictions about Native American Populations
> Learn about the Demise of the Buffalo - Predict Populations

Art/Music

> Learn Ceremonial Songs and Musical Instruments
> Create Bark Drawings
> Construct a Teepee
> Study Picture Writing and Draw Pictures on the Teepee

Religion

> Learn about Ceremonies
> Plan an Native American Powwow as a Culminating Activity

Physical Education

> Learn about Fitness and Analyze Native American's Fitness
> Play Lacrosse and Discuss its Origin

Teacher planners should keep in mind that the ideas produced during the second brainstorming session are just some of the possible projects and activities they can pursue with their students during a study. This list should be changed and modified as the study develops. The possibilities are endless!

Step Three: Student Outcomes

Whatever the topic or theme, it is most important to determine what students should know about a topic and the skills at the conclusion of the study. These are often called "student outcomes" and might be categorized as content, skill, and attitudinal outcomes. The teacher planners must decide:

1. What should students know? (Knowledge or Content)
2. What should students be able to do? (Skills)
3. What should students feel, learn, or believe? (Attitudes and Attributes)

The curriculum usually provides the basis for decision making regarding the selection of some of the student outcomes. Curriculum maps can also assist in reviewing disciplines. Students can become active participants in this decision making process. Curriculum planners

can conduct a survey that asks students to describe what they know and would like to know about a specific topic. This information can then be incorporated into the curriculum planning.

The content outcomes reflect the specific information or content teachers expect their students to acquire and master as a result of a study. Although students will learn additional information, these outcomes reflect the knowledge that will be assessed throughout the study. The content outcomes of the Native American study, as shown in the Planning Matrix in Figure 3, included:

1. The students will describe the culture of the Native Americans of the Plains.....
    - -way of life   -art and artifacts
    - -use of resources   -adaptation to the environment
    - -beliefs and customs
2. The students will list the factors that changed the Native American's way of life.

The process outcomes should reflect the primary skills the students will learn during this study. Once again, some or all of the skills selected may be required by a school district and included in the curricular documents. The teacher, as curriculum planner, determines which skills will be addressed and how to infuse them into the study. In making this decision, there are many things to consider. The new basic skills extend beyond reading, writing and arithmetic and should include: evaluation and analysis skills, critical thinking, problem solving strategies, organizational and reference skills, synthesis, application, creativity, decision making, and communication skills. Calvin Taylor's *Talent Totem Poles Extended Version*, 1986, delineates the following skills as important to the world of work: academics, productive thinking, communicating, forecasting, decision making, planning, implementing, human relations, and discerning opportunities.

Connecticut's Common Core of Learning (1987) includes skills and competencies that are included in the section entitled "Preparation for Life." Many states have similar competency instruments. The **Schoolwide Enrichment Model** (1985) includes a Taxonomy of Type II Enrichment Processes that includes the following categories: cognitive and affective training, learning how-to-learn skills, using advanced research skills and reference materials, and developing written, oral and visual communication skills. (See Appendix C). Deciding what skills to teach during any study is a complex process and needs to be given careful consideration.

The process student outcomes for the Native Americans of the Plains study included:

1. The student will compare and contrast the Plains, Desert, and Northwestern Coastal tribes.
2. The student will analyze the causes and effects of the Native American's conflict with the Europeans.
3. The students will learn and apply the ten steps of the independent study process.
4. The students will learn and utilize oral presentation skills.

The skills listed in the process outcomes are not the only skills taught during the duration of the study, but they are the most significant in terms of importance. The primary and secondary process outcomes should be outlined in the "Type II Process Training Lessons" column on the Planning Matrix.

The final student outcomes focus on attitudes and attributes. These outcomes are based on students' feelings, beliefs, values and emotions. The following two outcomes were used during the Native Americans of the Plains study:

1. The students will develop a sensitivity to and an understanding of the customs of the Native Americans.
2. The students will demonstrate a questioning attitude, curiosity, and independent thinking.

All of these outcomes provide a direction for the study and should be assessed in various ways prior to the conclusion of the study. Methods of assessment will be discussed later in this chapter.

Students should also be aware of what they are expected to learn in a unit of study. Before or during daily lessons, teachers should communicate the objectives to students. After this discussion with students, modifications can be made if and when necessary.

Step Four: Getting Started

Regardless of the theme or topic, the following tasks must be accomplished during the planning phase:

Designing and Conducting a Student Survey
Creating a Content Web
Establishing Student Outcomes
Constructing an Interest Development Center
Planning Type I or Introductory Activities
Locating Library and Human Resources
Writing Type II or Process Training Lessons
Brainstorming Possible Type III Training Activities

Two of these tasks, the Student Survey and the Interest Development Center, will be described in detail in this section and the other areas have been (Content Web and Student Outcomes) or will be addressed later in this chapter.

Student Survey

The purpose of the **Student Survey** is to gather information from students about the study. Students are asked to share what they know about the topic, what they would like to learn, how they would like to learn any new information, and if they have or know of any resources they would be able to share with the class. The survey is conducted when the study is being planned and the results can be used in many ways. For example, what students know about the topic and what they would like to learn will assist the planners when they are establishing appropriate and meaningful student outcomes and activities.

The question related to the students' learning style preferences will inform the teacher about the preferred and appropriate instructional styles for a given group. In the survey, students are asked to check their preferred learning style(s) based on the following learning situations: recitation and drill, peer tutoring, lecture, lecture and discussion, discussion, guided independent study, learning/interest center, simulation, role playing, dramatization, guided fantasy, learning games, investigative reports or projects, unguided independent study, internship, and apprenticeship. Students are also given the option to list any other ways they like to learn. Before completing the survey, teachers should explain each learning style and clarify any unknown terms.

The survey is designed for each specific study and modified according to the grade level. In the Native American of the Plains study, the students were asked what they already knew and wanted to know about the Plains culture. They were asked if they had any information (books, magazines, maps, posters, post cards, artifacts, or other memorabilia) related to the Plains tribes or any other tribes. Finally, they were asked if they knew any Native Americans or people who had visited or lived on a reservation and would be willing to talk to the class about their experiences.

This step has proven to be an invaluable component of the study, since it provides an excellent understanding of students' knowledge and areas of interest. The understanding of students' learning styles makes it possible to modify and adjust instruction in order to better meet the needs of a particular class. The students are invaluable contributors of resources, artifacts, and memorabilia for Interest Development Centers and save teachers hours of time in trying to locate resource people. See the Native Americans of the Plains Student Survey in Figure 6.

NATIVE AMERICAN OF THE PLAINS
STUDENT SURVEY

1. What are some things you know about the Native Americans of the Plains?

2. List at least three things you would like to know about this culture.

3. What is your preferred learning style? Please check all that apply.

   _____ Recitation & Drill
   _____ Peer Tutoring
   _____ Lecture
   _____ Lecture/Discussion
   _____ Discussion
   _____ Guided Independent Study
   _____ Learning/Interest Center
   _____ Simulation, Role Playing, Dramatization, Guided Fantasy
   _____ Learning Games
   _____ Investigative Reports or Projects
   _____ Unguided Independent Study
   _____ Internship
   _____ Apprenticeship
   _____ Other _____

4. Do you have any information such as maps, charts, books, magazines, posters, postcards, artifacts, or other memorabilia you would be able to share with the class during this study?

5. Do you know any Native Americans or individuals who have visited or lived on a reservation or know a great deal about this culture? Would this person(s) be willing to talk to our class?

Figure 6. Student Survey of Native Americans of the Plains

Interest Development Center

The primary purpose of the **Interest Development Center (IDC)** focuses on developing and creating interest and enthusiasm about the topic or theme that will be studied. Since student interest is a major motivational factor in the learning process, the importance of getting students actively engaged in all aspects of the study cannot be overly emphasized. Therefore, whenever possible, teachers should include interested students in the development of the centers. Parents are also an excellent resource and teachers may wish to invite them to contribute or create their own centers. A parent newsletter or special announcement about the current study might be effective vehicles for communicating with parents.

The Organizing Interest Development Experiences (Figure 7) is a valuable planning chart that can be used as the vehicle for the initial planning of the **Interest Development Center (IDC)**. This chart focuses the planners' thinking and helps in determining what should be included in the center. As shown in Figure 7, possible resources for general exploratory activities are checked and reviewed. Books, magazines and journals, audiovisuals, and display items are listed. Related curricular materials such as textbooks, resource books, journals, study guides, vocabulary lists, assessment instruments, manipulatives, etc. are recorded here. The names of potential visitors and speakers are recorded on the Organizer along with their names, addresses and phone numbers for easy reference. Finally, ideas for specific exploratory activities are generated and recorded. The Organizer, which can be used by individual planners or teacher teams, should grow and change throughout the course of the study and reflect students' interests and abilities.

The IDC helps to provide a focal point for unit activities. When creating a center, educators can use a bulletin board and display table or construct a foam core board display and locate it on a large table. (Foam core board is available at most art supply stores.) The center in Photograph 1 was constructed from a foam core board and was intended to catch the students' attention. The center had interesting pictures and designs as well as items in pockets for youngsters to explore. The three components of this center included "The Hunt," "Scouting," and "How! How? How!"

Inserted in **The Hunt** pocket were problem or question cards that were intended to generate student curiosity about the Native Americans and the many aspects of their life. A sample of the kinds of questions included in this pocket are listed below:

- What did the Plains Indians do in their leisure time? How does that compare with what you do in your spare time?

ORGANIZING INTEREST DEVELOPMENT EXPERIENCES

Content Area ___Social Studies___ (Interdisciplinary Study) Grade Range ___4-6___

TOPIC: | Survival: Native Americans of the Plains

General Exploratory Activities
(Check all that apply; star the most likely after reviewing resources)

X Visiting Speaker	___ Television
X Mini-Course	X Newspaper/Magazine Articles
X Demonstration	X Interest Development Center
___ Discussion/Debate	X Display
X Film/Filmstrip/Slides	___ Field Trip/Museum Program
X Tape/Videotape	___ Other

Books   **Indians of the Plains**, Ed. American Heritage
New York: American Heritage Publishing Co.,
1960

Magazines/Journals
Brandenburg, Jim. "The Land They Knew"
National Geography, October 1991.

Audio-Visuals
Videotapes: American's Indians Before the European
Settlement.
American Indian: Death of the Bison.

Display Items
Maps, Charts, Drums, Clay Pottery, Pipes, Bows,
Arrows, Headdress, Photographs, and Indian
Clothing.

Related Curricular Materials
Vocabulary Cards– Include new terms on one side and definitions on
the other.

Text: From **Sea to Shining Sea**
Unit 2, Chapter 5

Journal / Study Guide

Visitations/Speakers
Tamunk– Native American, Self-Employed
Marie Jones, Indian Potter, American Archeological
Institute, Washington, CT

Special Exploratory Activities
Mini-Courses:
Introduction to Sign Language
Indian Music and Songs
Why Totem Poles?
Problem and Product Cards
Current Listing of Plains Indian Tribes/Reservations

(Use the back of this sheet if you need additional space.)

Based on a form from The Schoolwide Enrichment Model:
A Comprehensive Plan for Educational Excellence. (1985).
J. S. Renzulli and S. M. Reis. Creative Learning Press. Inc.

Figure 7. Organizational Interest Development Experiences

Photograph 1. Native Americans of the Plains Interest Development Center

- Describe the Indian Shield Ceremony.
- How would you know who was the weakest member of the tribe? The strongest?
- What white men crossed the plains in 1541 and what was the reason for their presence? Were they successful and if so, how?
- How long have the Native Americans been in North America and where did they come from?
- Describe the weather and vegetation on the Plains.
- Who was George Catlin and what contribution did he make to this period in history?
- Explain the importance of the buffalo to the Native American and list their uses.
- Draw a picture of a teepee. What does it look like inside and outside? Why did the Indians live in teepees?
- What was the dress of the men, women, and children? Do we wear any clothing today that is similar to theirs?
- How did Native Americans use decoys when engaging in battle?
- What role did visions play in the life of a brave?
- What was the most important religious ceremony of the Plains Indians? Describe the ceremony.
- Why did it take until the mid 1880's for white men to settle the Plains?
- Who were the mountain men and what did they do on the Plains?
- In what ways did the missionaries affect the Indian way of life?
- What caused the violence and wars that began in the summer of 1855 and continued for almost forty years?

These questions were written on cards and placed in the pocket entitled **The Hunt** in the Interest Development Center. Students reviewed them and looked for answers to any questions that piqued their curiosity. In addition, these questions were used during an introductory research skills activity that was designed to acquaint students with the numerous resource books located in the IDC and help them learn how to locate information using a table of contents, index, chapters, and headings. During this lesson students selected a question, found the answer in one of the resources, and shared their discoveries with their peers in a small and/or large group setting. The information gathered during this activity also became part of a study guide for all students.

The questions in **The Hunt** pocket were written at various levels of Bloom's Taxonomy (1955) in order to accommodate the various

learning needs of the students. The wide selection of question topics were written to appeal to the many, varied interests of the students.

The **How! How? How!** pocket of the IDC included vocabulary cards featuring words and phrases that were new to the students. The words were written on one side and the students were encouraged to find and write the definition on the other side. Students were also invited to write words and definitions on blank cards. Both the completed vocabulary cards and the knowledge level **The Hunt** cards were used very successfully as a Jeopardy game midway through the study. Examples of some of the words and definitions used for this study included the following:

> **pemmican** - sun dried buffalo meat pounded into pulp and mixed with buffalo fat;
>
> **myth** - a story about Gods that explains something in nature;
>
> **symbol** - something that stands for something else;
>
> **sanka wakan** - "mystery dog" which is a Sioux name for a horse;
>
> **travois** - a primitive carrier hauled by a dog or horse;
>
> **chinvoh** - warm, dry wind of the Plains;
>
> **parfleche** - buffalo skin packet which looked like a giant envelope;
>
> **shaman** - tribal medicine man;
>
> **allotment** - United States government policy of the late 1800's that sought to divide land owned by a tribe into small tracts owned by individuals;
>
> **Dog Soldiers** - a group of Cheyenne men who were regarded as the tribe's most fierce warriors;
>
> **massacre** - the brutal killing of a group of people who are unable to protect themselves;
>
> **reservation** - an area of land set aside for use by Indians;
>
> **teepee** - a portable, cone-shaped house with a wooden frame and covered with animal hides;
>
> **treaty** - a written agreement between two or more groups of people.

The **Scouting** pocket contained cards and pamphlets listing the names, addresses, and phone numbers of present-day Plains Native American tribes. Students did their own scouting and wrote to numerous reservations requesting information. These letters were written approximately two weeks before the study and the students were pleasantly surprised when they received letters, pamphlets, postcards, pictures, maps, pouches, and other small memorabilia throughout the study.

Photograph 2 shows the Interest Development Center board on a long table, where it was displayed with many other items. The center

<u>Photograph 2.</u> Native Americans of the Plains Interest Development Center

included numerous fiction and nonfiction books that covered a variety of reading levels, drums, a headdress, a shield, student-made bow and arrow, several Native American artifacts, a bulletin board with several pictures of the people and places of the Plains, and authentic Plains Indians designs. Many of the items on the table belonged to the children.

The books on the display table and chalk rail were gathered by the teacher from the school library, local libraries, and state interlibrary loan. Students at this grade level should have easy access to resources in order to explore the topic being studied on a daily basis. Older students can be responsible for obtaining more resources, but the teacher should still play a key role in this area. Children should also visit libraries in search of additional resources as they pursue their own research topics.

Technology can play a key role in a study by helping teachers and students locate additional information about their topics. Computers, CD-ROMS, and modems can help students gain access to the myriad of facts and resources located on commercial on-line services and the Internet.

There are many variations and types of Interest Development Centers and educators should feel free to be resourceful and construct their own one-of-a-kind creations. One resource that may be especially helpful in developing centers is "Interest Development Centers: Land of Opportunity" (Burns, 1985). Keep in mind that centers are recyclable and many of their components can be used from year to year.

Step Five: Disciplines or Subject Areas

To the young mind everything is individual, stands by itself. By and by, it finds how to join two things and see in them one nature; then three, then three thousand . . . Discovering roots running underground whereby contrary and remote things cohere and flower out from one stem . . . The astronomer discovers that geometry, a pure abstraction of the human mind, is the measure of planetary motion. The chemist finds proportions and intelligible method throughout matter; and science is nothing but the finding of analogy, identity, in the most remote parts.

-Ralph Waldo Emerson

The *Enrichment Triad Model's* Type III investigations of real problems has provided the basis for an integrated approach to Triad in the Classroom studies. When students conduct their own in-depth investigations of problems or topics based on their interests, the studies naturally become integrated. Students learn to see connections among

the various disciplines and real life. For example, two students studied noise and its effect on behavior. They reviewed the literature on the topic, conducted an experiment with mice using a scientific method of inquiry, charted and graphed their findings, reported their findings in a written paper, created a visual display, and gave an oral presentation to their peers and parents. For a moment in time, they became the professional—the scientist, and like most professionals, it became necessary to combine several disciplines and skills in order to support the learning and processing of these disciplines. This study and hundreds of others like it clearly demonstrate the value and richness in making authentic connections during the learning process.

Many experts say that integrated approaches are also designed to help teachers surmount the problem of overcrowded curriculum. Interdisciplinary approaches offer a way of ranging over the disciplines without getting tangled in the maze of coverage. Another advantage of integrated instruction is that it fosters collaboration among teachers. This is especially evident in the middle school team concept where teachers from the major disciplines and special area teachers (art, music, and/or physical education) plan studies together.

Efforts to integrate the curriculum have a long history. In 80 studies carried out on the effectiveness of integrative programs, students in various types of integrative programs have performed as well or better on standardized achievement tests than students enrolled in the usual separate subjects (Vars, 1991).

Triad studies are designed to integrate disciplines or subject areas. Teacher-planned classroom studies are not unlike independent investigations. Both are integrated, so students can better understand the reasons why their learning has application to real life situations.

There are numerous ways to integrate the curriculum. Fogarty, 1991, describes ten models that can be used to connect the disciplines. She begins with an exploration within a single discipline and then demonstrates models that integrate across several disciplines by theme, topic, and skill. The Triad study uses a model similar to a webbed model which integrates all of the disciplines as appropriate within a specific topic or theme.

The existing curriculum or subject matter and corresponding content objectives often become the basis for establishing what disciplines will be included in any given study. For example, in the Native Americans of the Plains study, the content, presentation, and activities were designed to include all dimensions of the culture as they related to the various disciplines. Art, music, language arts, science, religion, and physical education all became a part of the study. By including the existing curricular objectives or student outcomes from the different disciplines in a study, students can benefit from learning

their required courses in an integrated manner. This is often done since teachers can accomplish integrated learning experiences in their classrooms without changing or restructuring the entire curriculum. However, it does not preclude the development of studies that may be of interest to students and not necessarily a part of the regular curriculum.

When using the Interdisciplinary Planning Matrix (Figure 2) only the disciplines that will be included in the study are written in the **Disciplines** column. The connections made among the disciplines should be authentic or else they should not be incorporated into the study. In some instances one or two disciplines may be more dominant than others and may require more space on the Matrix. This form is not designed or intended to restrict the number of disciplines or make it mandatory to include all disciplines. Although the Planning Matrix shows the four major disciplines of language arts, science, social studies, and math, it may be necessary to add other disciplines for the overall success of the study.

Step Six: Type I Content and Introductory Activities

To be interested is to be absorbed in, wrapped up in, carried away by, some object. To take an interest is to be on the alert, to care about, to be attentive. We say of an interested person that he has both lost himself in some affair and that he has found himself in it. Both terms express the engrossment of the self in subject.

-John Dewey, 1916

The Type I, content and introductory activities are the **most critical** aspect of the study since they involve developing student's intellectual curiosity about a topic and motivating them to WANT TO LEARN more about a given topic. As any educator knows, it is extremely difficult to teach students who are uninterested and passive about the subject matter. Although some teachers feel it is the student's responsibility to come to the learning situation ready to learn and work, we know that this is not the reality in today's classrooms. The teacher plays a key role in the Type I process and plans, organizes, and facilitates the experiences and activities that will set the stage for learning.

The Type I experiences are designed to "connect" to the regular curriculum or theme/topic currently being studied. They are the vehicle used to introduce the content to the youngsters in an exciting and meaningful way. The teacher is no longer the primary giver of

information or "sage on the stage." The resources of the entire school community are brought to bear upon the study. Professionals or experts in their respective fields bring their expertise into the classroom to share with students. With them comes the real world of ideas, thoughts, innovations, current research, unique happenings, and "opinions," all of which children will ultimately need to analyze, synthesize and evaluate the data they gather. Information is shared and exchanged in a multi-modal (visual, auditory, and kinesthetic) and multimedia (films, computer programs, interactive video) manner at a variety of intellectual levels in order to engage **all** students in the learning process. When educators consider the diverse learning needs in their classrooms, they will soon realize the far-reaching and profound implications and applications for Type I experiences in the regular classroom.

The most challenging aspect of a Type I experience is to locate the library and community resource people who might participate in the introductory activities. The Organizing Interest Development Experiences Chart (Figure 7), which was used during the planning of the Interest Development Center, is the first place to begin. Some of the resource people and materials listed on this chart can be recorded in the Type I Column of the Triad Planning Matrix adjacent to the appropriate discipline. For example during the Native Americans of the Plains study, the textbook **From Sea to Shining Sea** was listed as a resource in the Type I column of the Social Studies section. The name Francine Green was listed in the Art/Music section as a resource person for Native American ceremonial songs, music, and instrumentation.

Teachers who have implemented Triad studies have employed a variety of techniques to locate resources. Oftentimes, personal friends and colleagues are the best individuals to contact as possible Type I resources. These individuals are almost always the richest resource and the easiest to locate. Professional organizations and societies, colleges and universities, senior citizens, school and town film and video libraries, and the yellow pages of the telephone directory are also great places to look. However, if this task becomes too daunting, educators should look for some help.

The parent community is usually very helpful in assisting teachers in locating resources and resource people. Parent Teacher Organizations/ Associations often have a parent volunteer coordinator. Teachers should look for a classroom volunteer coordinator who can contact possible presenters, check their interest in speaking to a class, discuss their expertise or specific areas of interest, gather information about the nature of their presentation, and check their availability in terms of dates and times. After discussing this with the teacher, the volunteer can then schedule the presentation and do any necessary follow-up work, such

as creating a resource file. Although this seems like a great deal to ask of a volunteer, there are individuals who will welcome the opportunity to contribute to school programs in meaningful ways.

Students are also a great source of information. In the Student Survey, students are asked if they know of any individuals who have knowledge of the topic and would be willing to visit their class. Students are usually pleased to participate in this process and are more than willing to do so.

A more formal way of locating resources and resource people is to develop a Schoolwide Enrichment Team. An Enrichment Team is not a policy making body nor an advisory committee, but rather a working group of faculty members and parents who have specific responsibilities for organizing the enrichment effort of the entire school (Renzulli & Reis, 1985). **The Schoolwide Enrichment Model: A Comprehensive Plan for Educational Excellence** (1985) describes the procedures for developing such a team and explains who should be on the teams, how often they should meet and what they should accomplish, how they should determine the types of enrichment opportunities to offer, and other relevant information. This Team could be designed to assist individual classroom teachers in locating local resources and resource people.

It should be noted that the resource people who come into the classroom not only energize students, but they also add new dimensions to the teacher's own thinking! Many teachers who have developed and implemented Triad studies have attested to this fact.

There were numerous Type I activities developed for the Native American study. The following list contains descriptions of the Type I experiences. (These are not listed in the order in which they were taught. Please refer to the study's timeline later in this chapter.)

Type I Activities for the Native Americans of the Plains Study

Book Talks: The school librarian provided students with an introduction to literature titles available in the school library related to Native Americans and previewed several of the books.

Myths and Legends: The entire class read and discussed **The Gift of the Sacred Dog**, a myth written by Paul Goble. The teacher read the book, **Brother Eagle, Sister Sky, A Message from Chief Seattle** to the class.

Student-Created Topic Web: After the students had some knowledge of the topic, they created a class web based on the Native American theme. As they proceeded to learn new information about this topic, they expanded their web.

Student Survey: As mentioned earlier, all students were surveyed prior to the beginning of the study. (See Student Survey in Figure 7). It was valuable to survey them during this planning time since the teachers asked them to help locate resources.

Sign Language: A teacher from a neighboring school district taught a mini-course in Sign Language for the deaf. This four-session course taught the signs for the basic alphabet and common words and phrases. Although this was not a class in Native American Sign Language, it was hoped that this course stimulated one or more students to question the signs used by the culture they were studying.

Guessing and Dice Games: Students were introduced to a dice game that was similar to the "Button, Button, Who's Got the Button?" game, which was very popular among many Plains tribes. Since the dice used were not cubical in shape (sticks with different faces, plum stones, little pieces of bone, and similar objects), students used straws, small stones, and pieces of chicken bones to create playing pieces for this game of chance.

Ecosystems of the Plains: Students read the chapter in their science textbook about ecosystems of the Plains.

Indian Pottery: A speaker from a local Native American museum spoke to the students about the Indian Pottery she had created and fired in the kiln she constructed in her backyard. She explained that her process simulated one used by the Plains tribe and shared the results of her efforts with the children. Students then had an opportunity to make a small clay pot, which the potter fired and returned to them a week later. This speaker charged a fee that was paid for by the Parent Teacher Organization. Since the school had a small budget for visiting speakers, most presentations were given by volunteers.

The Native American Culture: Tamunk, a local Native American, visited the class and talked to students about his culture. He shared a great deal of information and numerous artifacts.

Interest Development Center-The Hunt: The Interest Development Center was introduced to students through an activity. Each student took a question card from **The Hunt** pocket of the center. Their challenge was to use the numerous books and other resources in the center to answer their question. The students worked in pairs helping each other to search for the answers. The answers were then written on the back of **The Hunt** question cards and shared with other children in a small group setting.

From Sea to Shining Sea: Students read **From Sea to Shining Sea** (Chapter 5 from Unit 2 of their textbook). The teacher was trained in how to teach reading in the content area and used this knowledge to assist students in reading and retaining the information.

Totem Poles: James Smith visited the class and talked to the youngsters about his totem pole carvings. Mr. Smith explained that he had been carving totem poles for thirty years and had carved hundreds of miniature replicas. He brought many of his totem poles with him and explained the origin and meaning of each one. He also showed children pictures of the life-size totem pole which stood outside his home.

Indian Art and Artifacts: This speaker, Edie Brown, was a teacher in the school district who had an intense interest in Native American tribes and had been collecting Indian art and artifacts for twenty years. She also dressed the part, by wearing and describing the dress of the Plains, Desert, and Northwestern Coastal tribes.

Videotapes: Students were given a historical perspective of this culture through two videotapes, which were shown to students and entitled "American Indians Before the European settlement" and "Indian Family of Long Ago." These films were found in the school district film library and provided a perspective not covered in any other part of the study.

Picture Writing and Painting: The art teacher introduced students to picture writing and painting through circle and bark drawings during two of their regularly scheduled art classes.

Quillwork and Beadwork: The art of quillwork and beadwork and how they were used to adorn ceremonial dress and clothing was presented through the use of several resource books and Native American clothing located in the Interest Development Center.

Ceremonial Songs, Dances, and Musical Instruments: The school's music teacher introduced students to Native American songs and dances. She also taught them how to play several of the musical instruments such as drums, rattles, and rasps, which were used to accompany their songs and dances.

Ceremonies and Rituals: Two students became intrigued with the unusual ceremonies of the Plains tribes. They read several books about them and taught the class about each one. They created a brief simulation to introduce the Sweat Lodge

Ceremony. However, since it was impossible and inappropriate to simulate the Sun Dance, this was shown primarily through pictures.

Lacrosse: The game of lacrosse originated with the Plains tribes. The school's physical education teacher discussed the origin of the game with the class and taught them the game as it is played today.

This is the manner in which students were introduced to the Native American culture. This deviates dramatically from a lecture and discussion format or the round-robin reading of a textbook, which are sometimes the only delivery system used to provide students with content. This approach has incredible benefits for the students. The most significant benefit is that **all** students in the class become actively involved in the learning process. No one is excluded because they read at a lower grade level and no one is bored because they are reading two or three grade levels above the class.

The primary reason this occurs is because the material is presented in a multi-modal manner by using oral, written, and kinesthetic modalities. The learners truly follow John Dewey's advice and "learn by doing." They play games, participate in simulations, sing, dance, draw, search for information in books which are easily obtainable and at all readability levels, create clay pots, draw pictures, question "experts" on the topic, view films and pictures of the culture, gather memorabilia for the Interest Development Center, and help locate resource people. This becomes their study and they are beginning to develop ownership and responsibility for their own learning experiences.

Even at this introductory level, there are opportunities for the very able learner to stretch. The Interest Development Center offers a wealth of resources on all topics and problem cards to stimulate thinking. Questions can be prepared for the speakers and interested students can be given the opportunity to interview and evaluate presenters following their presentations. If they locate information or an activity they would like to share with the group they can become the speaker or facilitator. These options are also available to every learner in the classroom.

The stage has been set for the study. Students will participate in their own learning, make decisions, solve problems, plan their own studies, develop their products, and find audiences for their work. All of this will occur in the regular classroom!

However, before we progress to the next step of the study we need to do some bookkeeping. It is very important to keep a record of the resource people who might be interested in assisting in the study or those who have already been resources for the classroom. The **Schoolwide Enrichment Model** (Renzulli & Reis, 1985) recommends several record keeping techniques. For the Native Americans of the Plains study, teachers used the Community Resource Record, Figure 8, which lists the names, topics, and types of assistance resource persons can provide, (e.g., Type I presentation, phone conference, private conference, mentorship, etc.).

The card number is cross-referenced with the Resource Directory Card for Resource Persons shown in Figure 9a. This card lists the card number, topic, and the name, address, and phone number of the resource person. Space is also provided to record successful contacts and additional comments. The second Resource Directory Card is used to list any other resources. The completed card in Figure 9b shows a listing of a videotape that was obtained from the school district's library. These forms can be filed in a general file or copied and filed with teacher notes and the Planning Matrix for the study. They can also be copied and shared with the Schoolwide Enrichment Team or interested colleagues.

In addition, the resource people and resources should be evaluated by both teachers and students. Once again, there are several examples of these forms in the **Schoolwide Enrichment Model** (Renzulli & Reis, 1985). The ones used most frequently for this study are shown in Figures 10, 11, and 12, and include the Type I Enrichment evaluation forms for students at the primary grade levels, students at the intermediate and secondary grade levels, and a teacher's form. Completed student and teacher forms for the Native American Study are shown in Figures 13 and 14.

Another form which has been used effectively is the Cumulative Speaker's Record. This form provides an annual summary or snapshot of the speakers who have visited the classroom, their topics, the results of the teacher and student evaluations, whether or not they are willing to return as a speaker, and additional comments. A blank form and a completed form for the Native Americans of the Plains study appear in Figures 15 and 16. Although this may seem like an overwhelming amount of paperwork, the forms are very easy to complete, and in the long run, save a great deal of time and energy.

As mentioned earlier, the primary purpose of the classroom Type I experience is to introduce content to students in a manner that is meaningful and engaging. If this aspect of the study is successful, it will pave the way for the more challenging process training strategies and independent learning opportunities.

COMMUNITY RESOURCE RECORD

NAME	TOPIC	Type I Presentation	Phone Conference	Private Conference/Interview	Visit at Place of Employment	Written Correspondence	Mentor	Evaluate Products	Mini-Course	CARD NUMBER	COMMENTS
Jane Smith	Native Americans	X	X	X			X		X	1	Plain, Desert, Northwestern and Northeastern tribes.
Mark Tangarone	Sign Language	X	X	X					X	2	American and Indian Sign
Ruth Jones	Indian Pottery	X								3	Demonstration of Pottery Making
Tamunk	Way of Life: The Native American	X		X					X	4	Brings Artifacts and Photographs
Francine Green	Indian Song, Instrumentation & Dance	X		X					X	5	Teaches Songs, Dances, and How-to-Play Instruments

AVAILABLE FOR:

Adapted from The Schoolwide Enrichment Model: A Comprehensive Plan for Educational Excellence. (1985). J. S. Renzulli and S. M. Reis. Creative Learning Press, Inc.

<u>Figure 8.</u> Community Resource Record

RESOURCE DIRECTORY CARD
Resource Persons

Card Number   <u>1</u>
Topic <u>Native American</u>

NAME: Jane Smith

TOPIC: Native Americans: A Comparison of Plains, Desert Northwestern, and Northeastern Indians

ADDRESS: 100 North Street, Anywhere, USA 12345

PHONE: (123) 123-4567

CONTACTS MADE: Type I Presentation 1/15/94

Note: Jane brings numerous artifacts from many tribes, Indian clothing, and other memorabilia. She also demonstrates Indian dances and then actively engages children in the dance.

Permission to reproduce this page granted by Creative Learning Press, Inc.

Reproduced from the Schoolwide Enrichment Model: A Comprehensive Plan for Educational Excellence. (1985). J. S. Renzulli and S. M. Reis. Creative Learning Press, Inc.

<u>Figure 9a.</u> Resource Directory Card—Resource Person

RESOURCE DIRECTORY CARD
Other Resources

Topic <u>Plains Indians</u>

TITLE: American Indian: Death of the Bison

MODE OF DELIVERY:

ADDRESS/CONTACT PERSON: Joe Jones, West Hartford Public Schools, Media Center

PHONE: (203) 233-9876

CONTACTS MADE: Ordered on 10/2/93 for 1/25/94

Notes: <u>Availability</u>: Must be ordered approximately four weeks before needed.

<u>Cost:</u> N/C

Permission to reproduce this page granted by Creative Learning Press, Inc.

Reproduced from the Schoolwide Enrichment Model: A Comprehensive Plan for Educational Excellence. (1985). J. S. Renzulli and S. M. Reis. Creative Learning Press, Inc.

<u>Figure 9b.</u> Resource Directory Card—Other Resources

TYPE I ENRICHMENT EVALUATION FORM

Student Form for Primary Grade Levels

Please help us plan future Type I's by filling out this form.

Speaker's Name_____   Your Grade_____

Topic of Talk _____

	Yes	No	Unsure
This Type I was really interesting.	☐	☐	☐
I learned about things I did not know before.	☐	☐	☐
This presentation was useful for students my age.	☐	☐	☐
This Type I helped me think of project ideas or ways to learn more.	☐	☐	☐

Was there something super-special about this Type I?
What was it?

What would you change about this Type I?

Please give this form to your teacher. Thank you.

Figure 10. Type I Enrichment Evaluation Form—Student Form for Primary Grade Level

TYPE I ENRICHMENT EVALUATION FORM

Student Form for Intermediate and Secondary Grade Levels

Please help us plan future Type I's by filling out this form.

Speaker's Name_____ Your Grade_____

Topic of Talk _____

	Yes	No	Unsure
The presentation was interesting.	☐	☐	☐
The speaker covered a topic not usually covered in my classes.	☐	☐	☐
This presentation was appropriate for my age and grade level.	☐	☐	☐
This presentation stimulated ideas for possible training I might need or follow-up studies I might conduct.	☐	☐	☐
The speaker gave me ideas for further exploration or possible projects.	☐	☐	☐

What did you like most about this Type I?

What would you change about this Type I?

Please give this form to your teacher. Thank you.

Figure 11. Type I Enrichment Evaluation Form—Student Form for Intermediate and Secondary Grade Level

TYPE I ENRICHMENT EVALUATION FORM

Teacher's Form

Resource Name _____

Topic of Talk _____

Date _____   Grade _____

	Low	Medium	High
Speaker's knowledge of topic.	1 2 3 4 5		
Organization of presentation.	1 2 3 4 5		
Use of AV or visual aids.	1 2 3 4 5		
Student interest or enthusiasm.	1 2 3 4 5		
Appropriateness for this age group.	1 2 3 4 5		
Suggestions for extension and further study.	1 2 3 4 5		

Overall success: Would you want to repeat this Type I next year?

Comments:

Figure 12. Type I Enrichment Evaluation Form—Teacher's Form

TYPE I ENRICHMENT EVALUATION FORM

Student Form for Intermediate and Secondary Grade Levels

Please help us plan future Type I's by filling out this form.

Speaker's Name _____*Mr. Smith*_____   Your Grade ___*4*___

Topic of Talk _____*Totem Poles*_____

	Yes	No	Unsure
The presentation was interesting.	☒	☐	☐
The speaker covered a topic not usually covered in my classes.	☐	☐	☒
This presentation was appropriate for my age and grade level.	☒	☐	☐
This presentation stimulated ideas for possible training I might need or follow-up studies I might conduct.	☒	☐	☐
The speaker gave me ideas for further exploration or possible projects.	☒	☐	☐

What did you like most about this Type I?

I liked the totem poles because he had so many and he told stories about them.

What would you change about this Type I?

I wanted him to stay longer and I wanted to be able to have time to look at all the totem poles and touch them too!

Please give this form to your teacher. Thank you.

Figure 13. Type I Enrichment Evaluation Form—Completed Student Form for Intermediate and Secondary Grade Level

TYPE I ENRICHMENT EVALUATION FORM

Teacher's Form

Resource Name *James Smith*

Topic of Talk *Totem Poles*

Date *November 15, 1993*   Grade *4*

	Low		Medium		High
Speaker's knowledge of topic.	1	2	3	4	(5)
Organization of presentation.	1	2	3	4	(5)
Use of AV or visual aids.	1	2	3	4	(5)
Student interest or enthusiasm.	1	2	3	4	(5)
Appropriateness for this age group.	1	2	3	4	(5)
Suggestions for extension and further study.	1	2	3	(4)	5

Overall success: Would you want to repeat this Type I next year?

This was a very successful Type I presentation and should be repeated next year. Ideas for further study could be expanded upon.

Comments:

Mr. Smith was scheduled to meet with the class for one hour but it extended to two hours. The children were mesmerized by the beautifully colored totem poles and Mr. Smith's vivid descriptions of their meanings. He is a wealth of information. We wanted him to stay even longer.

Figure 14. Type I Enrichment Evaluation Form—Completed Teacher's Form

TYPE I ENRICHMENT EVALUATION FORM

Cumulative Speakers Record 19_____   Annual Summary

Type I	Grade Topic	Teacher Level	Student Evaluation	Teacher Evaluations	To Return?	Comments
Jim Halpern	Oceanography	4	√+	√++	Yes	More appropriate for middle school audiences

Adapted from The Schoolwode Enrichment Model: A Comprehensive Plan for Educational Excellence. (1985). J. S. Renzulli and S. M. Reis. Creative Learning Press, Inc.

Figure 15. Type I Enrichment Evaluation Form—Annual Summary

TYPE I ENRICHMENT EVALUATION FORM

Cumulative Speakers Record 19____

Type I	Grade Topic	Teacher Level	Student Evaluation	Teacher Evaluations	To Return?	Annual Summary Comments
Jim Halpern	Oceanography	4	√+	√++	Yes	More appropriate for middle school audiences
James Smith	Totem Poles	4	√++	√++	yes	excellent - add more project discussion
Maria Jones	The Art of Indian Pottery	4	√+	√+	yes	Extend time - too rushed
Mara Smith	Sign Language for the Deaf	4	√+	√+	yes	Look for resource for American sign language
Tamunk	The Native American Culture	4	√++	√++	yes	Outstanding - valuable information/"feeling"
Edie Brown	Indian Arts and Artifacts	4	√	√	yes	Too much information too fast, needs organization
Jane Smith	Picture Writing and Printing	4	√+	√+	yes	Great work!
Francine Green	Songs, Dances	4	√++	√++	yes	Students loved this! It was wonderful addition to our pow-wow.
Jim Smith	Lacrosse	4	√	√	yes	Would need to spend more than one class.

Figure 16. Completed Type I Enrichment Evaluation Form—Annual Summary

Adapted from The Schoolwide Enrichment Model: A Comprehensive Plan for Educational Excellence. (1985). J. S. Renzulli and S. M. Reis. Creative Learning Press, Inc.

Step Seven: Type II Process Training Lessons

The "basics" of tomorrow include evaluation and analysis skills, critical thinking, problem solving strategies, organization and reference skills, synthesis, application, creativity, decision making given incomplete information, and communication skills through a variety of modes.
-Education Commission of the States, 1982

The skills needed to process and interact with the content presented in the Type I introductory activities are the focus of step seven's Type II process training lessons. These process training skills will blend and merge with the introductory activities and will be presented at appropriate times, sometimes even simultaneously, throughout the study. A Taxonomy of Type II Enrichment Processes (Renzulli & Reis, 1985), included in Appendix C, provides a comprehensive list of the specific process training skills such as creative thinking, problem solving, critical thinking, affective training, and learning how-to-learn skills such as interviewing and classifying data. This is an invaluable resource for the curriculum planner when determining the process training or skills necessary for a given area of study. This information, in addition to the school district's required curricular objectives in each discipline, provides the foundation for decision making regarding the appropriate skills for a given study. It is important to keep in mind that the process training that students need should not be limited to those prescribed in the regular curriculum.

When developing a Triad study, the challenge for the curriculum planner or teacher is to determine what skills to teach, to whom and when they should be taught, what instructional strategy to employ in the teaching of that skill, and what materials he/she should use.

The process training lessons and activities selected and taught in the Native Americans of the Plains study are shown on the Planning Matrix in the column entitled Type II Process Training Lessons (Figure 3). These specific lessons represent those selected by the teacher planner as necessary for this particular study. Some lessons are based on the school district's required curriculum and others extend beyond the scope of the curriculum. These generally include skills, such as planning, problem focusing, decision making, and creative problem solving.

A Lesson Planning Guide was created to assist the teachers in writing these lessons. This Guide (Figure 17) was designed to:

- assist teachers in documenting their lessons in an efficient, concise manner;
- provide teachers with an awareness of their teaching or

Interdisciplinary Studies
Lesson Planning Guide

Interdisciplinary Unit: _____   Lesson Title: _____

Teacher: _____ Grade: _____ Introductory _____ Midway _____ Follow-up _____

Instructional Strategies:

_____ Lecture
_____ Discussion
_____ Cooperative Learning
_____ Peer Tutoring
_____ Learning or Interest Center
_____ Simulation or Role Playing
_____ Learning Games
_____ Guided Independent Study
_____ Other _____

Disciplines Included:

_____ Language Arts
_____ Social Studies
_____ Mathematics
_____ Science
_____ Music
_____ Art
_____ Personal/Social Development
_____ Other _____
_____ Other _____

Instructional Objectives: Include content, process or skills, attitudes and attributes.

Description: Include any previous learning or necessary background material.

Resource Materials: Include chapter and page references to textbooks and/or other sources.

Assessment/Follow-up: List the method(s) you will use to assess mastery of objectives.

Figure 17. Lesson Planning Guide

instructional style(s) and encourage the use of a variety of instructional styles;

- demonstrate the curricular connections inherent in the lessons and enhance the inclusion of several disciplines within a given lesson or activity;
- ensure the establishment of clear content, process, and attitudinal lessons objectives (What do you want the student to learn? To be able to do?);
- provide a concise description of the lesson which other teachers can replicate;
- document all resources and resource materials needed for the lesson;
- record the manner in which student understanding will be assessed (Have they met the lesson objectives and how do you know?).

As a means of modeling how to use the Lesson Planning Guide and sharing the higher level thinking and creative and critical thinking lessons developed for the study of the Native Americans, lessons have been written for the majority of the activities listed in the Type II column on the Planning Matrix. Many of the lessons provide the teachers with access to the strategies necessary for independent learning. The lessons included in the Planning Matrix are marked with an asterick and appear in Appendix A.

Teaching and Learning Styles

Each lesson asks the teachers to determine the teaching or instructional style they are using in each of their lessons and to also consider their students' preferred learning styles. The Lesson Planning Guide requires the teacher planner to check the instructional strategy that will be used in each lesson. The purpose of including styles in the guide is to encourage teachers to employ a variety of instructional styles during their studies and extend beyond the lecture format. The list of 11 instructional styles is based on the **Learning Styles Inventory** (Renzulli & Smith, 1978) which is a research-based instrument developed to guide teachers in planning learning experiences that take into account their students' learning style preferences. The definition of learning styles is one or more of the following nine instructional strategies most preferred by individual students as they interact with particular bodies of curricular materials: projects, drill and recitation, peer teaching, discussion, teaching games, independent study, programmed instruction, lecture, and simulation.

There are entire books devoted to various teaching approaches and in-depth analysis of learning styles. Since a comprehensive discussion of this topic is beyond the scope of this book, we have

decided to include brief descriptions of the learning styles that appear in **The Schoolwide Enrichment Model: A Comprehensive Plan for Educational Excellence**, (Renzulli & Reis, 1985, pages 195-196).

Projects: The project method is characterized by a group of students working together to fulfill the requirements of an assignment. In most cases, the project results in a final work that can be shared with other students.   Students experience relatively little direct interaction with the teacher.

Drill and Recitation: This "traditional" approach to instruction involves a teacher asking questions and calling on students to respond with the appropriate information. Recitation typically entails questions that can be answered by statements of fact. The responses that students provide for these questions are evaluated in terms of the correctness of the facts.

Peering Teaching: This technique involves the use of students as teachers of other students. The tutoring situation can be highly structured (teacher assigns a tutor to a particular child and defines the content to be covered) or unstructured (students select their own tutors and cover the material that they decide upon themselves).

Discussion: Discussion is characterized by two-way interaction between teacher and students or among students. As opposed to the lecture method, group discussion involves a greater degree of active participation on the parts of students. Ideally, discussion as a technique requires students to think about the relationships among facts, weigh the significance of facts, and argue about them. Varying degrees of teacher domination are found, ranging from instances in which the teacher plays a non-directive, mediating role to instances in which the teacher asks most of the questions and provides the agenda and procedures to be followed.

Teaching Games: Teaching games are activities that are fun for students to participate in and at the same time involve content that the teacher wants students to learn. Games can involve the entire class or be geared to individual students or small groups of students.

Independent Study: This approach involves individual students pursuing topics or areas of study on their own. Independent study is characterized by freedom from constant supervision, although there is interaction with others as needed. Typically, the student chooses an area of study, develops his or her own approach to gathering information, and produces some kind of outcome.

Programmed Instruction: Programmed instruction is based on students working alone on material that has been sequenced to teach a particular concept. The material characteristically consists of short statements which end with a question or a blank to be filled. The

statements are presented by a teaching machine or in a textbook or workbook. Other features of programmed instruction include a provision for immediate feedback, student determination of own rate progress, highly organized content, and low rate of student error.

Lecture: Lecture refers to a verbal presentation in which the teacher or another individual perceived as an expert in a particular area communicates the ideas and concepts to be acquired. The lecture method is marked by a lack of discussion or interchange between teacher and students. The teacher "talks to" students. The lecturer organizes and presents the material in the sequence and style he or she prefers.

Simulation: This approach attempts to teach content and skills through role playing. Generally, a specific problem or social process is outlined for the simulation and students are asked to role play with this context. The student player must make decisions "on-the-spot." These decisions affect the next move of other players. Realism is a primary concern in the development of simulations. The more a simulation reflects real world circumstances, the more successful the learning experience will be. The function of the teacher in this context is generally to coordinate the proposed actions.

It is important to note that in any given classroom, students will have several preferred learning styles. If the teacher is aware of these styles, some of the instruction can be presented in a manner that matches students' styles. Student learning and motivation will very likely be improved as a result of this increased awareness. Students will also begin to develop skills that are not normally needed in a traditional lecture format. For example, self-directed and self-selected independent studies require students to make decisions, focus problems, determine objectives and direction, sequence tasks, access resources, use a wide variety of research skills, and develop final products.

Questioning

The important thing is never to stop questioning.
-Albert Einstein

A key component to the success of the Type II training and all other aspects of the study is the questioning strategies employed by the teacher. It is imperative that questions be asked at all levels of Bloom's Taxonomy (Bloom, 1955). These levels include:

Knowledge—Identification and recall of information
Comprehension—Organization and selection of facts and ideas
Application—Use of facts, rules, and principles
Analysis—Separation of a whole into component parts

Synthesis—Combination of ideas to form a new whole
Evaluation—Development of opinions, judgments, or decisions

All children need to be asked challenging questions on a regular basis. Through questioning, teachers are able to encourage their students to wonder, stimulate their intellectual curiosity, enhance their ability to connect disparate facts and information, assess the significance of situations, compare and contrast meaningful events past and present, and most significantly, provide a model that will enable them to ask questions of themselves without teacher prompting.

All children benefit from responding to questions at all levels. It is the challenge of the classroom teacher to determine when to ask students a question and at what level. Some students quickly master the content of a given discipline and need to be challenged to apply their knowledge, analyze the information by comparing and contrasting it with previous learning, synthesize the knowledge and create new and exciting possibilities, and assess the results of the effort. Teachers can use questioning to challenge all students in this manner by modifying their questions for each specific class and each unique student. It is not necessary nor is it possible for all children to be asked the same questions or to respond with the same answers. Questioning allows teachers to individualize learning and better meet the needs of their students.

One technique that has been used to assist teachers in this process is the use of question frames. These frames provide the teacher with question starters for all levels of the taxonomy and assist them in knowing the level of question they are asking and determining what question is most appropriate to ask. Some examples of these question frames are listed below.

Knowledge: Who, what, where, when _____ ?
     Describe _____ .
Comprehension: Retell _____ in your own words.
     What is the main idea of _____ ?
Application: Why is _____ significant?
     How is _____ an example of _____ ?
Analysis: Classify _____ according to _____ ?
     How does _____ compare/contrast with _____ ?
Synthesis: What would you predict/infer from _____ ?
     How would you create/design a new _____ ?
Evaluation: What criteria would you use to assess _____ ?
     Do you agree with _____ ?

These question frames can be put on a card and kept in a plan book. This provides a daily reminder of the importance of the manner

in which teachers question their students. In the development of a Triad study, questioning will also play a key role in the development of student products.

Selection of Type II Skills

The lessons teachers select for their Type II process training will vary greatly depending upon their curriculum and the needs of their students. However, there are several skills that are critical to the success of the study and MUST be included at some point. These skills are all detailed and written in the Lesson Planning Guides. The skills and the rationale for their inclusion is are described below:

1.   **Brainstorming**—Students will need to generate numerous ideas throughout the study. The development of fluency, flexibility, originality, and elaboration will provide the foundation for a more creative, dynamic study. The teacher is pivotal to the success of brainstorming and should always join the class as they think of ideas. It must also be kept in mind that students need to "play" with ideas and brainstorming is not a waste of time!

2.   **Webbing**—This skill is used extensively throughout the study in order to categorize thinking and ideas, expand and outline topics, and focus problems.

3.   **Decision Making**—This strategy allows students to become independent thinkers and rely more on themselves as decision makers.

4.   **Questioning**—Students will be asked to select a topic to research and create a product in conjunction with this study. They will need to ask themselves questions related to the topic and should have developed skill in asking themselves questions at more than a literal or knowledge level.

5.   **Creative Problem Solving**—During a study students may be presented with problems related to their independent investigations. The skill of problem solving is another life skill that will enhance students ability to think creatively and critically.

6.   **Planning**—The ability to plan a study is the final MUST skill. Students need to know how to determine the topic of their study, focus their problem, select an appropriate product, decide on an audience, and establish a sequence of tasks they will need to accomplish in order to complete the study.

Once students have learned these skills, the Triad studies become much easier to implement and facilitate. Without them, the students rely more on the teacher and have difficulty becoming independent

learners. The Lesson Planning Guides will assist the teacher/facilitator in teaching these skills and the Type III training activities will provide students with the application of many of these skills when they complete their own studies.

Step Eight: Type III Training Activities Interest-Based Independent Projects/Studies

For me, as their teacher, the benefits were many. First, problem solving with students throughout the unit helped me gain insights into the mental thought processes of sixth graders. Second, taking on the role as their facilitator and guide was rewarding. My gradual releasing of control to the student resulted in outcomes far surpassing all expectations. Finally, I am often reminded that empowering students is one of most effective maxims for education. Giving students the power and then watching them strive for excellence is an incredible teaching experience.

-Catherine Doane, 1993

This is the most dynamic part of the study and the most challenging for both teachers and students. Modeled after Triad's Type III independent and small group investigations of real problems, these studies have been renamed Type III training activities since they are designed to train **all** students in the development of an independent or small group study. Every attempt is made to duplicate the enthusiasm and motivation that students demonstrate during a Type III. Therefore, interest and choice continue to play a primary role, since students select their own studies, problems, and products based on their unique interests, talents or strengths. The primary difference is that the studies are limited to the theme, topics, areas, or units being studied instead of any area of interest. In addition, unlike the "real" Type III, the studies may not be as in-depth, may require less time, and students may not develop the same level of expertise.

In this step, the independent study process will be defined and an example of an authentic Type III investigation shared through the eyes of a young gifted student, Michael. The teacher's transition from "sage on the stage" to "guide on the side" or facilitator of student's learning will be explained and the strategies, techniques, and materials needed to accomplish this with all students will be described.

There are ten definable steps that need to be followed when conducting Type III investigations. These steps were outlined by Reis and Cellerino (Beecher) in an article entitled *Guiding Gifted Students Through Independent Study* (1983) and include:

1. Assessing student interest.
2. Exposing students to numerous interest areas.
3. Conducting personal interviews.
4. Developing a written plan.
5. Determining a direction and timeline.
6. Locating multiple resources.
7. Brainstorming the final product.
8. Providing necessary methodological assistance.
9. Identifying audiences.
10. Evaluating the study.

The following description takes the reader through the steps of a Type III investigation. Although the student discussed in this example is at the primary grade level, the process remains the same for students in kindergarten through twelfth grade and beyond.

Michael, a second grade student in the gifted program in Torrington, had indicated a strong interest in Tchaikovsky to both his classroom teacher and his teacher in the gifted program. An interview was conducted to assess his interest in the topic. Some of the interview questions included:

1. Michael, will you tell me a little about Tchaikovsky and how you became interested in knowing more about him?
2. Have you read any books about him and his music?
3. How long have you been interested in studying about Tchaikovsky?
4. Do you like looking in different books to find information?
5. Do you have any ideas about what you would like to do with the information you find?

Questions such as these will help to assess the student's interest as well as commitment to the topic. It is not uncommon, especially for younger children, to become interested in a topic for a very short period of time.

Through the interview process, the teacher learned that Michael was interested in the music of Tchaikovsky. When students come to their teacher with a genuine interest, it becomes the teacher's responsibility to help focus the interest into an investigation that the student can begin.

In Michael's case, certain steps were followed. When asked how he had become interested in Tchaikovsky, he replied that he had been practicing the *Nutcracker Suite* for a Christmas recital and began wondering how Tchaikovsky wrote music. When asked by his teacher what he was wondering about, Michael replied that he had noticed that

Tchaikovsky's music was often both sad and happy within the same piece. It is critical at this time in the process of problem focusing that the teacher become an active listener, combining an accumulated knowledge of this particular student's special talents and abilities with a simultaneous understanding of how much the student may already know about the topic. This enables the teacher to assist the child in setting realistic directions for the resulting study.

Michael's objective became answering several questions about Tchaikovsky's music through his independent study. In the problem focusing process, after several minutes of discussion, Michael decided that in order to know why Tchaikovsky's music was both sad and happy, he would have to study and learn about Tchaikovsky's life. With the help of his teacher, Michael brainstormed the following questions:

- When did Tchaikovsky live?
- Did he have a happy childhood?
- Did he love music?
- Was he a sad or happy person?
- What was his life like?
- Did Tchaikovsky write sad music when he was sad and happy music when he was happy?

Michael decided that he would like to write a "talking children's book" on the music and life of Tchaikovsky. He was encouraged to find out whether his school or town library already had a book suitable for children on this topic. He learned that neither one had a children's book like this, so he realized that his book could become a part of both libraries. This provided Michael with the incentive to do his best work.

When students find it difficult to decide upon a final product, teachers often encourage a group of students to help each other brainstorm a list of possible products. However, the final choice must inevitably be up to the individual. In Michael's case, the joy of knowing that his "talking book," which included a manuscript and a taped version, would become a part of the library was definitely a motivating factor. It also provided an essential part of Type III enrichment—an audience for his work.

Michael's product, a children's book consisting of thirty typed pages and a taped version that plays many selections of Tchaikovsky's music, is a reflection of his love for his topic, six months of hard work, and his own pride in his accomplishment. In the first page of his book, which follows, each of those traits is obvious.

Some of you may wonder why a second grader would want to write a book about Tchaikovsky. People get interested in different things

for different reasons. For example, I got interested in Tchaikovsky because I like his music. I play the piano and have a whole book of his music. At Christmas I saw the ballet of the Nutcracker Suite. His music can be both cheerful and sad at the same time. I wondered how music can be both happy and sad at the same time, so I decided to learn about Tchaikovsky's life.

I wondered if when he was sad he wrote sad music and if when he was happy he wrote happy music. In this book you will get to know a little bit more about Tchaikovsky, how he lived, and about the music he wrote.

Michael's rich, educationally rewarding, unforgettable experience through his Type III study of Tchaikovsky is the same experience that teachers are trying to replicate in the classroom setting during Type III training activities. It becomes evident that all children can benefit significantly from similar experiences. Therefore, the Type III study has been modified for the regular classroom and is presented at a level and in a context that is accessible to all students. The objectives of the Type III training activities are synonymous with those of the Type III studies, but are modified in order to provide all children with an opportunity to:

- Apply their interests, knowledge, creative ideas, and task commitment to a self-selected topic which is based on the content of their regular curriculum.
- Acquire more advanced understanding of the knowledge (content) and methodology (process) that are used in the topic being studied.
- Develop creative products for specified audiences.
- Develop self-directed learning skills in the areas of planning, organization, resource utilization, time management, decision making, and self-evaluation.
- Develop task commitment, self-confidence, and feelings of creative accomplishment.

Assessing and Stimulating Student Interest

The first step in this process is to assess and stimulate student interest in the topic to be studied. Interest is assessed by using the Student Survey described earlier and shown in Figure 6. This will provide the teacher with information about what students know or would like to know about a given topic. It gives students "ownership" of the study by asking them what they would like to contribute. Students can help the teacher gather a wide variety of valuable resources and locate many resource people. As one student said so simply, "Why didn't

you tell me you were looking for some people to come to our class and talk to us? I know lots of people and I'll find some for you!" And indeed he did!

Students need to be participants in all aspects of the study if they are to truly engage in the learning experience. The planning of the study's content, locating resources, deciding on topics to study, selecting projects to complete, finding an audience for their work, and evaluating their own studies are all part of the student's domain. This is the "modus operandi" of the Triad classroom studies which stimulates students to eagerly engage in the study.

Dimensions of the Study

In order to expose students to numerous dimensions of the study, a wide variety of information, ideas, and topics are presented during the Type I phase. The Interest Development Center (maps, charts, books, magazines, and posters), speakers, demonstrations, teacher lectures, and small and large group discussions contribute to the students' knowledge and understanding of the topic. In order to provide a comprehensive and panoramic view of the many dimensions of the study, the teacher and students create a content web. (See Lesson Planning Guide Number 6 in Appendix A.) This web is visually displayed in some area of the classroom and students add to it throughout the study. Whenever students locate new information, they are free to add to the web. Students begin to see the connections within the topic and the breadth of the study and become increasingly excited about the possibilities for their own studies. Thus, this simple web becomes much more complex and profound in its meaning to students.

Student-Selected Topics

When the web has been expanded sufficiently, students are asked what topic(s) they would like to study further. It is explained that the entire class has learned a great deal of information already, but that students will learn the topics they select in more depth and become the class expert in their areas. They are asked to review the web and select a topic from the web or any other topic of **interest** to them. When students have difficulty deciding between two or three ideas, they can be asked to use the decision making strategy and grid. (See Lesson Planning Guide Number 9 in Appendix A.)

Since students often want to study the same topics, they are also asked to write their first, second, and third choices for topics. The teacher will then decide which students will study each topic. In making this decision, it is important to keep in mind that students like to work together and this is acceptable if the students have the same interests. Only the teacher and students can determine how many students should

work together on the same topic. It is recommended that no more than two students work on a study together.

Another interesting phenomenon occurs when students, especially younger children, are allowed to choose their own study. Many students may want to explore the same topic since it is of high interest. For example, in the Native Americans of the Plains study, the class decided that they would like to construct a teepee and learn more about how it was made. When students had an opportunity to choose their topic, more than half the class selected the teepee. The teacher's solution to this dilemma was to have the entire class participate in studying and constructing the teepee. As a result, this was no longer one of the topics available for an independent study. Interestingly, the students felt this was fair and all enjoyed the group planning and constructing of the teepee.

Planning the Study

Once the topics are selected, students will need to begin planning their studies. Students are generally unaccustomed to and have had little training in this level of self-directed learning. The method which will be used in the study closely follows the method used to pursue a "real" Type III study. The **Management Plan for Individual and Small Group Investigations** (Renzulli & Smith, 1977), is the vehicle used to organize an entire Type III study. A smaller version of the Management Plan is reproduced in Figure 18. (The original plan is available from Creative Learning Press, Inc.) The students engaged in a Type III are required to determine the general areas of study, provide a brief narrative about their specific area, list the sequential steps needed to get started, determine their product(s) and audience(s), and record all resources used during the study. Finally, students must establish a timeline which shows deadlines for the completion of various phases of their work and a final completion date. Figure 19 provides an example of a completed Management Plan.

Planning is a critical component of a Type III investigation and offers a challenging task for both teachers and students. Without a clear plan most endeavors are doomed to failure. If students do not know and cannot articulate what they want to know, how will they begin their research? If they don't know where they are going or what they want to do with the information, they wander aimlessly and, oftentimes, fail to complete the study or complete it inadequately. In the hundreds of studies done with children, the completion of the Management Plan was the least favorite, yet most necessary task.

Whether these studies are authentic Type III investigations or Type III training activities, both require the same type of methodology. The teacher becomes the facilitator of the student's learning. The primary

MANAGEMENT PLAN FOR INDIVIDUAL AND SMALL GROUP INVESTIGATIONS

(Actual Size: 11" x 17")

Prepared by: Joseph S. Renzulli
Linda H. Smith

NAME _____ GRADE _____

TEACHER _____ SCHOOL _____

Beginning Date _____ Estimated Ending Date _____

Progress Reports Due on Following Dates _____

GENERAL AREA(S) OF STUDY (Check all that apply)

___ Language Arts/Humanities   ___ Personal and Social Development
___ Social Studies   ___ Science   ___ Other (Specify) ___
___ Mathematics   ___ Music   ___ Other (Specify) ___
   ___ Art

SPECIFY AREA OF STUDY
Write a brief description of problem that you plan to investigate. What are the objectives of your investigation? What do you hope to find out?

METHODOLOGICAL RESOURCES AND ACTIVITIES
List the names & addresses of persons who might provide assistance in attacking this problem. List the how-to-do-it books that are available in this area of study. List other resources (films, collections, exhibits, etc.) and special equipment (e.g., camera, tape recorder, questionnaire, etc.). Keep continuous record of all activities that are part of this investigation.

INTENDED AUDIENCES
Which individuals or groups would be most interested in the findings? List the organized groups (clubs, societies, teams) at the local, regional, state, and national levels. What are the names and addresses of contact persons in these groups? When and where do they meet?

1. _____
2. _____
3. _____
4. _____
5. _____

INTENDED PRODUCT(S) AND OUTLETS
What form(s) will the final product take? How, when, and where will you communicate the results of your investigation to an appropriate audience(s)? What outlet vehicle (journals, conferences, art shows, etc.) are typically used by professionals in this field?

GETTING STARTED
What are the first steps you should take to begin this investigation? What types of information or data will be needed to solve the problem? If "raw data," how can it be gathered, classified, and presented? If you plan to use already categorized information or data, where is it located and how can you obtain what you need?

A complete description of the model utilizing this form can be found in: *The Enrichment Triad Model: A Guide For Developing Defensible Programs For The Gifted And Talented.* Creative Learning Press, Inc., P.O. Box 320, Mansfield Center, CT 06250.

Figure 18. Management Plan for Individual and Small Group Investigations

MANAGEMENT PLAN FOR INDIVIDUAL AND SMALL GROUP INVESTIGATIONS
(Actual Size: 11" x 17")

Prepared by: Joseph S. Renzulli
Linda H. Smith

NAME _Annemarie Maccalous_   GRADE _Five_

TEACHER _Mrs. Cellerino/Mrs. Freminos_   SCHOOL _Harwinton_

Beginning Date	_Nov. 1_
Estimated Ending Date	_April 30_
Progress Reports Due on Following Dates	_Dec. 20_ _Feb. 1_ _March 3_

GENERAL AREA(S) OF STUDY (Check all that apply)

√ Language Arts/Humanities — Science — Personal and Social Development √

√ Social Studies — Music √ Other (Specify) _Genealogy_

— Mathematics √ Art √ Other (Specify) _Drama_

INTENDED AUDIENCES

Which individuals or groups would be most interested in the findings? List the organized groups (clubs, societies, teams) at the local, regional, state, and national levels. What are the names and addresses of contact persons in these groups? When and where do they meet?

1. _Channel 5 (T.V.)_
2. _TAG FAIR_
3. _Other Classes_
4. _School Visitors_
5. _TAG Room_

INTENDED PRODUCT(S) AND OUTLETS
What form(s) will the final product take? How, when, and where will you communicate the results of your investigation to an appropriate audience(s)? What outlet vehicle (journals, conferences, art shows, etc.) are typically used by professionals in this field?

1. _Videotape entitled: "A Living Genealogy"_
2. _Storyboard_
3. _Scrapbook_

SPECIFY AREA OF STUDY
Write a brief description of problem that you plan to investigate. What are the objectives of your investigation? What do you hope to find out?

I intend to study my ancestry and collect pictures and other information for my videotape and scrapbook. I plan to write, direct, and produce a play entitled "A Living Genealogy." In this play I will portray all the different generations from myself to my great-grandparents.

METHODOLOGICAL RESOURCES AND ACTIVITIES
List the names & addresses of persons who might provide assistance in attacking this problem. List the how-to-do it books that are available in this area of study. List other resources (films, collections, exhibits, etc.) and special equipment (e.g., camera, tape recorder, questionnaire, etc.). Keep continuous record of all activities that are part of this investigation.

Books:
Backyard History Book _Weitzman, David_
Boston: Little, Brown & Co.
Sutar Saga
Beechers: Saints or Sinners
Beecher Genealogy

Community Resources
Miss Calhoun, Torry Historical Society
Mr. Bentle, Raymond Harwinton Historical Society
Grandparents
Mother

GETTING STARTED
What are the first steps you should take to begin this investigation? What types of information or data will be needed to solve the problem? If "raw data," how can it be gathered, classified, and presented? If you plan to use already categorized information or data, where is it located and how can you obtain what you need?

1. _Write questions for interviews with my grandparents and/or other people._
2. _Begin writing script for my play._
3. _Do research in the city library-use microfilm and old newspapers._

Figure 19. Completed Management Plan for Individual and Small Group Investigations

reason teachers are challenged by the Type III process is because it represents a pedagogy that may be unfamiliar and/or uncomfortable to them. In traditional teaching, the teachers are the instructors or disseminators of knowledge. Teachers initiate, determine, and control the parameters of the learning. Feedback is provided in the form of grades based on normative criteria. The Type III study requires teachers to become the students' coaches, editors, resource procurers, and guides. Students, instead of the teacher, play a leading role in the topic or problem selection and pacing. Teachers and students become partners in formative evaluation based on progress toward self-selected goals (Renzulli, 1994). Thus, the goals, projects, and even assessment are not programmed and prescribed by the teacher, but mutually agreed upon by both. Teachers need to extend their existing teaching styles and change the roles they play (Renzulli, 1982).

To make matters more complex, students may also be moving into "unchartered territory." They may never have been asked to make choices which are this open-ended. This can be as threatening to the students as it is to the teacher. Students will need patience and guidance from the teacher. Educators need to remember that both the teacher and students are learning together and reaching new dimensions in learning. This can create excitement and energy, as well as apprehension and anxiety for all those involved in the study.

The planning of the study is guided by the Management Plan, which is used at the middle and high school levels. The Modified Management Plan (Figure 20), has been designed for use in elementary and primary classrooms and should be completed by all students doing an independent study. All of the plans should have the same key features as the original Management Plan and should be used to assist students in planning and organizing their studies. Since teachers are unable to plan individually with each student, as they do when planning authentic Type III's, each section of the plan is explained and modeled by the teacher prior to completion by students.

Students begin by completing the upper portion of the form while the teacher assists the group in selecting the beginning and ending date of the study. The areas of study which will be involved in this project will be checked at this time and expanded upon as the study progresses.

The first two questions asked to students include: **"What is the topic of your study?"** and **"What do you hope to find out?"** In order to respond to these questions, students will need to clarify the topic they will be studying. Since the topics selected by students are often too broad in scope, this is usually an essential step.

Lesson Planning Guide 20 in Appendix A demonstrates how webbing is used to locate a more specific area of study and focus a problem. As shown in this lesson, a student was interested in learning

MODIFIED MANAGEMENT PLAN

Name: _____ Grade: _____

Teacher: _____ School: _____

Beginning Date: _____ Estimated Ending Date: _____

General Areas of Study (Check all that apply).

_____ Language Arts   _____ Music
_____ Social Studies   _____ Art
_____ Mathematics   _____ Personal/Social Development
_____ Science   _____ Other: _____

What is the topic of your study?

_____

_____

_____

_____

_____

_____

What do you hope to find out?

_____

_____

_____

_____

_____

_____

List three things you will do to get started.

_____

_____

_____

_____

_____

_____

Figure 20. Modified Management Plan

List the resources that you will use during your study. This might include books, films, records, movies, maps, etc., and any people who might help you.

_____
_____
_____
_____
_____
_____
_____
_____
_____
_____
_____
_____
_____
_____
_____
_____
_____
_____
_____

What form will your final product take?

_____
_____
_____
_____
_____

With whom will you share your product?

_____
_____
_____
_____
_____
_____

Figure 20. Modified Management Plan (continued)

more about trains. When asked exactly what he wanted to know about trains he was unable to answer. He was asked to create a web about trains and include some of the key facts he had learned or already knew about the topic. Web #1 is an example of his first web. The student was then asked to select something from web #1 that was of particular interest to him. As shown, he selected "locomotives" and was asked if he could create another web or extend the topic. When he started thinking about how locomotives were powered and the possibility of future locomotives using solar energy to get that power, he quickly focused his study and became energized and excited.

The train webs helped the student to answer the two questions in this manner: *I plan to study locomotives and how they are powered. I hope to find out about photovoltaic energy and if this type of solar energy can provide the necessary power for a locomotive.*

Another student decided to study acid rain. When asked to create a web, she said she was unable to do so because she didn't have enough information. When other students were working on their webs, she decided to frame questions that she would like to research about her topic. Some of her questions included:

1. What is acid rain?
2. What are the causes and effects of this environmental problem?
3. What can I do to stop this?
4. What is our country doing to stop this?
5. Are scientists studying about this problem and trying to find solution?

Both techniques are effective strategies for focusing students problems or topics. Like many students, this step in the planning process may take more than one session. The important thing to realize is that students ultimately know what they want to find out and stay focused on their study.

As seen in the completed Modified Management Plan, Lesson 21 in Appendix A, the fourth grade student completing the plan clearly stated her topic and goals as follows:

What is the topic of your study?
I would like to know more about the myths and legend of the Plains tribes.
What do you hope to find out?
I would like to know why there are so many myths and legends and where they come from. I would also like to know more about the tribes' storytellers and the role they played in village life.

The next step asks students to list the things they will need to **get started**. Since every student will have different things to do to begin their studies, it is important that they learn to analyze the steps needed to complete their work. The first few things are the most important, since they help them to progress in a positive direction. As a whole group lesson, it is helpful to generate a generic list of things people generally have to do to get started. Students can then work in small, cooperative groups to help each other determine their individual and small group tasks. This will help students think of their specific tasks and complete this section of the Modified Management Plan.

In the completed Modified Management Plan (Lesson 21 in Appendix A), Maria Jones decided that she would need to do the following things to begin her study:

1. *Find books about myths and legends in the library and begin reading myths.*
2. *Call Tamunk, a Type I speaker, and ask him if he knows any storytellers I can talk to and where I can find information about them. I'll also ask him if he knows where to find authentic myths and legends.*
3. *Learn to tell a story.*

The list of resources that students will use during the study will be on-going and expanded upon throughout their studies. This will include books, magazines, films, videotapes, movies, maps, and other resources and community resource people. If teachers expect students to use a particular method when recording these resources, they will need to provide them with the necessary information. It cannot be assumed that they will know how to do this.

Students are also encouraged to use multiple resources when looking for information and answers to their questions: interviews, libraries, books, magazines, phone books, textbooks, globes and maps, yellow pages, travel agencies, hospitals, businesses, how-to books, radios, catalogs, field trips, newspapers, biographies, art galleries, encyclopedias, surveys, experiments, slides, films, videos, pamphlets, models, observations, games, stories, and whatever other resources they can think of and locate.

Since students will not have all of the research skills they may need, it is the teacher's responsibility to assess their current level of understanding. The school's media specialist would be most helpful to teachers in this process, since students will need a common core of understanding about how to locate information and resources. Depending on the students' grade levels, they may need guidance on how to use the card catalog, **Readers Guide to Periodical Literature**,

CD-ROMS, and on-line services.

The next question asks, **"What form will your final product take?"** This product is intended to go beyond the report stage and children are encouraged to develop a product which is unlike anything they have ever done before. Since many children have had very little experience in selecting their own topics and product, it is very important to take time to generate ideas for these projects. This usually takes the form of several brainstorming sessions and should follow the selection of the topic very closely. The topic and products are closely linked and need to be considered almost simultaneously. For example, a student may choose to create a game of chance based on the Native Americans' many recreational activities. The topic and product must be appealing to the student.

The fourth column of the Planning Matrix (Figure 2) is entitled Type III Interest-Based Independent Projects/Studies. In this column teacher planners can list various product ideas for possible Type III training activities. These ideas will help teachers when they begin brainstorming possible activity ideas with students.

When brainstorming ideas for products with students, it is often beneficial to begin with a generic list of product ideas (Chart 3). After students have had an opportunity to review the different product ideas, invite the entire class to hold a group brainstorming session. During this large group discussion, the teacher can add to students' ideas in order to make them relevant to the study.

For example, if a student shows interest in building a model, the teacher might suggest that he/she can replicate an Indian medicine wheel. Another student might piggyback on this idea and suggest another kind of model. The final list of ideas will reflect the thinking of both the students and the teacher. Keep in mind that students should list as many ideas as possible, develop their fluency and originality, and select an idea that will complement their interests and strengths. If students can't decide among several product ideas, they can once again use their decision making strategy. Once they have made a final decision, they record the exact product idea on their Modified Management Plan.

It is also most important to show students excellent models of other children's work. These products may or may not relate specifically to the topic currently being studied, but should include a wide variety of products completed by students at all grade levels. Students might be shown some of the following: published books, poems, and plays; historical walking tours; a simulation of an historical battle; results of scientific experimentation; a how-to booklet for baby-sitters; a model of a solar furnace; and a booklet of creative thinking lessons for children. They may also be shown exemplary products related to the topics they

Chart 3
Product Ideas

Choose an interesting way to present your information to an audience. This list of suggestions will help you think of ideas.

Design a crossword puzzle	Make a coloring book
Make a lithograph	Create a filmstrip
Write a short story	Design an illustration
Write a characterization	Create an advertisement
Write a computer program	Write and perform a skit
Create a dictionary	Make a mobile
Design needlework	Write a song
Make a picture dictionary	Make a collection
Construct a photogram	Make a speech
Create a game	Make a simulation game
Make a sequence story	Make a future wheel
Make an etching	Create a puppet show
Create a word-play game	Design an advertising campaign
Make an outline	Make a photograph album
Create a radio program	Prepare your work for publication
Create a bulletin board	Write a "Letter to the Editor"
Make a display	Draw a cartoon
Create a slide show	Make a comic book
Design a photo essay	Take a field trip
Teach a lesson to another class	Design a banner
Make a startling discovery	Write and produce a play
Write and illustrate a children's book	Create pantomimes
Make transparencies	Design and make costumes
Write a description	Create a collage
Write a book	Make a travel brochure
Create a film	Design a plaster of paris model
Create a model	Make an ammonia print
Write a new law	Patent an invention
Make a mural	Design an animated movie
Prepare and conduct a survey	Write and tape a conversation
Perform an observation	Make a time-line
Formulate a scientific theory	Prepare a TV program
Write a book report	Videotape a presentation
Plan and layout a newspaper	Design a brochure or flyer
Write a poem	Start a campaign

Chart 3 (continued)
Product Ideas

Design an experiment
Put on a demonstration
Make a splatter print
Make a diorama
Make a poster
Create a musical instrument
Design a mask
Make a finger puppet
Hold a press conference
Promote a cause
Make a clay sculpture
Create a paper mache object
Design a building
Draw a map
Create a painting
Make a diagram
Draw a chart
Do a comparison
Tape an interview
Design a flow chart
Hold a debate
Make a riddle
Create a slogan
Circulate a petition
Make a blueprint
Write a biography
Write an autobiography
Make a block picture story

Create a flip book
Make a bookmark
Design bumper stickers
Make a three-dimensional object
Write a cookbook
Make a crossword puzzle
Create a dance
Hold a discussion group
Write an editorial
Make an exhibit
Write a fairy tale or fable
Make a family tree
Design a flag
Create greeting cards
Make pop-ups
Start an interest club
Design a learning center
Create a project cube
Make a roller movie
Make a sandcast
Design a roller movie
Write secret code messages
Make a silk screen
Design a stencil
Make a terrarium
Start an aquarium
Hold a mock trial

are currently studying. All of these products help to provide students with models to follow, demonstrate high levels of quality in student work, and show them it is possible to do a project of equal quality. Since many of these products may be Type III studies, this is one way of promoting a "radiation of excellence" in the classroom and school.

In order to ensure this kind of quality work by all students, the teacher must provide guidance during the entire process of product development. This means that the majority of the project should be completed **in school**. The primary reason for this is that students generally require instruction in many of the skills needed to create their final product. For example, learning games often require game boards, cards, playing pieces, etc. If students select a product that requires this type of game board and have never created one, they will need guidance in the process. The game must have a specific purpose and connection to the content being covered; the skills of task analysis and sequencing are needed to write the directions; measuring, scaling, proportions, and ratios are often needed to construct the game board; and materials are needed for the actual construction. If teachers expect students to create quality products, they need to model how this is done. The learning that occurs during this process is well worth the time spent. Students will be learning life skills that will serve them well in their travels through school and into the world of work. They will be learning how to present their work and themselves to the outside world. We can't afford not to take the time to teach these skills.

Another factor to consider while students create their products is the technology, equipment, and materials needed to complete their projects. Students should be given an introduction to the various equipment and shown how it might assist them in their investigation and/or final product. For example, some students may need special training in how to access information from computer programs, CD-ROMs, *America On-Line*, *Prodigy*, *CompuServe*, *Electronic Classroom*, and fax machines. Students who are interviewing people for their study might need instruction in operating a tape recorder to record interviews. If the school has a book binding machine that is available for use, students should be aware of the machine and how to use it when binding their own books. The overhead projector provides an excellent vehicle for sharing certain types of information. Students can be shown how to make overheads and use them effectively in an audiovisual presentation. Other types of equipment that have been successfully used by students include: filmstrip projectors, video cameras and recorders, headphones, computers, cameras, film projectors, puppet stages, and laminators.

The final question of the Management Plan is, **"With whom will you share your product?"** Most students are unaccustomed to sharing

their projects with different audiences. Some students have only shared the results of their work with their teachers and other students in their classes. Once again, it is necessary to brainstorm and this time the idea-generating session should focus on possible audiences for their projects. This brainstorming session should occur after students have determined their topics and products. Chart 4 lists many possible audiences for the student work.

In the Native Americans of the Plains study, the class decided to have a powwow as a culminating activity and invite their parents to attend. Students planned to become "experts" in some aspect of this culture and share their knowledge and expertise in a meaningful way during the powwow. Maria's completed Modified Management Plan clearly states that she planned to become a tribal storyteller and tell the class myths and legends of the Plains Indian tribe. She shared the myths and legends with her class, other classes and parents during their powwow.

Although it is not essential, a culminating activity with a real audience is usually very rewarding for both teachers and students. Students are very proud of what they have accomplished and are ready and willing to share their work with other students, other classes, parents, and community members. This activity brings all students together to celebrate their efforts and, if others outside of the classroom are invited to attend, it usually makes the event more meaningful to students.

During this product development portion of the Triad study, the teacher/facilitator must also assess whether any students are interested in extending their research beyond the scope of this study and doing an in-depth investigation or Type III. One of the goals of a Triad study is to allow students to demonstrate "gifted behaviors" when they have a topic of interest they wish to pursue. Although this may not occur during every study or as an extension of every study, it will happen only when the teacher is receptive to the concept and encourages students to reach beyond the regular curriculum.

As mentioned earlier, during the Native Americans of the Plains study, one of the students decided to explore her genealogy in greater depth. This student wrote, directed, and produced a play entitled "A Living Genealogy," which was videotaped for a local cable company and became a national award-winning video. The classroom teacher, enrichment specialist, and parents all acted as facilitators and assisted the student in a variety of ways during the study.

However, what helped her most were the skills she had learned during the Plains Indians study. She knew how to brainstorm and SCAMPER in order to generate ideas, make decisions, locate resources, focus her study, take notes, plan and organize her study, and create an

Chart 4
Audiences

Ask students to think about who would be their most interested and available audience. Have them start with the suggestions written below.

architects	industries
art centers	libraries
artists	musical association
book stores	NAACP
builders	neighbors
clubs	nursery school
college	P.T.A.
companies	parents
counselors	parks
designers	photographers
environmental groups	police
farmers	post office
fire department	publishing companies
friends	school board
genealogical society	scientists
general public	senior citizens
government agencies	small business
government officials	students
highway department	superintendents
historical society	teachers
hospital	theater
humane society	writers

excellent, polished product. This demonstrates clearly one of the primary benefits of the Type III training activities: **To teach students to acquire how-to-learn skills and become independent learners.** When this is accomplished, teachers have given their students a wonderful "gift."

Step Nine: Resources

Many of the dynamic things that have been discussed about these Triad studies would not have happened if we didn't have resources available for students to explore topics, locate information, and learn interesting facts from people with expertise in the field. As shown in the Native Americans of the Plains Planning Matrix, Figure 3, numerous human and library resources were used for this study.

The most dynamic aspect of the study was the resource people that shared their knowledge and expertise with the students. These individuals, who were described earlier, added a valuable dimension to the study and instilled so many things in the students that would not have been accessible in library resources. They felt and understood Tamunk's love of the Native American culture, Maria's pride in her Indian Pottery, Mr. Smith's lifetime commitment to his work with his totem poles, Mark's need for sign language because of his hearing impairment, Mrs. Brown's enjoyment of a culture that was not her own, and Francine's rhythm and song. It's impossible to measure the extent of the value in these experiences, but many of their reflections appeared in the student's own projects and final culminating activity.

In addition, one of the speakers, Mrs. Green, became the mentor to two students who, with her guidance, knowledge, and expertise, wrote their own songs and a drum accompaniment. She worked with the students three times a week for three weeks until their project was completed. Mentors have played a significant role in many Type III investigations and can also play a role in the classroom with Type III training activities.

The role the mentors play is a unique one and unlike that of a teacher, facilitator, or Type I speaker. They are community members who take time from their busy schedules to facilitate the learning process for children. They seem to find a sense of fulfillment in watching children learn and grow, sharing their knowledge, and becoming an integral part of the children's learning experiences. The following three narratives of mentor/student relationships will more clearly illustrate the significance of their work and how their role is unlike that of a speaker or classroom visitor.

Raymond G. Bentley: He wants to share his love and enthusiasm for his childhood town. Richly laden with knowledge and memories, 87 year old Mr. Raymond G. Bentley, cane in hand, eyes full of yesterday, relates with acute clarity the names and places of roads, now concrete webs, and hills where children used to sled, now house burdened and cluttered with signs of progress. Mr. Bentley's homemade ginger cookies in hand, the four children chew and listen intently, absorbing each word. With each new image, they watch the past unfold. All senses alive, they taste the flavor of yesterday, by viewing his photographs, listening to the flow of his words, and sampling his recipe.

Paula, Kristen, Betsy, and Christopher are deeply involved in a study with Mr. Bentley, their mentor. A written tour of Historical Harwinton, Connecticut becomes their goal. Many visits to Mr. Bentley's home, where he shares his book entitled **The History of Harwinton**, old maps, slides, photographs, and other memorabilia, provide the bulk of the resources. Visits to Harwinton's old homes and numerous interviews with town residents bring the children closer to their ultimate goal, the formation and completion of the book.

Numerous ginger cookies into the past, the children acknowledge Mr. Bentley's commitment by presenting him with their first copy of "A Tour of Historical Harwinton." The remaining copies are donated to the Harwinton Historical Society where tourists and residents of Harwinton can see the past revisited through four pairs of young eyes that managed to use the expertise of age as their looking glass into the past.

Robert Kenney: Two youthful athletes, flushed from recent activity, toss their baseball caps into a nearby chair and immediately change roles. Brian and Tim systematically begin their day's work with white Swiss Webster laboratory mice. At exactly 2:30 p.m., middle school science teacher Robert Kenney rushes into the room and enthusiastically greets his young proteges. They are already busy weighing their experimental subjects.

Brian and Tim are learning how it feels to be scientists and practicing professionals. With the help of their mentor, they are learning a scientific method of inquiry in order to investigate animal behavior. Their experiment is designed to determine the effects of noise on hybrid mice and is entitled **Mice, Boys and Noise**.

Once a week Mr. Kenney observes the progress and procedures the boys are using to obtain and review their research. With his guidance, they have established a specific purpose, developed a hypothesis, and outlined their procedure. The room is filled with hard rock music as heavy metal pours out of a small tape recorder in the corner of the room. One by one, the ten tiny mice are placed in a boy-built maze and their performances are timed. All data is recorded carefully on charts designed especially for this experiment.

<u>Dr. Mario D'Angelo</u>: For eight months Dr. Mario D'Angelo, a local optometrist, has spent Thursday mornings working with Todd and Michael, two sixth grade students. They are grinding lenses, watching carefully to make sure they are following Dr. D'Angelo's earlier instructions. The two boys are far beyond their earlier discussions of light and refraction. They are now well on their way to constructing their very own telescopes with Dr. D'Angelo's assistance.

As demonstrated by these dedicated individuals, the mentor has a commitment to act as an advisor, a consultant, a specialist, and a critic (Cellerino (Beecher) 1983). The teacher's tasks are to define the mentor's role, become familiar with the student-mentor endeavors, and find time to act as a liaison between student and mentor. The teacher arranges schedules between mentor and student and assists the student in the development of the study. This cooperative effort between mentor, student, and teacher results in a new shape, form, and meaning for students' learning process.

Since mentors are involved and busy in their own careers, they do not have the time or inclination to receive in-depth training in how to facilitate a Type III study. Yet, it is necessary for them to have a general understanding of their role. In an attempt to facilitate and streamline the process of mentor orientation, a pamphlet was designed to clearly and concisely delineate the roles of the mentor, the student and the teacher. The contents of the pamphlet, entitled *Guiding the Gifted,* is shown in Figure 21 and has been successfully used by teachers in efficiently and effectively training mentors.

In addition to human resources, the Native Americans of the Plains study also utilized the social studies textbook, videotapes, and magazines. The teacher reference books were numerous and only a sampling of these books were listed on the Planning Matrix, Figure 3. Student's resource books were obtained from both school and public libraries through interlibrary loan. These library resources covered many grade levels and topic areas.

How-to books also have played a role in both Type III investigations and Type III training activities. These books provide valuable methodological assistance to the facilitator by providing step-by-step instruction on how-to do numerous things. Some topics include how-to write a play, conduct an experiment, give an oral presentation, conduct various types of research, conduct an interview, become an amateur archeologist, and many others. A listing of these books appears in **The Schoolwide Enrichment Model: A Comprehensive Plan for Educational Excellence** (Renzulli & Reis, 1985) and a sample list is also shown in Figure 22.

Librarians are usually invaluable resource people throughout these

The Mentor's Role

The Student

When pursuing an Independent Study the student will be expected to. . .

Establish Goals and Objectives

To narrow the topic and focus on a specific problem

Determine Direction

To decide how to begin the investigation

Locate Related Resources

To find library and community resources relating to the topic

Plan a Time Line

To specifically state the length of time of the investigation

Create a Final Product

To determine the form of the final product

The Mentor

"The mentor is a wise and trusted counselor."

When working with a student the mentor will. . .

Act as a Guide

To become a guide and a facilitator of the child's learning, allowing independence and self-direction

Share Knowledge

To know the subject well and freely share information with the student

Demonstrate Method of Inquiry

To provide guidance in the method of inquiry appropriate to the specific area of study

Give Direction

To give the child some direction in locating relevant resources

Provide Continued Support

To be committed to the student and provide guidance as long as needed

The Classroom Teacher

The classroom teacher will. . .

Acquaint Mentor with Program

To acquaint the mentor with the goals and objectives and the nature of the Independent Study

Know Student's Topic

To be familiar with the student's study and to give assistance when needed

Coordinate Efforts

To act as a liaison between the mentor and the student

Guide Student in Planning Study

To help the student develop a management plan

Plan Schedule

To arrange the student-mentor schedule

Prepared by: M. Cellerino (Beecher)

Figure 21. The Mentor's Role

Sample List of How-To Books

Acting and Directing
Russell J. Grandstaff
National Textbook Company Publishing Group
1993
ISBN: 0-8442-5132-1
$8.95
Grades 7-12

How to Make Pop-Ups
Joan Irvine
Beech Tree Books
1991
ISBN: 0-688-07902-4
$6.95
Grades 1-8

How to Write & Sell Greeting Cards, Bumper Stickers, T-Shirts, and Other Fun Stuff
Molly Wigand
Writer's Digest Books
1992
ISBN: 0-89879-471-4
$15.95
Grades 6-12

Kid Vid: Fun-damentals of Video Instruction
Kaye Black
Zephyr Press
1989
ISBN: 0-913705-44-6
$16.95
Grades 5-12

Making Books: A Step-By-Step Guide to Your Own Publishing
Gillian Chapman and Pam Robson
The Millbrook Press
1991
ISBN: 1-56294-840-7
$6.95
Grades 2-5

Roots for Kids: A Genealogy Guide for Young People
Susan Provost Beller
Betterway Publications, Inc.
1989
ISBN: 1-55870-112-5
$8.95
Grades 4-12

So You've Got a Great Idea: Here's How to Develop It, Sell It, Market It, or Just Cash in on It!
Steve Fiffer
Addison-Wesley Publishing Company, Inc.
1986
ISBN: 0-201-11536-0
$10.95
Grades 7-12

Stamp Collecting
Neill Granger
The Millbrook Press
1994
ISBN: 1-56294-734-6
$9.95
Grades 3-6

Where Do You Get Your Ideas? Helping Young Writers Begin
Sandy Asher
Walker Publishing Company, Inc.
1987
ISBN: 0-8027-6691-9
$12.95
Grades 3-9

Worms Eat My Garbage: How to Set Up and Maintain a Worm Composting System
Mary Appelhof
Flower Press
1992
ISBN: 0-942256-03-4
$8.95
Grades 5-8

Figure 22. Sample List of How-To Books

studies. They help not only in locating relevant resources, but also in recommending resources they feel would enrich the study. They add to their usefulness by assisting students in locating materials for their independent investigations.

It is important to record the teacher and student reference materials that are of particular value to the study. This will enable the teachers to locate them the next time they engage in this study. The Planning Matrix provides a limited amount of space for this and teachers may want to record other books on the reverse side of the matrix.

Step Ten: Student Assessment

One of the most current trends in education is the use of performance-based assessment and portfolios. Since performance assessment covers many different types of testing methods that require students to demonstrate their competencies by creating an answer or a product, this type of assessment fits naturally into the Triad studies. These types of assessment include: constructed-response, writing, oral presentations and dialogue, exhibitions, experiments, and portfolios.

The constructed-responses require students to produce answers to a question rather than to select from an array of possible answers as in multiple-choice tests. Questions may have just one correct answer or may be more open-ended and allow a range of responses. These include filling in a blank; solving mathematics problems; writing short answers; and completing a figure such as a graph, illustration, or diagram. Another common type of assessment is an essay in which students write a description, analysis, explanation, or summary in one or more paragraphs. An extension of this type of assessment is writing. This is probably the most common subject tested by performance assessment methods. Guidelines are developed for both analytical and holistic scoring in the form of rubrics and checklists. Both the mechanics and the writing process are assessed in this manner through these two scoring methods. Oral presentations, exhibitions, and experiments can also be evaluated by developing rubrics and checklists.

As shown on the Planning Matrix (Figure 3) of the Native American of the Plains study, student writing was scored in both a holistic and analytic manner. Students played an active role in scoring the writing by participating in peer editing. Students were trained in both scoring techniques and were familiar with the value of each holistic score. In this same study, rubrics and accompanying checklists were developed for oral presentations. Students helped to establish the criteria used in the checklist and also had an opportunity to assess themselves on their presentations. The primary goal was to have students become experts at assessing their own presentations and those of their peers.

Journal entries allowed for a more informal assessment of student understanding. The journal became a diary for the students' study and they imagined themselves as a Native American. They tried to "walk in the shoes" of that young Indian and write the type of diary they thought the child would have written.

The content of the study was assessed through the end of chapter test which included multiple choice questions, fill-in the blanks, short answers, and paragraph-long essays. The test was administered at the end of the chapter and at they conclusion of the study. The items tested also included information students had shared with each other as a result of the study.

The final step was the **assessment of student products**. In addition to teacher assessment, students should also assess their own work and participate in the establishment of the criteria that will be used in this assessment. The *Student Product Assessment Form* (SPAF) (Renzulli & Reis, 1985) was developed in order to assess both individual aspects as well as overall excellence of products of high ability youngsters and is shown in Appendix C. A modification of the overall assessment section of SPAF is recommended for most Triad classroom studies. The criteria might include some of the following:

- Originality of the Idea
- Achieved Objective(s)
- Used Multiple Resources
- Quality of Work
- Care and Attention to Detail

This list can be transferred to a checklist and a specific number of points given for each criteria. Students can score themselves on each item and the teacher can award points. If there is a difference between the two scores on any item, the student and teacher can discuss these differences and decide on the appropriate score. If it is necessary to grade the projects, the total score for each project can be translated into a grade. This is an excellent example of performance-based student self-assessment.

A Triad study does not require teachers and curriculum developers to immediately change their present methods of evaluating students. However, because of the nature of the studies, students will create products that will be difficult to score by more traditional methods of evaluation. Rubrics and classroom checklists let children know exactly how they will be evaluated prior to the beginning of their studies. If students are allowed to participate in the establishment of the criteria and allowed to assess their own work, they generally become more actively engaged in the entire process. At the same time, they are

developing the higher level thinking skills of analysis, synthesis, and evaluation.

Step Eleven: Timeline for Implementation

The best plans are doomed to fail unless a timeline is established for the implementation of the study. A timeline enables the planners to determine when the various speakers, activities, and lessons will be taught and when independent projects will begin and end. It enables teachers to make appropriate connections among the disciplines and activities, quickly view the entire spectrum and sequence of the study, and plan effectively and efficiently with other teachers if they are working as a team.

A Timeline for Implementation (Chart 5) was created for the Triad studies. This chart provides space for the planners to record the discipline and the specific activities or lessons on the week and day they will be taught. The Planning Matrix provides the data that will be recorded on the timeline. The contents of the matrix are reviewed and decisions made about the sequence of events. The information is then transferred to the timeline by discipline. Chart 5, pages one and two, provides adequate space for planning an eight week study. The chart can be modified in any way to better meet specific timeline requirements and can also be enlarged to provide more space for ideas. A completed timeline of the Native Americans of the Plains study is included in Chart 6.

A Logical Sequence

The logical sequence for a Triad study is shown in Chart 7. This will provide the implementers with a listing of the primary activities that are included in all Triad studies. This is also an attempt to simplify the process from beginning to end and to guide teachers throughout the study.

Step Twelve: Evaluation of the Study

At the conclusion of the study, it is important to spend time evaluating the study from the point of view of both the students and the teachers. A Student Evaluation Form and Teacher Evaluation Form were developed specifically for these studies as shown in Figures 23 and 24. The results of these evaluations are synthesized and analyzed and the study is modified and adjusted in order to improve it the next time it is implemented.

Chart 5
Timeline for Implementation

Teacher(s) _____ School _____ Grade Level (s) _____ Topic/Theme/Unit of Study _____ Duration of Study _____

WEEKS		WEEK 1					WEEK 2					WEEK 3					WEEK 4				
DAYS		DAYS:					DAYS:					DAYS:					DAYS:				
DISCIPLINE/ SUBJECTS		1	2	3	4	5	6	7	8	9	10	11	12	13	14	15	16	17	18	19	20

Timeline Developed by Margaret Beecher

Page 1

Chart 5
Timeline for Implementation

Teacher(s) ————— School ————— Grade Level (s) ————— Topic/Theme/Unit of Study ————— Duration of Study —————

DISCIPLINE/ SUBJECTS	WEEKS DAYS	WEEK 5					WEEK 6					WEEK 7					WEEK 8				
		DAYS:					DAYS:					DAYS:					DAYS:				
		21	22	23	24	25	26	27	28	29	30	31	32	33	34	35	36	37	38	39	40

Timeline Developed by Margaret Beecher

Chart 6
Timeline for Implementation

Teacher(s) Margaret Beecher **School** Smith School **Grade Level(s)** 4 **Topic/Theme/Unit of Study** Native Americans--Plains **Duration of Study** Eight Weeks

DISCIPLINE/ SUBJECTS	WEEK 1 (Days 1–5)	WEEK 2 (Days 6–10)	WEEK 3 (Days 11–15)	WEEK 4 (Days 16–20)
Social Studies	Text: **From Sea to Shining Sea**, Unit 2, Chapter 5; Tamunk: The Culture; Video 2	Smith: Totem Poles; Video 3; Letters to Reservations	Brown: Arts and Artifacts--Debriefing Presentations; Create Topic Web; Decision Making--Topic	Notetaking
	Review Content Area Reading Strategies; Interest Development Center			
Language Arts	Student Survey; Myths and Legends; Smith: Sign Language Mini-Course	Book Talks	Reading Myths and Legends	Writing Myths and Legends
Math/Science	Text: **Ecosystems of the Plains**; Chance and Probability	Indian Guessing and Dice Games	Jones: Indian Pottery; Video 1; Estimation--Buffalo Past and Present	Plains Ecosystem Simulation; Brainstorming: Teepee Activity
Art/Music	Smith: Picture Writing and Painting; Green: Mini-Course: Indian Songs and Dances (Twice a week)	Quillwork and Beadwork	Ceremonial Dress and Clothing Design	Construct Teepee
Religion				Design Personal Shield; Ceremonies and Rituals: Sun Dance
Physical Education	Smith: Origin of Lacrosse/Playing Lacrosse			

Chart 6
Timeline for Implementation

Teacher(s) __Margaret Beecher__   School __Smith School__   Grade Level(s) __4__   Topic/Theme/Unit of Study __Native Americans--Plains__   Duration of Study __Eight Weeks__

DISCIPLINE/ SUBJECTS	WEEK 5 — DAYS: 21 22 23 24 25	WEEK 6 — DAYS: 26 27 28 29 30	WEEK 7 — DAYS: 31 32 33 34 35	WEEK 8 — DAYS: 36 37 38 39 40
Social Studies	Compare and Contrast Dwellings and Plains, Desert and Northwestern Tribes →	→	Causes and Effects of Conflict	Self Assessment
Language Arts	Decision Making-Product; Descriptive Writing (Expository)	Modified Management Plans; Research Skills; Research and Investigation	Oral Presentation Skills	Study Completion; Presentations
Math/Science	Maintain Terrarium; Creative Problem Solving Simulation		Product Development and Completion	
Art/Music	Sing Indian Songs and Play Instruments	Prepare for Powwow	Individual Student Products	
Religion	Role Play Sweat Lodge Ceremony	Prepare Skits for Powwow	Rehearse	
Physical Education		Plan Teams for Lacrosse Game for Day of Powwow		Play Lacrosse
All Disciplines	Begin Planning Powwow	Group Management Plan; Divide Tasks	Invitations to Parents	Culminating Activity--The Powwow

Timeline Developed by Margaret Beecher

Chart 7
TRIAD IN THE CLASSROOM
A LOGICAL SEQUENCE FOR A STUDY

<u>Sequence</u>	<u>Activities</u>

1st	Type I Enrichment and Content
	    Interest Development Center
	    Speakers
	    Videos, Filmstrips, Films, etc.
	    Textbooks

2nd	Type II Process Training
	    Brainstorming
	    Webbing
	    Decision Making

3rd	Selection of Individual Project Topics
	    Individual Interest Areas Determined
	    Research Begun
	    Problem Focusing

4th	Product Selection
	    Brainstorming Specific Product Ideas
	    Decision Making
	    Selection of Product

5th	Modified Management Plan
	    Specific Area of Study
	    Getting Started
	    Resources
	    Product and Audience

6th	Product Development
	    Edit, Revise, Rewrite, Polish
	    Product Completion
	    Presentation Preparation (Oral or Written)

7th	The Audience
	    Explore All Possibilities
	    Contact Group, Association, Societies, News Media
	    Share Product

ENRICHMENT TRIAD IN THE CLASSROOM
STUDENT EVALUATION FORM

Please answer these questions the best that you can. There are no right or wrong answers. It is not necessary to write your name on the paper.

1. Did you enjoy working on this unit?   Yes No
2. Were you able to choose your own topic?   Yes No
3. Were you able to research and study on your own?   Yes No
4. Did you use more than one book or resource in your study? Yes No
5. Did you have enough time to work on your project?   Yes No
6. Are you happy with the work you have done?   Yes No
7. Would you like to do this kind of study again with a different topic? Yes No
8. How much did you learn through this unit and your studies?

   _____

   _____

9. What were the most important parts of this study?

   _____

   _____

10. What did you enjoy most about this study?

   _____

   _____

11. How was this study different from studies you usually do?

   _____

   _____

12. In what ways could we make the study better the next time?

   _____

   _____

Developed by Mary Brackett Sullivan, 1983

Figure 23. Enrichment Triad in the Classroom—Student Evaluation Form

**THE ENRICHMENT TRIAD IN THE CLASSROOM
TEACHER EVALUATION FORM**

In an attempt to make the Triad studies in the regular classroom a valuable experience for both teachers and students, we are seeking feedback on the effectiveness of the study that was recently completed. Will you please answer the following questions:

1. What did you, as the teacher, gain from the experience?

2. What do you think your students gained?

3. What are the strengths of this approach?

4. Is there anything you would like to see changed? If so, what?

5. Additional comments:

Developed by Mary Brackett Sullivan, 1983

Figure 24. The Enrichment Triad in the Classroom—Teacher Evaluation Form

Conclusion

The purpose of the step-by-step description of an Enrichment Triad classroom study has been to provide the curriculum developer or classroom teacher with all of the information, methodologies, strategies, lessons, and forms necessary to successfully and independently implement this model. The hundreds of teachers who have received training in this model and are implementing it in their classrooms, have requested this type of how-to book to use as a resource. Although an elementary study was used as the primary example, this model has been implemented at all grade levels. In the next section, examples from the primary, elementary, middle, and high school levels are presented and briefly described.

CHAPTER 4

GRADE LEVEL MODIFICATIONS

Grade Level Modifications

Section 1: Primary Triad Study

The Enrichment Triad studies employ many of the same teaching methodologies currently recommended and developmentally appropriate for early childhood and primary grade levels. Whole language, integrated language arts, experiential learning, authentic assessment, developmentally appropriate learning experiences, and flexible grouping are all concepts that fill the literature related to young learners and are incorporated into the Triad studies. When these concepts are brought to life in the Triad studies and translated into classroom practice, they excite children into becoming engaged in meaningful learning experiences. This is what was taking place in one primary classroom as they learned about their southern neighbors in Mexico. They were literally using all of their senses to hear, see, taste, smell, and touch another country. The Planning Matrix in Figure 25a clearly outlines all aspects of the study of Mexico. Several areas will be highlighted here, especially those that require modifications from the original model described in Chapter 3.

Challenging Activities

Some studies at the primary level become just a series of activities with no clear direction or definable outcomes. Children seem to be engaging in many activities and enjoying what they are doing, but when teachers begin to examine exactly what is happening, they sometimes see very little learning taking place. Although it is valid and critical for students to enjoy school activities, teachers know students can enjoy learning and that the two are not mutually exclusive.

In planning the Triad study of Mexico, the teachers clearly defined what they wanted their students to know, what they wanted them to accomplish, and the attitudes and attributes that were important for the students to acquire at the conclusion of the study. Thus, the activities were well-planned, purposeful, developmentally appropriate, and FUN.

The lessons employed a variety of instructional strategies which accommodated the different learning styles of the students. The students were challenged in many ways and were continuously learning new information and skills. Triad studies are always intended to challenge students, regardless of grade level.

Type I Speakers

The Mexican study included many speakers who taught children about deserts, animal habitats, iguanas, Mexican songs and dances, art and artifacts, and foods. Others taught them how to pronounce their names, numbers, colors, and basic phrases in the Spanish language. Several people came bearing foods for children to taste or prepare themselves. When students could not read or were limited in their ability to read, the speakers played a significant role in the students' acquisition of knowledge. Speakers provided a wealth of background information, which allowed all of the children to contribute to classroom discussions and actively participate in all aspects of the study.

The idea of Type I speakers was discussed in detail earlier in this book. It is mentioned again here to reinforce its effectiveness with children at the primary grade level. Teachers are sometimes hesitant to have speakers at the primary level, because they are concerned that the presentations will be too sophisticated. Likewise, speakers are often reluctant to visit primary classrooms, because they are unsure how to address the young students. In reality, speakers prove to be excellent resources and add a richness to the study, as long as teachers have paved the way for their visit. Teachers can accomplish this task through a discussion with the speaker prior to the presentation, in which the teacher gives him/her some understanding of the students' general listening levels and the kind of information to share.

Interest Development Center

An Interest Development Center is a MUST at the primary grade level. This center immediately provides a critical hands-on dimension to whatever topic is being studied. During the study of Mexico, the room was filled with Mexican picture books, musical instruments, pinatas, toys, pottery, clothing, pictures, photograph albums, etc. that children could look at and touch. All of these things were there throughout the study to stimulate interest and curiosity about Mexico.

Webbing

As illustrated in the study of Native Americans of the Plains study, webbing plays an important role in the Triad studies. However, this strategy takes on a new dimension in a Kindergarten classroom if most of the students cannot read. The teacher may choose to create a word

Interdisciplinary Unit of Study
Planning Matrix

Teacher: Michele Griffith & Hannah Shapiro   School: Duffy   Grade Level: K-1   Topic/Theme/Unit of Study: MEXICO   Duration of Study: Four Weeks

Student Outcomes	Disciplines	Type I Content and Introductory Activities	Type II Process Training Lessons	Type III Interest - Based Independent Projects/Studies	Resources Needed:
Content: The student will: • describe the following components of the Mexican culture: - clothing - houses - flag - language - crafts - foods • identify the three biomes in Mexico: desert, rain forest, and mountain region. **Process:** The student will: • compare and contrast the culture of Mexico and the United States through a series of hands-on activities. • locate Mexico on a map of North America and the world. **Attitudes and Attributes:** The student will: • develop an appreciation of the Mexican culture.	Language Arts	Interest Development Center: Musical instruments, clothing, picture books, toys, pottery, etc. Read: **Mexico: The Land and the People** Introduce Spanish Language: Basic phrases, colors, numbers Speaker: Otelia Bonner*	Writing postcards home from trip (use temporary spelling) Learning colors, words through games Compare and Contrast U.S. and Mexico: clothing, flags, foods, language, crafts, houses (using graphic organizers) Webbing the topic: "Write and Say"	**CULMINATING ACTIVITIES** ** Trip to Local Mexican Restaurant - Buffet (Taco Bar) ** **Mexican Fiesta** **"A Taste of Mexico"**	**Resources Needed:** **A Sampling of Fiction and Non-Fiction** (Read to Students and Displayed) **Books:** **Mexico in Pictures** (Geography Series) **Journey Through Mexico**, Barbara Thomas **Hill of Fire**, Thomas Lewis **Mexico, The Land and It's People,** John Hubbard **Count Your Way Through Mexico**, Jim Mashins **Arroz Con Leche - Popular Songs and Rhymes from Latin America,** Lulu Delacre **Gus was a Mexican Ghost**, Jane Thayer **Pepito's Story**, Eugene Fern **A New True Book- Mexico**, Karen Jacobson **Passport to Mexico**, Carmen Irizary **Resource People:** See Type I listing on Matrix and Classroom Resource File for addresses and phone numbers
	Math	Measurement: Creating a unifix cube snake Counting to ten in Spanish What is an Aztec Calendar? Patterning using Mexican flag Read: **Count Your Way Through Mexico** Probability: **Mexican Jumping Bean Math**	Graphing favorite Mexican foods Creating simplified Aztec Calendars Play number game with Mexican Hats Make flags: Compare with American Flag Patterning on snakes and belts	Fiesta included: Simulated desert and rain forest in the school hallway with students work: unifix snakes, clay iguanas, monkeys and parrots, sloths, jaguars, humming birds	**Video Tapes:** Introduction to Mexico Kids Explore Mexico **Cassette Tapes:** Grandes Ecitas Amigos Cantando El Club de Mickey Mouse

	Social Studies	Videotapes: **Introduction to Mexico** and **Kids Explore Mexico**
		Life in Mexico/Mexican Dances
		Speaker: Jack Perez
		Slides and artifacts of Mexico
		Mexican foods: A buffet
		Speaker/Chef: Dr. Smith
		Geography: deserts, mountains, rain forest / location on map
			Simulated trip to Mexico:
			Make passports, tickets, suitcases
			Map reading:
			  Locating Mexico on map of North America and the World
			  Finding Geographic Regions
			Decision Making: What to bring on trip!
				Classroom Displays:
				Bark Paintings
				Papel Picado
				Mexican Flags
				Suitcases & Postcards
				Woven Belts
				Mexican Paper Dolls
				Lacquerware
				Paper Mache Pinata
					Big Books:
					Enrico's Project
					Mexico - written by teachers Michele and Hannah

	Science	Read: **Hill of Fire** to introduce volcanoes Desert terrain and animal habitats Speaker: Francie Brown Visit by "live" Iguana Presenter: Pat Droney The birth of chickens	Create clay adobe village Make a volcano/Create eruption Create a rainforest environment in terrariums Make a cactus garden Construct pyramids Create clay iguanas Hatch baby chickens	Performance in Auditorium ABC's of Mexico (Class song written by teachers) Friendship and other Mexican songs Mexican Hat Dance Breaking a Pinata	**Student Assessment:** Daily Performance: Observation Projects: Informal Assessment

	Art/ Music	Mexican Songs/Spanish Names
		Speaker: Susan Rodriguez
		(Students learned names in Spanish)
		Mexican Songs and Dances
		Singer/Dancer: Cheryl Jones
		Art Projects introduced with book and/or artifact
			Learn Mexican Hat Dance
			Learn and sing songs
			Create decorative paper hangings
			Papel picado
			Make sombreros and serapes with Mexican designs
				Mexican Foods:
				(Made by parents)
				Tortillas and Tortilla Chips
				Nachos
				Guacamole
					- Trip to Mexico
					  • Suitcases, Tickets, Passports
					
					- Temporary Spelling
					  • Write and illustrate something you learned about Mexico

Getting Started Locate library and community resources Develop an Interest Development Center Create a content web Acquire the Mexican Artifact Box from the district resource center Contact resource people and schedule presentations Develop a timeline for the study Begin planning lessons Schedule auditorium for culminating activity			Decision Making/Group Planning: Students plan and set-up a classroom Mexican restaurant and market Students plan field :trip to restaurant Students plan "Fiesta" foods to serve songs to sing		

*Name Changed

Matrix Developed by Margaret Beecher

Figure 25a. Interdisciplinary Unit of Study—Planning Matrix (Mexico)

Mexico Web

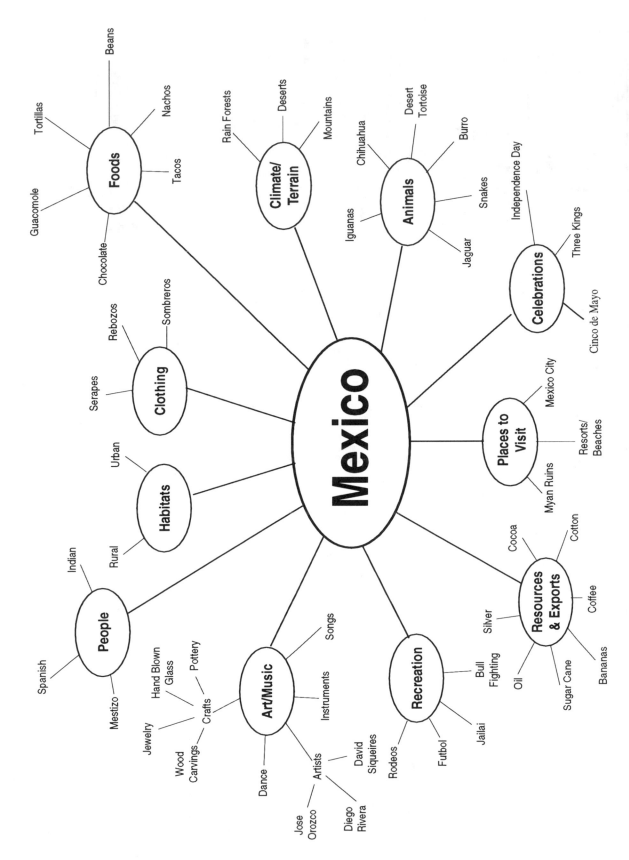

Figure 25b. Curriculum Web (Mexico)

web, a pictorial web, or combine words and pictures in a web. Students can either draw, color, or cut pictures out of magazines and then categorize them on a bulletin board. If a study is taught to children who have some reading ability, a simplified version of a web can and should be created and placed somewhere in the classroom. Interested students can add to the web if and when they choose to do so. Figure 25b illustrates the web used in the Mexico study.

Simulations

A trip to Mexico was simulated during this study. Students made passports and tickets, decorated their suitcases, packed, boarded the plane, and were ready to go. Since teachers cannot actually take students to all of the places they study, the next best thing is to imagine themselves there. This is particularly effective with younger children, although it certainly can be effective at all grade levels.

This is a wonderful time to develop the students' visual imagery by having them close their eyes and travel with the teacher as he/she narrates their trip. In preparation for the trip students can view a video, listen to some picture books, and watch slides. They will need some background knowledge just as any person would like to have before he/she takes a trip. There are many opportunities for simulations during a study. Simulations are designed to help students develop their creative thinking and, as a result, bring them to new and exciting places.

A different kind of simulation was experienced by students when they created a rain forest environment in individual student terrariums. This helped the children have a hands-on experience with the rain forest and get a miniaturized view of this biome. They learned about the topography, animals, and weather in a rain forest region. A small lizard enjoyed its home in the terrarium for the remainder of a school year.

Group Versus Independent Work

Group work is the hallmark of the primary Triad studies since most students do not conduct independent studies based on their own interests at this level. Since many of the skills and experiences are new to the students and require more of the teacher's guidance than at the upper grade levels, the activities are introduced to the students as a whole group. In the Mexico Triad study each student in the class made a Mexican flag, designed their own sombreros and serapes, and created replicas of Mexican crafts such as paper picados, bark paintings, lacquer ware, and other Mexican crafts.

Many of the skills of independence are modeled in this group process. For example, on several occasions, the students participated in group decision making. They decided as a whole class what would be displayed in their classroom desert and rain forest environments.

The students also helped teachers plan a Fiesta for their parents. This group work was modeled on chart paper for the students and used as a guide when they completed the tasks they planned.

However, there will be some kindergarten students and first graders who are reading several grade levels above their classmates and have strong interests in specific areas. These students may wish to explore their interests and other new and exciting topics. If given the opportunity, students may want to conduct Type III independent investigations and extend beyond the present curriculum. With the assistance of teachers, enrichment specialists, and/or mentors, primary students can and should be allowed to pursue their interests.

Higher Level Thinking

One of the objectives of the study was to compare and contrast certain aspects of the cultures of Mexico and the United States. This was done at the conclusion of the study when students were asked to use higher level thinking and analyze the information they had learned. The teachers assisted students by creating a bulletin board that provided a visual comparison of the two cultures.

The Fiesta

The Fiesta was a very successful event. Parents were invited to walk through the student-created rain forest and desert and see the numerous displays in the classroom, including the living terrarium and newly hatched chicks. The children wore sombreros and serapes and performed for their parents in the school's auditorium. They sang an ABC song about Mexico, written by their teachers, and performed skits which captured the essence of the culture. A Mexican buffet prepared by students and parents was the evening's finale.

The teachers made this culture come to life for their students. They skillfully integrated the concepts discussed in Chapter 3 into the studies, and as a result, children enjoyed a variety of unique and exciting learning experiences. "Sombreros" off to them for making learning real!

Section 2: A Modified Elementary Model

The teacher who developed the Triad Immigration study, in Figure 26, is truly talented at developing and implementing Enrichment Triad studies. The study, as outlined on the Planning Matrix, has been taught in a third grade classroom for several years. Several unique modifications from the original study will be highlighted and explained in this chapter.

Chapter 4

Interdisciplinary Unit of Study
Planning Matrix

Teacher: Nancy Thurmond   School: Huckleberry School   Grade Level: 3   Topic/Theme/Unit of Study: IMMIGRATION   Duration of Study: Eight Weeks

Student Outcomes

Content:

The student will:
- explain why people immigrated to the United States.
- describe the immigration process and how an individual becomes a citizen.
- identify and list contributions made to the United States by immigrants.
- explain the history and symbolism of the Statue of Liberty.

Process:

The student will:
- learn the following research skills:
  - using encyclopedias
  - locating information from reference books
  - using the library
  - compiling information from many sources into a report
- compare and contrast the Immigration process past and present.

Attitudes and Attributes:

The student will:
- appreciate the similarities and differences in people around the world.
- establish connections among diverse people.

Getting Started

Gather resources from school and town libraries.

Locate, contact, and schedule Type I speakers.

Develop Interest Center with students.

Plan trip to Nursing Home.

Plan Process Training Lessons including Talents Lessons.

Disciplines	Type I Content and Introductory Activities	Type II Process Training Lessons	Type III Interest-Based Independent Projects/Studies
Language Arts	Trade Books (Multiple Copies) Call Mr. Charlie - Black American; Caesar Chavez - Migrant Workers; Felita - Child's Adjustment Tools. Interest Development Center Books from libraries, students and teachers; realia from other countries; ethnic clothing.	Webbing Topic: Six Categories complete following speakers, timeline and video. Decision Making: Selection of Topic Category/Group. Reports of Famous Immigrants. Notetaking: Facts from Visiting Speakers	Create Statue of Liberty Birthday Cake "100 Candles". Write a recipe book of Ethnic recipes. Oral History & Video Tape: An Interview with Grandfather. Simulate the Process of Becoming a Citizen
Language Arts	Pictoral - Timeline Immigration Key events and people (Sequenced on hallway wall). Immigration to the United States Presenter: Immigration Official, State of Connecticut. Video: Statue of Liberty	Creating Skits: All students combine facts with fiction "Coming to America". Writing newspaper advertisements for ethnic restaurants. Following directions/extending vocabulary	Construct a model of a tenement house. Write original poems. Create fate cards for Irish fortune cakes. Make Mobile on Immigration - green card, citizenship papers and photographs
Social Studies	Textbook: People of the World "Contributions of Immigrants". Experience of a Cuban Immigrant (Foods: Black Bean Soup) Speaker - Mr. Rivera. Russian Music, Songs and Food Speaker - Ms. Mabose	Creating personal timelines on adding machine paper. Researching their genealogy ancestry booklets family trees. Ukrainian egg dying	Write a storybook for a talkshow host interviews with recent immigrants. Make a paper mache model of Statue of Liberty - "Lighted". Write comic book (cartoons) & explain why people would come to America
Social Studies	Immigration by Luxury Liner from Hungary Speaker- Mr. Roth. Puerto Rican Immigration: A Feeling of Homelessness Speaker- Mrs. Roberts. Life in India - Music, Foods Dance, Songs, Customs	Data collecting sessions/cooperative groups collect and share information (usually three sessions). Interviewing skills/forming questions (prior to visit to Nursing Home)	Design and sew ethnic costumes. Write newspaper editorial. Write a rap song about Immigrants' feelings and adjustments. Create a living diagram - Setting Ellis Island - A brief snapshot of an event through a skit.
Social Studies	Speaker- Mrs. Nukhenee. Slide Presentation: Adoption of Philippine Children Speaker - Ms. Mabose. Immigration from Saudi Arabia Differences in Customs, Foods. Speaker - Mrs. Fokhouri	Learning Ethnic Dances - "Dutch Shoes" Presenter - E. Sister. Song: "Coming to America" Neil Diamond. Playing Ethnic Games	Write a rap song about Immigrants' feelings and adjustments. Use visual imagery to create a picture of the long trip across the Atlantic. Construct a model of a steamship
Social Studies	Field Trips to Nursing Home All students interview residents about their ancestry. Children create country banners. Weekly Reader Skills Books: Statue of Liberty, Selected Articles	Talents Lessons: Communications similes. Productive thinking. Forecasting: Causes and effects of Immigration. Planning the studies	Create a game using Immigration facts and timeline. Design a law that would help immigrants and adjustments. Become a storyteller and tell stories about your own imaginary immigration

Resources Needed:

Textbooks:
Peoples of the World, Osbourne
Cities and Suburbs, Economy
Statue of Liberty, Weekly Reader Skill Builders

Resource Books By Country:
India:
Karl, the Elephant, Dhang Opal Mukerj
A Little Princess, Francis Burnett
Sweden:
Klara's New World, Jeanette Winter
Norway:
Viking Adventure, Clyde Robert Booth
China:
Yeh-Shen, Ai-Ling Louie
Egypt:
The Winged Cat, Deborah Lattimore
France:
Linnea In Monet's Garden, Christina Bjork and Lena Anderson
Denmark:
The Ugly Duckling, Hans Christian Andersen
Israel:
Purlon, Molly Cone
Bar Mitzvah, Howard Greenfield

Other Resource Books:
Immigrant Girl, Brett Harvey
Onion John, Joseph Krumguld
Immigration I, Cobblestone
Immigration II, Cobblestone
Children of the World

Speakers:
See Content and Introductory Activities

Student Assessment:

Language arts/social studies worksheets
Reports of famous people: (Scored holistically and analytically)
Teacher-made tests: fill-in the blank, short answer, and essay. (Information based on tests, speakers, and other student and group reports.)
Student projects and oral presentations (Scored by teacher based on an established ratio)

Matrix Developed by Margaret Beecher

Figure 26. Interdisciplinary Unit of Study—Planning Matrix (Immigration)

Immigration Web

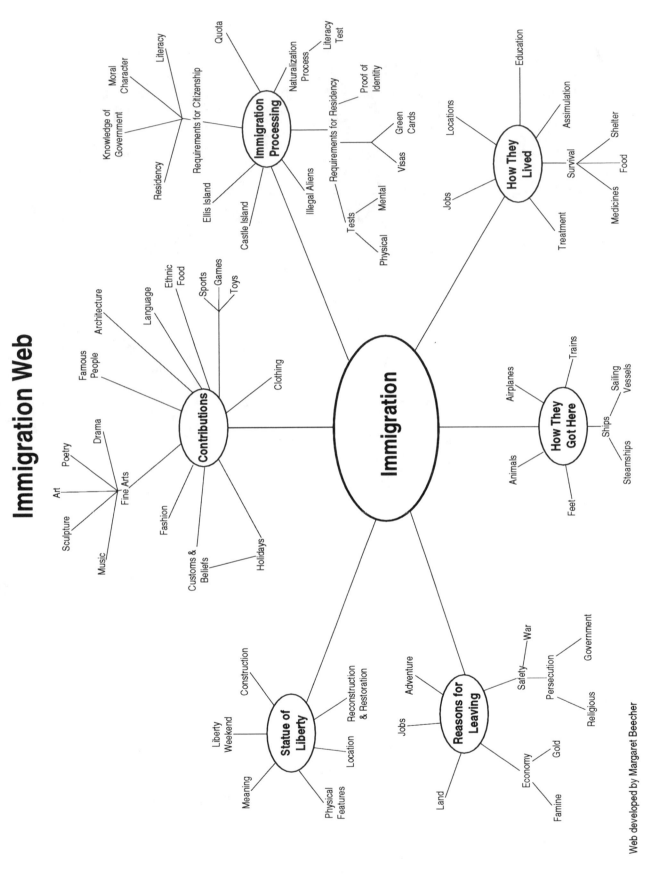

Web developed by Margaret Beecher

Figure 27. Immigration Web

Integrating Two Disciplines

As mentioned earlier, a Triad or integrated study does not have to include all of the disciplines. The study of Immigration combined the language arts and social studies curricula in a creative, innovative manner. Authentic connections were made between these two disciplines and they were taught in a completely integrated (Fogarty, 1991) rather than a parallel fashion (Jacobs, 1989). Writing, vocabulary, grammar, and other process training lessons, as well as fiction and nonfiction reading material, were directly related to the study of Immigration.

Remarkable Resource People

This study included many resource people who visited the third grade classroom and shared a wealth of information in both the cognitive and affective domains. All of the speakers, with the exception of the State of Connecticut Immigration Officer, were immigrants who came to the classroom to share the trials, tribulations, rewards, and joys of emigrating to the United States. They also brought their native countries into the classroom in the form of favorite ethnic foods, clothing, and other memorabilia. They often taught the children songs and dances that they remembered so well from their homelands. The classroom came to life with a rhythm and beat that energized the students and made their learning fun.

Some of the presenters dispelled stereotypical beliefs about immigration. Many people believe that immigrants travel to America in unpleasant conditions aboard large, crowded, uncomfortable ships. Mr. Roth described his trip on a luxury liner and the elegance of his surroundings. Another common belief is that people feel grateful and joyous to be in our country. Mrs. Roberts told students that she had a feeling of homelessness and felt that she didn't belong anywhere. She no longer felt she could return to her homeland and she didn't feel a sense of "belonging" to the United States. Orphans from other countries that were adopted and emigrated to the United States added yet another perspective for the students. By bringing so many speakers into the classroom, the teacher truly made her students' learning REAL.

Locating Resource People

Many people often ask the teacher of this study, Nancy Thurmond, how she finds individuals to visit her classroom and she quickly replies, "They're everywhere!" She tells a story of waiting in line at the bank and listening for people with accents. Although she laughs as she tells this story, it does indicate the commitment she has to finding people who will share with her students.

Nancy finds speakers all around her. The speakers are mostly the

parents of her students past and present. She conducts a survey of all parents at the beginning of each school year and her resource file has grown over the years. She also asks colleagues and friends to visit the class if they have an area of expertise that would enhance a study. The yellow pages of her telephone directory are also tattered from using them to find other people and places.

Sometimes she takes her class to the resources. During the Immigration study she made arrangements for her class to visit a local Nursing Home. The students and interested residents met in a large meeting room. The students made large banners with the names of many countries on them and held them up in different parts of the room. The elderly people went to the part of the room that represented the country where they were born. A small group of students waited in each section to questions and conduct interviews. The residents and students certainly learned a great deal about each other that day!

Webbing and Small Group Organization

Nancy used a slightly modified method of webbing that has proven to be very effective. Webbing was conducted after students had been exposed to the speakers, established a historical timeline of Immigration, and viewed a video of the students' presentations from previous years. Students then began to brainstorm all the words that related to Immigration. During this process, the students browsed through resource books and added words they thought were important or meaningful to the study. As the children were brainstorming, the teacher wrote the words on the chalkboard. At this time, they were not in the form of a web.

When the students finished brainstorming, they categorized the words on another chalkboard. The teacher facilitated this process and guided students to organize the ideas into six categories. The teacher used the six categories to help students select their independent projects. They used decision making to determine the categories they liked best. The teacher asked them to list their first and second choices and placed them in groups based on this information. Each student selected a sub-topic within a category that did or did not appear on the web. This was a unique way of grouping students and modifying a Triad study. Figure 27 illustrates the web used in the Immigration study.

Pictorial Timeline

An excellent teaching strategy was used in order to provide the students with knowledge and understanding of the sequence of important events and famous immigrants involved in this Triad study. Students searched through resources and resource books in the classroom and, with the help of the teacher, located enough information to create a pictorial timeline. Students selected events or people and illustrated, labeled, and dated them. These pictures were hung in sequence by date in the hallway outside the classroom. The students used this timeline as a reference throughout the study.

Data Collecting Sessions

Several data collecting sessions, which were also unique to Nancy's studies, were held during the study prior to the beginning the actual project work. The students' primary goals were to gather information about the category their group had selected and find facts about the topic they were planning to explore. The teacher's goal was to have students become researchers and find the information they were seeking in order to become teachers for the other students.

Students worked in their cooperative, categorical groups and collected and shared information with each other. This information was sometimes written on charts, shared with the whole class, and then hung on one of the walls as a reference for the class. The facts were also written on study sheets and given to members of the other groups. The purpose of this activity was to pass information on to other students because **all** of the students were responsible for knowing the information which had been gathered by each group. The teacher used this as the basis for student quizzes that assessed students' content knowledge of the topic. A Study Sheet for the Immigration Unit and two student quizzes are shown in Figures 28, 29, and 30.

Independent Projects

The project or independent work began following the class webbing of the study. Students selected the category of their choice from the six categories in the web. Based on this selection, they were placed in small groups. Once again they used the web as a reference and students within each group then selected their own topic to study in that category. Children were allowed to work individually, in pairs or triads, but their topics and tasks had to be clearly defined.

The teacher gave each group a portion of the room in which to work and ultimately display their work. It was interesting to watch groups share the space with each other and work "cooperatively." They were very successful! The tables, walls, floors, and ceilings were covered and filled with student work. They all took pride in their sections of this learning classroom.

Audiences

The students in this class had many audiences for their work. At the end of each study they invited parents to visit and made presentations of their work to the whole group. Parents, grandparents, and friends

STUDY SHEET: IMMIGRATION UNIT
UNITED COUNTRIES OF AMERICA

NAME: ROOM:
DATE: SOCIAL STUDIES:

All Americans are immigrants or are descendants of immigrants.

Reasons for Leaving:

1. Personal freedom and economic opportunity are the two main reasons people enter the United States.

2. Many people immigrated to America to escape famine. For example, many Irish came during the potato famine.

3. Many people immigrated into America to escape persecution. For example, many Jews left Hungary in 1956.

4. Many came to own land. Many peasants were not allowed to own land in their native countries.

5. Some wanted to get rich quick and discover gold.

How They Got Here:

1. Many had to save money for passage.

2. Until 1850, the immigrants traveled in sailing vessels.

3. The average trip from Liverpool, England to New York took 40 days.

4. After 1850, many came by steamship.

5. Steerage was confined space below deck.

6. One in ten failed to survive the crossing due to harsh conditions.

7. Indians migrated by walking from Asia to America 20,000 years ago.

8. Today many immigrants travel to the U.S. by plane.

9. Many Cubans migrated to the U.S. by rowboat.

Figure 28. Study Sheet: Immigration Unit—United Countries of America

Immigration Processing: Page 2

1. Immigrants must pass tests to show they are physically and mentally healthy.

2. Immigrants that traveled in steerage passed through Ellis Island.

3. Immigrants cannot have contagious diseases.

4. Immigration laws allow only 20,000 people per country each year to enter the U.S. This is a quota system.

5. An alien must live in the U.S. for five years, read and speak English, have good moral character and understand U.S. government to become a United States citizen.

6. The process of an alien becoming a citizen is called naturalization.

7. Immigrants receive visas to allow them to be residents or to live in the U.S.

8. A refugee is a person who leaves his country because of a real fear of his/her government.

9. Today many immigrants are processed at airports.

How They Lived:

1. All new ethnic groups met with prejudice from people that were already settled in the United States. The Ku Klux Klan and the Know Nothing Party were two groups that reacted to immigration.

2. Chinese and Irish immigrants built many railroads.

3. Many immigrants from Scandinavia worked as lumbermen in Oregon.

4. Many Welsh and Poles worked in coal and steel industries.

5. Many Italian immigrants took jobs in heavy industry or on the railroads.

6. Many immigrants settled in their Lower East Side of New York City.

7. Many lived in tenement homes and worked in sweatshops.

8. Germans and Scandinavians turned millions of acres of wilderness into productive farm land.

9. Sometimes immigrants return to their native land.

10. Many Cambodian refugees live in Danbury, Connecticut.

11. Many immigrants join ethnic clubs or groups so they can remember their native language and customs. Two such groups include the Sons of Portugal and the Hibernians (Irish).

Figure 28. Study Sheet: Immigration Unit—United Countries of America (continued)

Statue of Liberty:

1. The Statue of Liberty was a gift to the U.S. from France to honor our friendship.

2. Frederic Auguste Bartholdi is the French sculptor who designed and engineered the building of the statue.

3. The Statue of Liberty symbolized the immigrant's search for freedom.

4. Emma Lazarus, a Portuguese Jew, wrote the poem on the base of the statue.

5. Liberty Weekend, July 3-6, 1986 celebrated the 100th birthday of Miss Liberty.

6. 40,000 boats had planned to be in the New York Harbor.

7. Up to 200 aircraft flew overhead.

8. The largest fireworks display in the history of the U.S. burst from 32 barges.

9. More than 2,000 immigrants were sworn in on Ellis Island as new citizens.

10. 20,000 more immigrants were sworn in via satellite.

Contributions:

1. All Americans have been immigrants or are the children of immigrants.

2. Immigration has greatly enriched the American vocabulary.

3. All the major American faiths were brought to this country from abroad.

4. Foods from many countries can be found in the U.S. English muffins came from the England, goulash came from Hungary, and lasagna came from Italy.

5. Many holidays and customs celebrated in the U.S. have come from other countries. St. Patrick's Day came from Ireland and St. Valentine's Day from Rome.

6. Many famous immigrants have contributed to American growth. Some of the most famous immigrants are Albert Einstein (from Germany), who made advances in physics and Alexander Graham Bell (from Scotland), who invented the telephone.

7. Many toys, games, and sports played in the U.S. originated from other contries. Checkers came from ancient Rome, karate from Asia, Jai alai from Spain, stack dolls from China and Russia, and trouble dolls from Guatemala.

8. Many different kinds of ethnic music can be heard in the U.S. Bagpipes are from Scotland and drums are from Africa.

Figure 28. Study Sheet: Immigration Unit—United Countries of America (continued)

Immigration
Reasons Immigrants Migrated

NAME: ROOM:
DATE: SOCIAL STUDIES:

Directions: Read each statement carefully. Choose the best word from the word bank to complete each statement.

1.   Many people left Ireland to escape the potato _____ .

2.   The United States offers more _____ than most countries.

3.   Many immigrants wanted _____ opportunity.
      They wanted to be able to earn more money.

4.   Some people came because in America they could buy acres of
      _____ for less money than in their native country.

5.   When _____ was discovered in California,
      many people wanted to get rich quick.

6.   Very little food and _____ are famine.

7.   Some wanted to escape religious _____ .

8.   Many Jews wanted to escape _____ terror.

9.   Some people want to leave their country because of a real fear of
      their government. These people are called political _____ .

10.   When a country has been at war, some people leave because they
      want to live in _____ .
      _____

Word Bank: economic, land, Hitler's, famine, freedom, gold, peace, persecution, starvation, quota, refugees, steamships.

Figure 29. Immigration—Reasons Immigrants Migrated

Immigration
How Immigrants Lived

NAME: ROOM:
DATE: SOCIAL STUDIES:

Directions: Read each statement carefully. Choose the best word from the word bank to complete each statement.

1. Many _____ helped to build the transcontinental railroad in the west.

2. Many _____ helped to build the transcontinental railroad in the east.

3. Poorer buildings where many immigrants lived in crowded rooms were called _____ .

4. Many immigrants settled in the _____ of New York City.

5. Many immigrants worked in factories called _____ where workers worked in unhealthy conditions.

6. Many Mexicans who cannot obtain visas enter the U.S. _____ .

7. A group of people who did not want any immigrants to enter the U.S. were called the _____ .

8. Germans and Scandinavians turned millions of _____ of wilderness into productive farmland.

9. Blacks were not allowed to attend school or learn to read until after the _____ War.

10. Each new group of immigrants faces _____ .

_____

Word Bank: Civil, world, acres, Chinese, Portuguese, sweatshops, prejudice, Irish, Cambodians, Lower East Side, tenements, illegally, Know Nothing Party, Vietnamese.

Figure 30. Immigration—How Immigrants Lived

filled the room and, for a moment, they were brought to another place and time.

Other classes in the school were also invited to an Open House in the third grade classroom. In order to allow for a more intimate interaction among the presenters and visitors, students presenting their work were grouped by the categories of their studies and the visitors were also placed in small groups. Children circulated from group to group when the teacher rang a bell. The invitations used for parents and other classes appear in Figures 31 and 32.

At the conclusion of the Immigration study, when the presentations were made for parents, flags from all countries were hanging in a circle from the ceiling in the center of the classroom. The children's work was displayed all over the room. The children were both the presenters and the teachers on this day. They shared a tremendous amount of knowledge on a wide variety of topics with energy, enthusiasm, and pride. After their projects were shared, they stood in a circle and used sign language to visually illustrate Neil Diamond's song "Coming to America."

The moment was magical, as those times are, when teachers see students engaged in learning and loving what they were doing. They were in charge of their own learning and now were doing the teaching. They knew what to do and when to do it and THEY WERE ONLY EIGHT YEARS OLD!

Section 3: Implementing Triad Studies in the Middle School

The Triad studies fit easily and naturally into the "new middle school" with its most current national focus being directed toward curriculum and specifically differentiated curricular experiences for all children. These new initiatives call for interdisciplinary teacher planning teams, block scheduling, new and innovative teaching strategies, and integrated or interdisciplinary curriculum. The Triad studies meet all of these criteria, but will require some modifications in both planning and implementation at the middle school level.

The interdisciplinary planning teams have presented a unique challenge to middle school teachers. Not long ago teachers were departmentalized and compartmentalized and worked independently of each other. The interdisciplinary teaming concept requires just the opposite of the teachers, especially when they are asked to engage in the development of interdisciplinary studies.

Teachers come together with differing philosophical beliefs, professional and experiential backgrounds, and teaching methodologies. They may have spent their careers teaching one discipline and may not

Parent Letter

April 15th

Dear Parents,

Your children have been studying immigration for several weeks. They brainstormed a web, which was divided into six main areas:

1. Statue of Liberty
2. Why Immigrants Left
3. Immigration Processing
4. How They Lived
5. How They Got Here
6. Contributions

Each child has chosen an area to research and has been gathering facts. These facts will be presented in product form on Friday, May 1st. Attached is a list of suggested products.

Parents may help with encouragement and support. The student's understanding of his or her project is part of the evaluation.

You are invited to a presentation on Immigration on Friday, May 15th. Miss Brownwell's class will present at 10:30 a.m. to 11:45 a.m. Ms. Thurmond's class will present from 11:10 a.m. to 11:45 a.m.

In the afternoon on May 15th, students will celebrate their success and completion of hard work at an ethnic feast. Any parents wishing to donate any ethnic foods are welcome to contribute.

_____

I _____ have chosen to gather facts on _____ . I will complete a product on this topic and share it with my class on May 1st.

Student's Signature: _____

I am aware of the due date and the invitation.

Parent's Signature: _____

Figure 31. Parent Letter

Teacher Invitation

May 21st

Dear Migrant Fact Collectors,

Some points of interest along the halls to Room 404 include: an immigration comic time line that starts 20,000 years ago with people walking across the Bering Strait into North and South America; personal time lines that include important events in students' lives; family shields; limericks about immigration; reports on contributing immigrants; pictures of flags and aliens of other worlds; stories about aliens; and a scene of immigrants coming to America via sailing vessels, steamships, and planes.

Students will present facts on six main areas of immigration:

1.   Reasons Immigrants Left
2.   Statue of Liberty
3.   Immigration Processing
4.   How Immigrants Lived
5.   How They Got Here
6.   Contributions of Immigrants

Please divide your class into six groups. Each group will then be paired with a group of student presenters. Groups will rotate at the sound of a bell.

Please remind your students to be good listeners. Thank you.

Sincerely,

Ms. Nancy Thurmond

Schedule:

9:05	Jacobson
10:20	Zaborowski
10:45	Shanley
11:15	Gordon
12:40	Ryer
1:20	Nelson
2:30	Ross
2:50	Pettigrew

Figure 32. Teacher Invitation

be familiar with the content and skills taught by their colleagues. They may be enthusiastic about meeting with their team members to discuss concerns they have with students and other topics, but not receptive to the concept of discussing their curriculum and developing interdisciplinary studies.

Administrators cannot assume that just by bringing these individuals together all of this will happen naturally. On the contrary, they must first be aware that developing interdisciplinary studies may be a significant problem and that specific strategies, such as staff development for team building techniques may need to be employed before some teams will be successful. Obviously, curriculum development will be difficult to implement if a team is not functioning effectively and efficiently.

A thematic study of Survival: Shelter, which was planned and implemented by an excellent seventh grade, five-member teacher team, provides a model for our discussion of the middle school Triad classroom. The study, shown on the Planning Matrix in Figure 33a and the web in Figure 33b, was developed by the Stone team.

Selecting the Theme or Topic for Interdisciplinary Studies

The first modification for the middle school Triad study is the process of selecting the theme or topic. When developing an interdisciplinary study at the middle level, teacher teams must first decide on the theme or topic that will provide the foundation for the study. In order to do this in a valid and meaningful manner, teachers **must** know what is taught in all curricular areas and must attempt to see connections among the various disciplines. One way of doing this is to review and analyze the school district's existing curriculum guides in all disciplines. Since this is such a time consuming task, teachers seldom have the time, energy, or opportunity to do this review.

Curriculum mapping, which was described in detail earlier in this book (Figures 4 and 5), provides a valuable vehicle for reviewing the "taught" curriculum in a clear, concise and timely fashion. Since all curricular areas including the arts, music, technology education, health, and foreign language, are mapped, the teacher teams will be able to see connections from many perspectives. They usually analyze the maps prior to their team meetings and then discuss possible themes, topics, and ways to integrate their curricula.

These "connections" might be made by a two to five-teacher team. The number of teachers is not the most important aspect of the study. The critical element in an integrated study is that: (1) the connections are authentic and not "forced" and (2) the teachers involved see these links and can demonstrate them to the students in a meaningful way. Once teachers have had an opportunity to discuss their curricula

Interdisciplinary Unit of Study
Planning Matrix

Team Leader: Don Stone- Social Studies
Teachers: Bob Evenski- Science
Nancy Horton- Language Arts
Monique Petty- Mathematics
Lucy Read- Spanish

School: King Philip Middle School   Grade Level: 7   Topic/Theme/Unit of Study: SURVIVAL: SHELTER   Duration of Study: Four Weeks

Essential Questions

1. Why do animals and humans build the shelters they do?
2. What do humans learn from animal construction of shelters?
3. How are a people's values reflected in their shelters?

Student Outcomes

Content:
The student will:
- identify the basic characteristics of shelters, e.g., storage, materials, and protection.
- understand that animals and people share a fundamental need for shelter.
- explain how geography, climate, and resources impact shelters in various parts of the world.
- recognize how technology impacts construction of shelters.

Process:
The student will:
- use the following writing genre as they relate to shelter:
  comparison and contrast
  description
  persuasion
- make qualitative observations and describe both human and animal shelter.
- to review and apply: scales, ratio, measurement, decimals & percentages.

Attitudes and Attributes:
The student will:
- demonstrate open-mindedness and sensitivity toward other people who live differently yet have the same basic needs.
- appreciate diversity.

Disciplines	Type I Content and Introductory Activities	Type II Process Training Lessons	Type III Interest - Based Independent Projects/Studies
Language Arts	Attend book talk about books with unconventional shelters. Brainstorm the topic: "Requirements for Survival" *Hatchet*, Gary Paulson; **Call of the Wild**, Jack London; **Adrift**, Stephen Callahan (non-fiction)	Describe your "Dream House" Persuade an audience to purchase a home (Employ writing process) (Keyed to writing outcomes) Webbing the Theme/Topic Shelter Web - Whole Group	Create a "Dream House" Advertising Campaign; Research famous survival stories and give individual or group presentation; Create a children's book about shelters (ABC, Pop-up, Other)
Math	Tower Simulation: Cooperative Construction of a Structure; Student Survey/Focus Groups (Assess what students want to learn about shelter); Speaker: Mr. Hughlett, Architect	Create a blueprint of a shelter using scales, ratio, and measurement; Learn about and develop a household budget using decimals and percentages	Construct a shelter of your own design; Create a dwelling for the year 2000; Design the interior of a structure
Social Studies	Opening Ceremony (Unit Overview) All Staff/Student Participation; Text: **World Geography: People Places**, Merrill, 1989; Film: **Yankee Sails Across Europe**; Brainstorm: "Shelters Around the World"	Research a specific shelter by responding to key questions; Analyze types of shelters as they relate to their geographic locations; Maps: Identifying types, making, and reading; Brainstorming product ideas	Construct a model of an existing shelter; Produce a videotape about shelters; Make a collage entitled: "World Shelters or Unusual Shelters"
Science	Field Trip: Observe animal and human habitats on neighborhood campus walk. Review multiple resource books related to shelter.	Record observations of homes around the campus and compare and contrast them; Research shelters of a particular group of animals and share findings; Locate computer programs; Compare human and animal architecture	Design an animal habitat, e.g., terrarium, herbarium, etc.; Produce a slide presentation of a specific habitat and write a critique to accompany slides; Produce a photographic essay about shelters
Spanish	Habitat for Humanity: Presentation related to homes being constructed for needy people. Presenter: James Lacock	Create a floor plan for an imaginary home; Describe home in complete paragraphs in Spanish	Design a topographical map of a specific region/habitat; Develop a landscaping plan for a home and provide a rationale for your selection of specific plants, etc.
Art	Creating a Two-Point Perspective of a Human Dwelling; Art Teacher: Joyce St. Jermaine	Create a commercial advertisement for a Spanish newspaper; Create a skit with a partner - Buying a home (buyer/seller)	
Social Studies/ Language Arts	Shelters Around the World Slide presentation by: Karen Golebiewski; Library research skills and book talks. Media Specialist: Muriel Gaynor	Record journal entries of campus walk, class novels, and unconventional environment book. Decision making strategies for selection of topic/project; Planning the Studies/Modified Management Plan; Problem Focusing	Debate environmental issues, i.e., wetlands; Construct an underwater dwelling

Getting Started:
- Review summer curriculum work.
- Write essential questions.
- Establish student outcomes.
- Determine content and introductory activities.
- Plan appropriate process training lessons.
- Brainstorm possible topics for independent or small group studies.
- Determine the timeline.

Resources Needed:
Textbook: **World Geography, People and Places**, Merrill, 1989.

Resource Books (A Sampling):
Brower, Carol, **The Children's Book of Houses and Homes**
Silverstein, Shel, **The Giving Tree**
Macaulay, David, **Unbuilding**
Camesasca, E., **History of the House**
Bodains, David, **The Secret House**
Kohl, J., J., **The View From the Oak**
Thorndike, Joseph, **The Magnificent Builders: Their Dream Houses**
Stevens, Peter S., **Patterns in Nature** (W.H.P. Library)
Siberall, Anne, **Shelters from Prehistoric Times to Today**
Flegg, Dr. Jim, **Animal Builders**
Fisher, Timothy, **Huts, Hovels, Houses**
Weiss, Harvey, Shelters: **From Tipi to Igloo**
Giblin, James Cross, **Let There Be Light**

Films:
"Yankee Sails Across Europe"

Resource People:
See Type I Activities

Student Assessment:
Writing Assignments:
Holistic and Analytic Scoring
Student Survey
Dream House Ads:
Holistically Scored with Rubric
Student Projects:
Scored by Teacher Team with Rubric

Matrix Developed by Margaret Beecher

Figure 33a. Interdisciplinary Unit of Study—Planning Matrix (Survival: Shelter)

Survival: Shelter Web

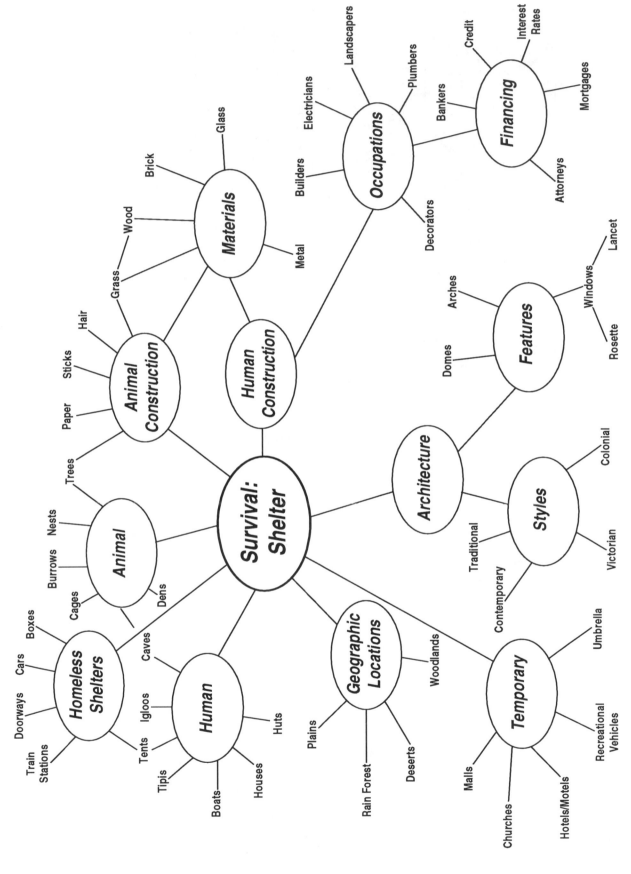

Figure 33b. Curriculum Web (Survival: Shelter)

amongst themselves, the number of disciplines and teachers to be included will become more apparent.

It is also most important to know if the studies must be based on the regular curriculum. In the event that they don't, the content portion of the curriculum maps is less significant, but the process or skills covered in each discipline may still provide a necessary basis for the study. These are all considerations that need to be evaluated when selecting a topic or theme in a team setting.

In order to select the theme, many different ideas are explored. The work of Beane (1990) and Fogarty (1991) are both rich sources of themes. The Stone team's theme came from yet a different source. The team was asked to think about developing an interdisciplinary study based on a project that had been very popular with many students several years earlier. This was called the Home Project, and during the study, students had learned how to construct a model home. The team's challenge was to use this as the basis for their planning. During their early planning, they realized the constraints of limiting the topic to just the Home Project and thought of ways to develop the study into an interdisciplinary study that included five major disciplines and demonstrated authentic connections for the students. The theme which was finally selected was Survival with a primary focus on Shelters.

Academic Teacher Teams and Special Area Teachers

It should be noted here that the Stone team was a five member team which represented the five major disciplines of science, social studies, language arts, math, and foreign language. This team's schedule allowed for a team planning session every day for one period and also a personal planning session each day for one period. The team was unable to meet with special area teachers in art, music, physical education, technology education, and health during their team planning time, because their students were with these special area teachers during that time. This made it difficult to involve the special area teachers in the planning of the study, which is reflected in the limited number of connections made with these areas.

Essential Questions

As the reader may have noticed, the Planning Matrix has an additional section entitled essential questions. This demonstrates another modification to the Triad study and one that is appropriate at all grade levels. Although the concept of essential questions is not a new one, it added a valuable dimension to this study and the Planning Matrix was redesigned to accommodate this change. If teachers are interested in developing essential questions for their study, the following definition and criteria will help guide them.

Essential questions and problems go to the heart of a discipline. They can be found in the most historically important problems and topics in the sciences: What is adequate "proof" in each field of inquiry? Is light a particle or a wave? Is evolution fact or theory? Does mathematics always require numbers? Each study is designed to explicitly address and answer the essential questions, using textbooks, lectures, exercises, and other resources.

Essential questions have no one obvious "right" answer: essential "answers" are not self-evidently true. Even if there are truths and essential theories in a discipline, the student comes to know that there are other plausible theses and hypotheses to consider.

Essential questions are higher order, in Bloom's sense- matters of analysis, synthesis, and evaluative judgment (Bloom, 1954). The student is always asked in assignments and major tests to "go beyond the information given." Because essential questions involve higher-order answers, the questions and answers usually undergo change and refining as the work progresses.

Essential questions allow for personalized interest. They provide opportunities for creative approaches. There is not one correct way to do things or to prove that mastery of the question has been achieved. Students can thus be more like the professional researcher.

Jacobs (1989) provides the following guidelines to use when structuring questions for interdisciplinary and discipline-based curriculum. Essential questions . . .

> Highlight conceptual priorities for your specific target population.
> Fulfill learning outcomes.
> Use umbrella-like language for organizing purposes.
> Are limited in number - usually two to five questions.
> Embrace a distinct section of the activity/study.
> Are non-repetitious.
> Are realistic for the time frame.
> Are posted by all participating teachers.
> Connect a range of disciplines.
> Have a logical sequence.
> Are understood by all students.

Jacobs also recommends that teachers ask themselves this fundamental question when designing essential questions: "Given the amount of time we have to spend on this particular study, what is essential for the learners in our care to explore?" An example of essential questions related to flight (Jacobs, 1989) are: What flies? How and why do things in nature fly? What has been the impact of flight on humans? What is the future of flight?

After reviewing and discussing this information and following an in-service program, in which two of the team members were present, the Stone team decided on the following three essential questions that would be posted in all four classrooms for the duration of the study:

1. Why do animals and humans build the shelters they do?
2. What do humans learn from animal construction of shelters?
3. How are a people's values reflected in their shelters?

Student Outcomes

The essential questions are generally written prior to the development of the student outcomes. It is important to note that they are not one and the same. The content and process student outcomes must be measurable and aligned with student assessment.

The modification necessary in the development of student outcomes at the middle school level is that all team members must have input in this process. When a team is developing outcomes, each member explains what is critical for students to know and accomplish in their discipline. This information is discussed, reviewed, and critiqued and a decision is made about the outcomes that will be included in the study.

In the implementation of the study, each outcome is not necessarily addressed by only one of the disciplines. For example, one of the content outcomes for the Survival study was: "The students will identify the basic characteristics of shelters, e.g., storage, materials, and protection." These characteristics were discussed in language arts through literature, in social studies when they learned about shelters in different parts of the world, in science when they studied animal shelters, and in math when they designed their own shelters. This is true of most of the outcomes and is critical to the connections that are necessary for an effective, integrated study.

Getting Started

Once again this is a team effort and the group must decide what group members will take responsibility for getting started. In many cases the entire team engages in the activity. The tasks and participants are outlined below:

Task	Participants
Review Summer Curriculum Work	Entire Team
Write Essential Questions	Entire Team
Establish Student Outcomes	Individual & Team
Determine Content & Introductory Activities	Individual & Team
Plan Appropriate Process Training Lessons	Individual & Team
Brainstorm Possible Topics of Independent Studies	Entire Team
Determine Timeline	Entire Team

The reader will notice that in some cases the team members first plan individually and then share their ideas, lessons, and activities with the entire team. The Planning Matrix assists in this process since each member completes their section of the matrix and then adds other team member's information. At the conclusion of the planning, all team members have a completed matrix and an excellent understanding of what their colleagues will be doing throughout the study. Without this kind of planning, many connections would never be made and studies would really just parallel each other rather than truly integrate.

Block Scheduling

Many middle schools and junior high schools have a period-by-period day with bells ringing and students moving from class to class every forty-five minutes. The students' days are compartmentalized and segmented with no connection among classes and disciplines. This type of learning and instruction is not conducive to interdisciplinary studies or differentiated learning experiences for young adolescents.

The concept of block scheduling is in keeping with the new restructured middle school. This type of schedule provides opportunities for classes to meet and make the curricular connections that are necessary if integrated learning is to occur. This does not usually include the special areas of art, music, physical education, health, and technology since the team meetings are generally scheduled when the students are in class with these special area teachers.

With the knowledge, expertise, and guidance of Paul Berkel, an innovative school principal, the King Philip Middle School in Connecticut implemented a block schedule that allowed the teacher teams to break the boundaries of the period-by-period day and combine classes when there was a need to integrate the curriculum or whenever there was a need to have students come together in large groups. During their Shelter study, whenever a speaker visited the team, classes came together and met in a large group setting. A sample of their block schedule is shown in Figure 34.

Middle School Type I and Type II Highlights

The Stone team had an effective way of beginning their Triad study. On the first day of the study, all of the classes met together and the teachers introduced the interdisciplinary unit to the students. All teachers who participated in the study provided students with a brief overview of the activities that were planned. Students worked in small groups assisting teachers in their on-going planning by brainstorming ideas for content and activities. Students were then asked to individually complete a student survey. They were asked what they wanted to know and would like to know about the topic. They were also asked if they

King Philip Middle School
West Hartford Public Schools, West Hartford, CT
BLOCK SCHEDULE

Time	DAY 1	DAY 2	DAY 3	DAY 4	DAY 5
Homeroom					
1	ATPM/H*	ATPM/H	ATPM/H	ATPM/H	ATPM/H
2					
3					
4					
5	ATPM/H	ATPM/H	ATPM/H	ATPM/H	ATPM/H
6					
7					
8					

*ATPM/H = Art, Technology Education, Physical Education, Music, and Health

Form Developed by Paul Berkel

Figure 34. King Philip Middle School Block Schedule

had any information or memorabilia they would be willing to share with the class and if they knew anyone who had lived in a different kind of shelter and would be willing to speak to the class about their experience. It was a very worthwhile session and a great kickoff for the study.

One of the most interesting Type I experiences was a speaker from Habitat for Humanity. The presenter was one of the officers of the organization and explained how the habitat functioned and engaged children in estimating the cost of constructing a home. In addition to sharing a great deal of information, he also presented the class with an interesting proposal: If they wanted to help build a home, they could collect old and used eyeglasses and sell them to earn enough money to build the home. This was an opportunity for students to really make a difference and several students met the challenge.

The science teacher engaged students in a unique field trip. In order to teach his students to do qualitative observations and describe animal shelters, he brought them on a tour of their own school grounds, which was basically a young forest.

The English teacher blended the school district's required literature and writing genre into this study in a more meaningful way. The novels students read enhanced their knowledge and understanding of the theme. The two required writing genre were descriptive and persuasive writing. Students were asked to describe their dream house and, after researching and critiquing home advertisements, they were asked to persuade an audience to purchase their home.

Mathematics was brought into the real world during the Type II lessons when students created blueprints of the dream houses they had described and persuaded someone to buy in language arts class. An architect explained the tools of his trade and students combined this knowledge with their own and used scales, ratios, and measurements to make their own architectural drawings. Once the houses were designed, students were asked to determine how much it would cost to maintain their dream dwellings.

Management of Type III Training Activities

The research project presents new challenges to interdisciplinary middle school planning teams. Questions such as the following present themselves and must be resolved before proceeding:

What teacher will be responsible for which projects?
Who will grade the projects? In what subject will students receive the grade?
Will students assess themselves? Who will establish the rubrics and checklists? Does everyone need to agree on this criteria?

How long will students have to complete the projects?
Will the projects be done at home, in school, or both?

The responses to these questions rest with the team of teachers and the decisions must be made during the planning of the study. The Stone team decided that two of the teachers would be responsible for the projects since the others felt they could not devote the necessary time to this task due to time restraints and other responsibilities. These same two teachers evaluated the projects with the students and the results became part of their language arts grade. The students had three weeks to complete the projects and the work was done both at school and at home. This was obviously a challenging task for these two teachers since there were 125 students on this team.

Skills of Independence

All students were given training in decision making, problem focusing, management and organization of the study, and library research in order to assist them with their study and further develop their independent study skills. This was also critical to the two teachers who were responsible for facilitating all of the Type III studies.

The topics and products selected by students were unique and diverse. They included dwellings located on the side of cliffs, on mountains, in cities, in boxes, underwater, in space, and in numerous other places in and out of this world. They studied homelessness and shared the consequences of having no shelters. A sampling of the products completed by the students on the Stone team included: an illustrated short story written for younger children, a book explaining how to construct shelters in natural settings with no man-made materials, charts demonstrating the most efficient use of bedroom space, models of a wide variety of new and original dwellings, a song composed and sung about homelessness, and a written tour and description of West Hartford's animal homes. The students responded very well to having an opportunity to choose their own topics and they became more motivated, self-directed and independent in their learning styles.

Grouping Patterns

It is important to note the grouping patterns that existed in this sixth, seventh, and eighth grade middle school. All students were heterogeneously grouped in all disciplines and subjects with the exception of seventh and eighth grade honors English and mathematics. Modified classes for children below grade level had been eliminated. Special education students including the mentally handicapped were mainstreamed into the regular classroom. Special education teachers,

teaching assistants, and paraprofessionals provided support for the classroom teacher through planning and supporting classroom instruction. The school district did not have a program for gifted and talented children at the middle school level.

Student Assessment

The performance-based assessment employed by the team included many types of testing methods that required students to demonstrate their competencies in a variety of ways. One type of assessment used the constructed-response format, which required students to produce an answer for a question rather than select from an array of possible answers. Students solved math problems, wrote short answers, and completed diagrams and graphs.

Another type of assessment was used in scoring student's writing. Students were required to write in three different genre which included description, persuasion, and comparison and contrast. The writings were scored both holistically and analytically. The students' knowledge of composition, which included inventing, revising, and clearly stating ideas to fit the purpose and audience, as well as their knowledge of language, syntax, and grammar was assessed by both the students and the teachers. Students wrote in all curricular areas.

The performance criteria for the student projects was established by the teachers and shared with students prior to the beginning of their projects. Students were graded on their overall performance based on these criteria. The students also assessed their own work. Teachers met with individual students only when there was a significant difference in the teacher and student scores.

Section 4: Stretching the Secondary Curriculum

The model presented in this section closely parallels all of the others. However, unlike the middle school model, the planning and implementation was done by a single teacher rather than a teacher team. When this study was developed and taught, the high school did not have an interdisciplinary team structure. Teachers focused their instruction on their respective disciplines and planned and worked independently. They met periodically with their peers who taught the same discipline.

The Planning Matrix (Figure 35a) and the web (Figure 35b) reflect the efforts of Mimi McKenna-Hostetter to integrate her discipline, social studies, with language arts, art, and music. As shown on the Matrix, the information or content was presented in more than lecture format. Videos, a field trip, speakers, and multiple resource books in the school

Interdisciplinary Unit of Study
Planning Matrix

Teachers: ___Mimi McKenna-Hostetter___ School: ___Conard High School, West Hartford, CT___ Grade Level: ___9___ Topic/Theme/Unit of Study: ___MIDDLE AGES___ Duration of Study: ___6-8 Weeks___

Essential Questions

What are the forces that make a civilization change and grow?

How does the interaction of one civilization with another affect its development?

How did the Medieval culture emerge and evolve as a result of the collapse of the Roman civilization?

Student Outcomes

Content:

The students will...
- describe the following components of this culture...
  - way of life
  - economics
  - political structure
  - use of resources
  - resourcefulness
  - geography
  - religion
  - vernacular languages
- know which European culture developed by the end of the Middle Ages

Process:

The students will...
- develop a timeline and a chronology of the period
- complete an expository writing assignment
- develop the thinking skills of cause and effect, compare and contrast, analysis, and evaluation

Attitudes and Attributes:

The student will...
- assume primary responsibility for their learning.
- demonstrate a questioning attitude, open mindedness and curiosity.
- demonstrate independence of thought.

Disciplines	Type I Content and Introductory Activities	Type II Process Training Lessons	Type III Interest - Based Independent Projects/Studies	Getting Started:
				Create Essential Questions Establish Student Outcomes Determine Content and Introductory Activities Contact Resource People Plan Field Trip Locate Multiple Library Resources Determine Study Timeline
Language Arts	Biographies/Biographical Sketches Charlemagne St. Francis Joan of Arc Eleanor of Aquitaine Novels: St. Peter's Fair, Ellis Peters Saint Joan of Arc, V. Sackville-West Ivanhoe, Sir Walter Scoll Saint Joan, George Bernard Shaw	Expository Writing: • Evaluate the government from feudal to monarchy • How trade changed business structures, language, goods Biographical sketches of prominent monarchs/figures from the 10th to 15th Century	Write and perform a monologue based on the play Saint Joan by George Bernard Shaw Design a banner from Richard III's coat of arms Design a coat of arms	**Resources Needed:** *Teacher Resource Books* **The Crucible of Europe**, Geoffery Baraclough **Culture & Values, A Survey of Western Humanities**, Lawrence Cunnington & John Reich **Feudal Society**, Marc Bloch **Life in a Medieval Castle**, Francis & Joseph Gies **Women in the Middle Ages**, Francis & Joseph Gies
Language Arts	Student Survey: Assess students present knowledge, what they want to learn, and what they can contribute in terms of resources, and resource people	Cause and Effect Effect of the crusades on Western Europe (Use Graphic Organizer) Journal Entries Writings related to videos, speakers, field trip and other readings Reading in the content area/oral reading- sections of text	Create a simulation or board game about the crusades Design a tapestry depicting a significant battle Write a poem glorifying a battle, event, or someone's life	**Women's Lives in Medieval Europe**: A Source Book, Emilie Amt. ed. **Women of the Renaissance**, Margaret L. King **The Oxford History of Medieval Europe**, George Holmes, ed. *Student Resources* **Books:** **Castles**, David Macaulay **Cathedral**, David Macaulay
Social Studies	Text: **History of the World**, Houghton Mifflin, 1990. Video Tapes: -Charlemagne: Holy Barbarian -The Castle -The Cathedral -The Peasant Rebellion -The Crusades	Maps and Mapping • Locate and label cities and geographic areas in England and France • Trace travel routes- the crusades and trade maps showing movement of products	Create a mobile demonstrating the hierarchy of the social system of the Middle Ages Write a short story, biography, characterization, or perform a dramatic reading about the life of a woman of the times or another topic of interest	**Novel:** **St. Peter's Fair**, Ellis Peters **Video:** "Becket", Richard Burton, Peter O'Toole "Lion in Winter", Peter O'Toole, Katherine Hepburn "Ivanhoe", with Elizabeth Taylor and Robert Taylor
Social Studies	Primary Sources: Feudal Relationship Magna Carta Field Trip: Higgins Armory Museum • Creating and using armor	Analysis of Feudal Documents Conclude how people felt about the serfs Evaluate the effects of the Magna Carta on the monarchy	Create a photographic essay about castles and how they have changed Draw your own etchings or simulated grave rubbings Develop a slide show of Medieval life	**How-to-Book:** **Picture the Middle Ages**-Higgins Armory Museum, Owl Publishing Co.

Social Studies	Speakers/Topics:
	- Medieval Architecture
	- The Medieval Church: Monks and Nuns
	- Church Manuscripts: Calligraphy
	- Medieval Reves
		Compare and Contrast
		• Medieval Art and Renaissance Art
		• Government in England and France in 12th Century (use graphic organizer)
		Decision Making
		Topic/Project Selection
			Write and perform a play depicting life in the times and events such as: Joan of Arc on Trial, Henry II and Becket, Eleanor of Aquitaine and Henry II, Richard the Lionhearted or another famous figure of this time	**Student Assessment:**
				Chapter Tests
				  Short Answer and Essay
				Maps
				Writing
				  Development and Structure
				  Content Accuracy
				  Grammar and Punctuation
				Independent Projects
				  Teacher Assessment and Student Self-Assessment
				Homework and Readings

Art/ Music	Introduction to Medieval Art Instrumental music and songs from this period	Management Plan • Problem Focusing • Sequencing the Study • Resources • Product and Audience	Design and create a bust of a famous figure Compose a musical piece for flute and violin Prepare a Middle Ages menu	

Matrix Developed by Margaret Beecher

Figure 35a. Interdisciplinary Unit of Study—Planning Matrix (Middle Ages)

Middle Ages Web

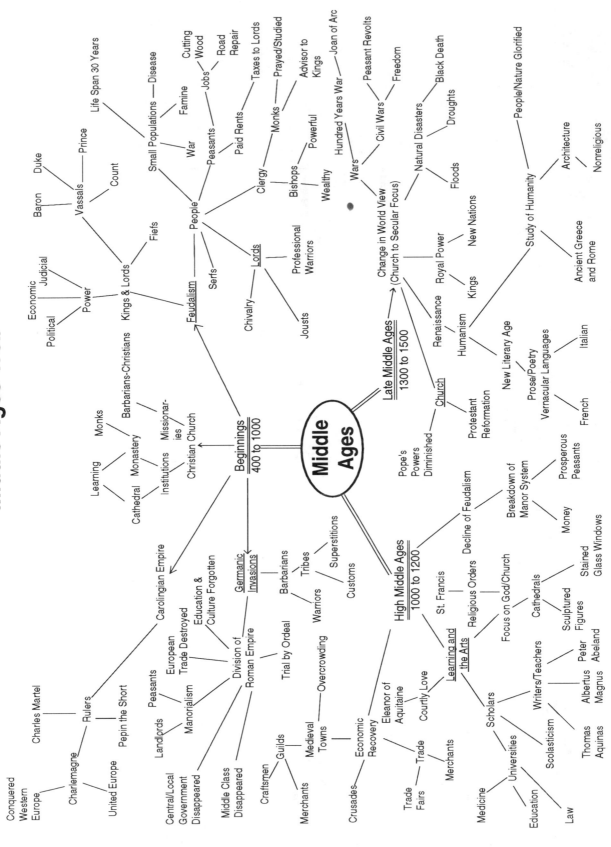

Figure 35b. Curriculum Web (Middle Ages)

library provided students with information from a wide variety of sources and at varying levels of readability. Once students had begun to digest and comprehend the knowledge, rich discussions and debates ensued.

Higher level questioning was common classroom practice as students compared and contrasted characters and historical events and analyzed their causes and effects on history and the present. The essential questions, which were posted in the classroom, provided a consistent focus and stimulated student thinking. Many of these discussions were preceded by writing assignments that allowed students to focus and clarify their thinking.

Students at this level had the prerequisite skills to conduct their own independent studies. The challenge was to brainstorm as many topic and product ideas as possible, in order to extend and stretch students to a Type III level and provide an opportunity for any student to become an actual historian or practicing professional in a field. The open-ended nature of interest-based independent projects required students to take risks. When ideas were generated, the teacher added the ideas to the Matrix in the column entitled, Interest-Based Independent Projects. These ideas, which were generated by the teacher during the planning phase of the study, were never actually shown to the students, but were added to their ideas as the teacher and students brainstormed together. The number and diversity of ideas were very meaningful in determining the students' decisions.

Students at this level had more opportunities to locate library and community resources since they often had transportation. Interviews with local experts, visits to historical societies, museums, and libraries were now within their reach. This added another valuable dimension to their studies.

When the projects were completed, students had an opportunity to assess themselves and contribute to the criteria that were used to evaluate their work. This was consistent with the concept of performance-based assessment and an excellent addition to any program, especially the secondary level. Traditional means of assessment were combined with short answer and essay tests. The creation of maps, holistic and analytic scoring of writing by both teacher and students, student and teacher ratings of projects using student-established criteria, and homework and readings were used to produce the students' final grades.

This study provides an excellent example of the authentic and meaningful ways in which many secondary teachers integrate their curriculum. Although they work independently in their respective disciplines, they create opportunities for their students to explore all dimensions of specific themes and topics. However, high schools are

beginning to experiment more frequently with the same interdisciplinary teaming concept that has become the hallmark of the middle school movement.

CHAPTER 5

A GIANT STEP BEYOND

A Giant Step Beyond

Do not train youth to learn by harshness, but lead them to it by what amuses their minds. Then you may discover the peculiar bent of the genius of each.

-Plato

During my years as an educator I have had the opportunity to interview hundreds of students. One of the most commonly asked questions I asked them was, "What is the most memorable and significant experience you have had in school?" The students' responses have been amazingly consistent and surprising to me. The vast majority of students stated that a certain field trip, class celebration or party, or extra-curricular activity was most significant. Very few students recalled a specific study or anything related to curricular experiences as being memorable.

However, once a student has had an opportunity to pursue a Type III small group or independent investigation of a real problem, the experience is never forgotten. Some of my former students have called or written to express their feelings about these studies years after their completion and have shared how the studies had impacted their college selections and career decisions.

These Type III studies were conducted in the resource room setting with a teacher of the gifted and talented as the facilitator. Students had an opportunity to pursue a topic of interest and select and create an original product to share with a real audience. Their studies were always several months in duration and were primarily completed in the resource room setting, although some portion of the final product may have been done at home or in other locations. Students sometimes had a mentor who worked with them on a consistent basis for the entire study. In these Enrichment Triad programs the teacher of the gifted and talented was not responsible for teaching the regular curriculum. This was usually considered the domain of the classroom teacher. Students were generally in the resource room approximately three to five hours

each week if they were developing a Type III study.

Because of the time involved, the individualized nature of the studies, and the resources which needed to be located and gathered, these studies were not designed to occur in the regular classroom. It was generally felt that all students may not be interested in studying one specific topic in depth for an extended period of time. In addition, the topics were not generally connected to the curriculum. Therefore, the Type III studies were designed to be optional and included only those children who were interested in doing a study.

However, there are teachers who want all of their students to experience this type of a study and are willing to go a GIANT STEP BEYOND in order to make this happen. One of these teachers is Beverly Favreau, a third grade teacher in Dalton, Massachusetts. The following is a description of Bev's experience with what will be referred to as Modified Type III studies for the regular classroom.

Beverly had taken a course related to educating the gifted and talented that I was teaching at a local college. During the course, she was introduced to the *Enrichment Triad Model* and became very interested in the Type III studies. As her instructor, I explained the process in detail and showed examples of Type III studies. In her pre-service training, graduate courses, and subsequent staff development, Beverly had never studied this Type III process.

She became energized by the types of things students at her grade level had accomplished and felt that she had two or three students who would benefit from conducting their own Type III study. She felt that she now had some knowledge about this process and could facilitate this type of learning in her classroom. Nancy Harrington, the teacher of the gifted and talented was in her school one day a week and offered to help Beverly implement Type III studies in her classroom.

She decided to forge ahead and one Monday morning said the following to her entire class, "Children, I now know how to help students who have a strong interest in a specific topic and would like to study about that topic. For example, if someone is interested in the Vikings and collects a great deal of information about them, that person might be interested in writing a skit or a play about the Vikings. Someone else may be interested in sources of energy and want to know how we can get energy from plants. Whatever your interest, if you want to do a real, in-depth study anytime during this school year, please let me know and I will help you in any way I can." She then waited to see if anyone would approach her.

Within a few days, about ten students had approached her and mentioned an interest they would like to pursue. Because so many had come forward, she again asked her class how many thought they would be interested in completing a study. Beverly had a class of twenty-three students and every hand was raised. Beverly was speechless for a moment and then asked them what topics they might want to study. The topics ranged from nebulae to helicopters to modern jazz dancing. At that point, she wondered what she had gotten herself into and how she could possibly facilitate all of these studies.

Her class was heterogeneous and she had several students with special needs as well as students with very high ability. She was pleased that all of the students wanted to participate and didn't want to disappoint or dampen their obvious enthusiasm. Thus, Beverly entered into a very new learning experience with her students. One that she would later say was a PEAK EXPERIENCE IN HER CAREER and one that she would repeat times with many different classes.

Beverly's first task was to get organized. She knew the **Management Plan** (Renzulli & Smith, 1977) was too sophisticated for her third graders, but also knew the steps involved in an independent investigation. She used the Plan and these steps as a guide in developing an "I Wonder" booklet for her students. This would enable all students to progress in a sequential manner through the study and, at the same time, allow Beverly to monitor their progress.

The first section of the booklet entitled "First Thoughts" was for students who had not identified what they wanted to study. It asked them what they have been wondering about or what they were interested in learning. It clearly stated that they did not have to include topics related to what they learned in school. "Second Thoughts," assisted students in determining a topic to study, by listing numerous topics. Students were asked to check those of interest to them and narrow their interests to two items of particular interest. Students were then asked if they liked to work alone or with another person, a small group of people, or an adult. It also asked them if they liked being a leader or a helper and if they liked to be on-stage or backstage. These questions helped Beverly guide them in their selection of projects.

There were spaces provided throughout the booklet for student/ teacher conferences and recommendations. The purpose of the first conference was to discuss interests and decide on one or two broad topics. The first recommendations were to review books, magazines, or any other source of information, related to the topic and search for specific areas that really turned them on. They were asked to start a resource list and were taught how to use it. She then wrote specific suggestions for each student as appropriate.

Prior to the second conference, students were asked to look at the material they had gathered and think about answers to the following questions. They were not asked to write the answers:

1. How long have you been interested in this topic?
2. When were you first interested and why?
3. How many books or articles have you looked at concerning this topic?
4. How many books or articles have you actually read?
5. What else have you done with this topic?
6. How much do you already know about this topic?
7. Are there lots of things you still want to know about it?
8. Do you know anyone who knows a lot about it?

During the second conference, Beverly attempted to determine if there was a genuine interest in the topic and aid the student in narrowing and focusing the topic. During this interview, her primary goal was to listen to the student. She recommended that her students find at least three resources about their topics, review them, and write them on their resource list. They were then asked to make a list of at least ten to fifteen questions about the topic and write them on the appropriate pages. Once again, space was provided in each student booklet for Beverly to write specific suggestions.

The third conference provided an opportunity for Beverly to determine if the interest had sustained itself; help categorize, organize, and add questions; and finalize exactly what the research will cover. If the interest had vanished, students were encouraged to return to the beginning pages of their booklet and start again. Irrelevant questions were discarded and pertinent ones were added. At this point, Beverly recommended that they search everywhere to find the answers to their questions, e.g., libraries, museums, filmstrips, interviews with people, etc. Students were also expected to write answers to their questions in their own words. They were to write any other information which was important to the topic on the additional space in their booklet and were reminded to keep track of every resource they used. They were asked to see the teacher as soon as they had finished answering the questions or whenever they became confused.

Lists of possible project ideas and audiences were written in the booklet. Students reviewed the lists and checked five or less project ideas that were of interest to them. They were asked to bring this information to the fourth conference, at which time Beverly checked on their research and brainstormed project and audience possibilities with them. Together they developed the steps needed to complete their project and timeline. Beverly asked the following questions:

1. Did you find a lot of exciting information? Tell me about it.
2. Do you need more information about your topic? If so, what do you need to know?

3. Do you need anyone's help? If so, who might help you obtain this information?
4. What project(s) are you interested in doing?
5. Do you need information about ways to prepare your project? If so, what do you need to know?
6. Do you need materials? If so, what and where can you get them?
7. With whom would you like to share your project?
8. Do you need any help in locating this audience?

Lists of things needed to complete the project and specific dates were then listed by Beverly and her students on the page in their booklets entitled, "Steps and Timeline." Research that needed to be completed, steps needed to plan and complete their project, time needed to plan and rehearse their oral presentations, and project evaluations were listed on this timeline.

The fifth and sixth conferences were for the purpose of checking student progress and facilitating their learning. Beverly asked how they were doing and provided progress forms for students to complete.

The "I Wonder" booklet also provided the students with guidance in preparing their oral presentations. Beverly suggested they answer the following questions about their project when making this presentation:

1. What is your project about?
2. Why did you want to know more about this topic?
3. What did you learn? Please include enough detail here.
4. What special things happened as you did your research? Include interviews, trips, problems, enjoyable events, etc.

Students were expected to practice at home and then rehearse it with Beverly. They knew they were to spend the most time on the third question.

The project evaluation for both the student and teacher was the final section of the booklet. Beverly developed the following criteria which was used to assess each study:

- You chose a good topic that wasn't too big and kept you interested.
- You used many and different resources, gathered much information, and organized it well.
- Your project shows you put in lots of time, work, and care.
- Your oral presentation was well-prepared and delivered.

A four-point scale was used: a "4" was considered outstanding, a "3" very good, a "2" fine, and "1" meant it could be better. Both she and each student rated the criteria and discussed where they agreed and disagreed.

It should be noted that the conferences were not all formal and particularly time-consuming tasks. Most of the conferences were conducted at the students' desks as Beverly circulated around the room. Others were held before and after school and during lunch and recess times.

Beverly had excellent organizational skills and the booklet provided a clear direction for her students. This was their first experience with doing an independent investigation based on their own interest and they needed the guidance that Beverly provided. The conferences that were held with each student throughout the studies had remarkable benefits for the students. They learned how to research a topic using multiple resources and create a new and unique project. During the conferences Beverly guided them, stretched their thinking, and allowed them to reach beyond existing parameters.

A brief discussion of some of the products completed by these third graders will provide a better understanding of the magnitude of their efforts. Although students were allowed to work in small groups or with a partner, they each opted to create their own individual projects. A sampling of some of the topics and projects created by these third graders include the following:

Skiing A video entitled, "How-to Learn to Ski" was created on the slopes of the Berkshires by one of the students who was an avid skier.

Paper-Making A slide show was created on how paper was made at a local paper mill. Paper-making was one of the major industries in this small eastern Massachusetts town and the creator's father was employed at this company. He requested permission to give his daughter a tour of the plant and she was allowed to take pictures of the process.

Nebulae A 3-Dimensional display of nebulae was created by a student who had read about them and wanted to know more. In the course of her study an article appeared in the local paper about an expert in the field who was visiting a local college. Without

prompting from her teacher, she called the college and made an appointment to see the professor.

Treehouse   A student designed and constructed a small model of a treehouse that she and her father were planning to build in her backyard. She also listed the materials that were needed and determined the approximate cost of the project.

Fraction Fun   A game that would help students learn about fractions was the focus of one of the projects. This student loved mathematics and wanted others to like it as much as he did.

Fishing   "How to Make and Use Fishing Lures" was the topic of one student's projects. This booklet was created for children who enjoyed fishing and wanted to improve their skills in this area.

Helicopters versus Airplanes   A student built a model of a helicopter and an airplane, analyzed the two flying machines, and then compared and contrasted them.

History of the Acquisition of the United States   This student demonstrated the acquisition of our country through colorful maps, which were created on transparencies and shown on an overhead projector during an oral presentation.

Main Street   A model of the Main Street of Dalton, Massachusetts with miniature buildings lining the street was the focus of this student's study. He learned about the buildings and created a tape recorded tour of "A Walk Down Main Street."

Wheels on the Bus   This slide show was done by a special needs student. She had her own special ride on a school bus and took pictures of the bus and scenes from the window. She then shared the slides which were accompanied by the song, "The Wheels on the Bus Go Round and Round."

Dance   One student who had taken dance lessons for several years choreographed her own dance using a favorite piece of music.

'Twas the Morning of Monday   This student studied the brain and some of its primary functions. She was also interested in helping students with special needs. In addition to her research and display board about the brain, she wrote a poem which reflected her concern for children with disabilities.

This sampling of products is most impressive for a heterogeneous third grade class and the success of the students can be attributed to their wonderful teacher. Beverly always maintained high standards for all of her students and this was certainly true of their final products. Whatever the completed product was, it had to be neat, clear, accurate, and well done. She showed them how to make a display board by following the following steps: select colors and pictures, cut and trace letters, and place materials on the board. She demonstrated how to make overhead transparencies and use the overhead projector. She allowed students to use her camera and showed them how to create a slide show. On some occasions the entire class learned a process and at other times only a small group was given instruction on a specific skill.

When the projects were completed, students shared with classmates, other classes, and parents. The students knew they were expected to give an oral presentation about their projects. Therefore, it was necessary for Beverly to provide direct instruction in how-to make an oral presentation. As mentioned earlier, the guidelines for making the presentation appeared in the "I Wonder" booklet and included four questions to be answered. Since students had been accustomed to reading reports, there was a "no reading" rule that they all agreed upon. In order to help them remember the sequence of what they were to say, Beverly wrote the four key questions on a large chart and put it high on the wall on the opposite end of the room. This allowed the children to simply glance at the questions if they needed some assistance. They also learned the importance of eye contact with the audience, speaking clearly and loudly, making certain the visual aides could be seen by everyone, and showing enthusiasm for their studies.

Beverly included the parents in this activity since its inception. She wrote them the following letter:

Dear Parents,

We are beginning something very, very exciting in our room and I'd like to ask for your support. We are doing optional independent individualized research projects for these reasons:

1. It seems to me that we're always telling the children what they're going to study. I think it's time I asked them what they would like to learn about and provide time for them to do so (mostly in class). I know that some of the topics they are interested in are not school-related, but I believe they can learn a great deal by pursuing their interests.

2. I think the children need an organized and exciting method of study that they can apply to all future projects in years to come.

All of children were asked to participate and have chosen topics and narrowed them down. Your child has decided to study about _____ and his/her project might be _____. At this time all of the students have written a list of questions which we have edited and are now in search of answers. I'm asking parents to help their children obtain the information they will need. They may need a ride to a library or a local museum. They may need your help in locating other resources such as magazines, videotapes, or resource people to interview. You may be able to get copies made for them of some of their findings such as charts, pictures, and longer readings. The answers to the questions will be used to create projects which will be done in school.

I realize that these projects will be challenging for everyone involved, but I believe your child will grow in many ways as a result of this effort. I will sincerely appreciate any assistance you can provide and thank you in advance for your support. If you have any questions please call. If you don't wish to have your child participate, please let me know.

Sincerely yours,
Beverly Favreau

Most parents did assist their youngsters in a variety of ways. If the parents couldn't help them, Beverly did, and all students were supported in their efforts. As Beverly said, although the research and fact finding was done in a many places, all of the projects were completed in school.

At the conclusion of the study the parents were invited to an evening of celebration, and I would like to share my reaction to this event with you.

At the time of this program, I had been a teacher of the gifted and talented for seven years. I had also been Bev's instructor in the course she had taken related to this special population of students. Bev was an enthusiastic member of the class and seemed to embrace many of the concepts presented. The individual who had made the course possible was Central Berkshire Regional School District's teacher of the gifted and talented, Mrs. Nancy Harrington. In this capacity Nancy was not only an outstanding teacher, but also did a great deal to encourage teachers to implement new strategies in their classrooms and actively supported their efforts. When Beverly wanted to attempt the individual projects, Nancy was there to support her.

When I arrived that evening I was not expecting to witness what unfolded. I felt briefly transported to my own gifted and talented product celebration, but these weren't only students identified as gifted and talented. This class contained a heterogeneous group of children with varying academic abilities. One by one, they presented their studies with the ease of a practicing professional, and only occasionally, was a head raised to look at the prompt card on the back wall. They knew their topics very well and used a wide variety of methods to share their information. Slide presentations, models, graphs, diagrams, transparencies, and many displays all graphically illustrated the extent and quality of their work. The children were extremely proud of their projects and wanted very much to share their results with their audience. They somehow seemed older than their years and I became very aware that I was experiencing a "radiation of excellence" (Ward, 1961).

Beverly brought what she had seen others do in a gifted and talented program and adapted these ideas into her own classroom. She presented the challenge and an entire class responded positively and enthusiastically. When everyone asked to participate, she developed strategies that would allow all students to become actively involved and successful in their pursuits.

The educator in me changed that evening and I have never been quite the same. In a resource room setting I had experienced what gifted children could do when given the opportunity to pursue a topic. I had been working in the regular classroom to develop Triad studies based on the curriculum that allowed all children to create a product based on their interest. I had often seen children do projects such as I-SEARCH, but I had never seen what occurred in that classroom during the development of these studies. It was a synthesis of individualized learning, cooperative learning, performance-based assessment, interdisciplinary studies, creative and critical thinking, learning how-to-learn skills, and much more. Students were working and learning together and were energized by what they were doing. This is what education should be about!

Beverly felt that in her entire career as an educator, this was the most outstanding experience she had ever had. She readily admitted that it was a tremendous amount of work and that it was certainly a scary venture with lots of risk-taking on her part and on the part of her students. She felt the rewards of her tireless efforts in the students' response to this challenge. They had learned so many valuable skills and lessons. They stretched beyond the classroom walls for resources and learned how to manage their studies, solve problems, make decisions, share with their peers, develop a quality product, and reach meaningful audiences.

Although these are life skills that need to be repeated in order to be mastered, this was the beginning for these youngsters. Students came much closer to understanding that they were capable of doing more than they ever thought they could do! These studies became PEAK EXPERIENCES for Beverly's students. Some day if someone asks them to share a memorable school experience, I'm sure they'll quickly remember their third grade year when their teacher allowed them to discover their own unique gifts and talents.

CHAPTER 6

MOST COMMONLY ASKED QUESTIONS ABOUT THE MODEL

Most Commonly Asked Questions About the Model

1. **I would like to implement this kind of study in my heterogeneous intermediate classroom and have students with very high, average, and below average ability. I also have special education students and students who have not yet mastered the English language. Is it possible for me to successfully implement a Triad study?**

When Triad studies were first developed and implemented, one of the primary goals was to assure that gifted and talented children were challenged in the regular classroom setting. However, it became apparent during the first implementations of these studies that they truly met the needs of all students. The Type I activities, especially the speakers, provide all students, regardless of their reading level, with knowledge about the topic which allows them to engage in class discussions and successfully participate in other activities. The Interest Development Center contains books at a wide variety of reading levels, artifacts, photographs, slides and narrated filmstrips, and other memorabilia that help children at all levels gain knowledge and understanding about a given topic. Type II training is appropriate for all levels since all children must learn and are capable of developing their creative and critical thinking skills, oral and written communication skills, and research skills.

The Type III training activities provide the most latitude for individualized learning. Each student has the opportunity to select a topic and a project based on his/her own interest and the teacher assists individual students in choosing projects based on his/her strength areas and at the correct level of difficulty. This allows each student to be challenged and not overwhelmed at the same time. This has been one of the most successful components of the Triad studies and has been

effectively implemented with all students in heterogeneous and homogeneous classrooms.

2. **I've read about flexible grouping and would like to know if and how this type of grouping is used in this kind of study?**

Students are flexibly grouped within the classroom when there is a need to do so. For example, during a Triad study students are taught how to focus their study or problem. Some students may need more assistance than others in learning this process. This group of students would be brought together in order for the teacher to provide additional instruction in problem focusing. A similar procedure would be used with any other skill that needs reinforcing.

Some students who have already mastered some of the skills would form a flexible group and have an opportunity to pursue an aspect of the study which would be more challenging to them. They might also participate in other enrichment opportunities available in the classroom. This strategy is called curriculum compacting and is used in order to assure that all students are functioning at an instructional level that is commensurate with their ability.

3. **I am currently on a four member team of middle school teachers. Although I employ many of the strategies presented in the Triad studies in my classroom, I am interested in working with my colleagues in planning an interdisciplinary Triad study. Only one other member of the team in interested in doing this. How can we get the others to participate?**

I would first recommend that those of you who are interested in developing a Triad interdisciplinary study do just that. As we know, there are many ways to integrate our curriculum and to make meaningful connections for our students. It is not mandatory that all disciplines be represented in each study or that all four members of your team participate in the study. Additionally, the teacher of a given discipline is not the only one who has the knowledge or ability to include the subject matter in a study.

As shown in the text of this book, you and your partner should review your curriculum, determine how authentic connections can be made, select a theme, and begin planning. When you implement the study, it will be done in only your two classes. There are many occasions in middle schools when two-member teacher teams work together and it is appropriate in your situation to do so.

Almost certainly after you complete your study, the other two members of the team will probably become interested in getting involved. This frequently happens when teachers are uncertain about how to do something and are unwilling to take a risk. Rather than admit this, they find numerous excuses not to try. However, once they have seen you successfully implement a study, they may be more willing to become involved. You will become role models and that will help your colleagues grow.

Of course this does not always work! There are those individuals who have little desire and motivation to do anything differently and feel their modus operandi is the best. The statement they usually make goes something like this, "I've done it this way for twenty years and it seems to work for me and my students. So why change?" In this case the only thing that will work is to move on and work with teachers who are interested in creating a truly effective integrated study.

4. **I am presently teaching in a rural community and am concerned about obtaining an adequate number of library resources for my students. Locating speakers is also a problem. Do you have any suggestions?**

Locating both library and community resources is one of the most often asked questions regarding Triad studies. Teachers from urban, suburban, and rural communities are all concerned about reaching into a community and finding no response. I always did the following things when I was in a new school community and knew I'd be needing resources.

1. Survey the parents of my students at the beginning of the school year and ask them about their professions or occupations, skills, hobbies, and interests. Determine if they would be willing to speak to the class and when they would be available to do so. I also let them know I would call them only if I felt they could assist is some way.
2. Visit the school and community library or libraries, get to know the librarians, and become acquainted with the resources available to students and teachers. Explore other possible local resources such as museums, historical societies, clubs, an organizations.
3. Create a Schoolwide Enrichment Team (See Chapter 3, Step 4).

4. Survey the interests of my colleagues either formally with a survey or informally through casual conversations and interviews. These individuals always have proved to be valuable, willing, and able speakers and mentors.

5. Locate one individual, usually a parent, who is willing to volunteer their time to call and locate specific speakers. This should generally be an individual who has been in the community a number of years and has many acquaintances.

I first used this procedure in a rural community, but it has also been successful in both urban and suburban settings. I have always been surprised at the enthusiastic response from individuals who are interested in working with students and contributing to classroom studies.

5. The area of creative thinking is relatively new to me. How can I gain more experience when I am unable to participate in any formal staff development training at this time?

I would highly recommend the book **Creativity is Forever**, written by Gary Davis, which was published by Kendall-Hunt Publishing Company in 1986. This book is an excellent starting point and provides the reader with definitions and theories of creativity, a description of the creative process, techniques of creative thinking, types of tests of creativity, tips for developing personal creativeness, and other related information. There is also a list of references that will direct you to other sources of information.

6. I'm exited and somewhat intimidated by the concept of all of my students selecting different topics based on their own interests for their independent studies. Although I know my subject well, I'm concerned they will be studying aspects of certain topics that I will know little about. How will I deal with this?

If the study is developed as intended, your students may very well stretch beyond your knowledge level and into new and meaningful directions. This is one of the most dynamic aspects of the study and certainly can be one of the most challenging and intimidating parts of implementing a new study. I always felt exactly as you are feeling when I entered new domains and disciplines with my students.

However, the key to this process is the new role you will now be playing. You will become the facilitator of your student's learning in the truest sense. You are not expected to know every detail of every topic or have mastery of your students' studies. You are becoming the "guide on the side" and will ultimately have mastery of the independent study methodology. The skills of independence which you will teach your students will include but not be limited to: decision making, problem focusing, problem solving, locating and utilizing both library and community resources, planning the study, notetaking, outlining, time management, brainstorming, and determining products and appropriate audiences.

It is essential that you are patient with yourself and your students during this learning process. As you learn new skills with your students, they will start to take ownership of their own learning experiences. They will be making their own decisions and solving their own problems. You are always there to direct and redirect as needed, nurture their new interests, and help them extend and reach beyond the boundaries of their existing knowledge and abilities.

Although you want your students to go as far as they can, it is never intended that you or your classroom will be out of control. You are still in the driver's seat and are monitoring the student's learning and adjusting the process as necessary. When I first began implementing these studies, I was not comfortable with my students moving in so many different directions and often brought the class together to assess where they all were and where they were going. Although I still do this, I have more confidence in their ability to work independently.

It's really like any new thing. You just need to DO IT! This book has given you all of the tools you will need to get started.

7. When we brainstorm ideas for topics and projects my students think of the most outlandish things. How can I modify their ideas without discouraging them or dampening their enthusiasm?

My own rule of thumb on this point is to never say no to any idea! I should qualify this statement by saying that I refrain from saying no to an idea until the student and I have had time to think about the idea and its possibilities. I have found that students can do the most remarkable studies if I don't limit their thinking.

A few examples may serve to clarify my rationale. One of the teachers I had trained remembered my "never say no" philosophy when one of her second grade students said, "I know what I am going to do for my study. I am going to find a cure for cancer." Although this was

obviously impossible, her first reaction was not a negative one. She asked the student about her interest and discovered that her grandmother had recently died from cancer. They then talked about her need for more information and she visited the local Cancer Society. Following this visit she realized that the society had no information for kids her age to read. She decided to write a small booklet about cancer and donate it to the Cancer Society. Her topic had modified itself and although she did not find a cure for cancer, she made a significant contribution to other children.

8. **After brainstorming project ideas with students and inviting them to create any project they want, I still have students who select typical project ideas such as dioramas, posters, and reports. How can I get my students to pursue other project ideas?**

We have not generally given children the opportunity to choose the topics they will study and the projects they will do. If they are allowed to choose, there are usually very specific criteria which are established for them, e.g., a list of topics or projects from which to choose, a specific number of pages for a report, or the defined format for a project, such as a chart, report, mobile, diorama, etc.

When the task of selecting a project is open-ended and new to the learner, we need to show them how to take risks and make decisions. Many youngsters will not be comfortable with this kind of task. They probably know exactly how to be successful with traditional assignments and aren't sure what to do to achieve the same degree of success with open-ended tasks.

I remember two fifth grade students who were planning to study about schools during Colonial times. They decided to write a play that would take place in a Colonial classroom. Two weeks after they began the study, they said they had changed their minds and were going to write a report instead of the play. When I inquired about their rationale for changing projects, one boy nudged the other and said, "Show her!" Out of the desk came a pile of papers which was the beginning of their play. This was their first experience with writing a play and they needed my support, training, and validation of their efforts. I read what they had written, made suggestions, reviewed some of the resources that were available to them, and gave them a small book on how to write a play.

As a class, we also established a rubric and checklist of criteria on which the projects would be evaluated by both student and teacher. Sometimes we also used peer evaluation. This helped students know

what needed to be included in their projects. An excellent example of this is the *Student Product Assessment Form* (Renzulli and Reis, 1985) which can be used to successfully evaluate student products (See Appendix B).

9. **When I assign a project to my students, I usually give them a few weeks to complete the project at home. You suggested that these projects or at least a portion of them be done in school. What aspects of the study must be done in school and how do I find the time to do this?**

The best case scenario is to have all students complete their projects in school with you acting as the facilitator. However, since this may not be possible all of the time, one part of the study which must be done in school is the planning. This includes students determining the topics they will study and what they want to learn, listing what they must do to get started, locating relevant resources, and deciding on their products and audiences.

Students may need direct skill instruction for tasks such as conducting an interview, writing the dialogue for a play, accessing information from a computer, etc. In most cases, students often need assistance in creating a final product and presenting information to an audience. Very seldom have they been trained to create a display, use overhead transparencies, make filmstrips, draw a mural, make a mobile, etc. My students always needed assistance in how to present an oral presentation that will engage an audience. Instead of simply reading reports, my students needed to learn skills for effective public speaking such as projecting their voices, maintaining eye contact, and speaking slowly and loudly.

The list of needs will vary depending on your class and the topics and projects they choose to pursue. Although some of the actual doing of the project may be done at home, the skills students need to be successful in the study fall in your domain as teacher and facilitator.

10. **I feel overwhelmed with the management of so many independent studies. How do I keep all my students on task and monitor what they are doing?**

This aspect of a Triad study usually does seem overwhelming especially the first time you attempt it. However, you will have all the tools you need to work through this process with your students. Perhaps the most significant adjustment you will need to make is giving your

students more freedom to explore their studies and use this freedom to their advantage. If we program and strictly orchestrate all the activities of our students, they will never learn to direct themselves or know what to do when given time to pursue interests.

The *Management Plan* provides the direction students need, as well as an opportunity for teachers to provide necessary feedback during the learning process. A timeline helps to keep everyone moving at approximately the same pace. Students are more likely to stay on task if they are interested in the topic they are studying and excited about the project they will be creating. This should be the focus of your efforts. As the students get more and more involved and enthused about their studies, their feelings and attitudes will become contagious.

Obviously some students will have more difficulty than others and will need more guidance from you. As with all teaching, we monitor and adjust as needed.

11. I am a very traditional teacher and my primary instructional style is that of lecture and discussion. I have never used many of the methods and strategies included in the Triad studies and although I'd like to try, I'm afraid I'll fail. What would you suggest?

I have found that this concern is a common one and has been voiced by many teachers. One option is to begin slowly and try one new strategy at a time, since many of them are new to you. For example, you might begin to use speakers when introducing new topics to your students, create an Interest Development Center for one of your studies, or teach your students decision making and other strategies that are new to you. Once you become more comfortable with several aspects of the study, you may feel more comfortable trying to do the entire study.

Many teachers have thrown caution to the wind and JUST TRIED IT! Everything may not be perfect, but it will get better each time you do it. It usually is a wonderful learning experience for you and your students. You certainly won't be the same person after you try implementing one of these exciting studies in your classroom.

12. How much staff development is needed before teachers are able to implement a Triad study?

Teachers have been trained to use this model in graduate courses, one and two-week training sessions, one and two-day training sessions, and many other time frames. However, there seems to be a direct correlation between the amount of time devoted to the training and the quality of the studies and the comfort level of the teachers. The more time spent on training, the better the studies, the more comfortable the teachers, and the more successful the students.

The amount of training can be decreased if an enrichment specialist or teacher of the gifted and talented is available to support the teachers' efforts and if the *Schoolwide Enrichment Model* is being implemented in the school. The training needs to be personalized for each school district based on their individual needs.

13. What role do computers and other technology play in the Triad studies?

Computers play a key role in the development of Triad studies and should be used whenever possible. Type I experiences can be brought into the classroom through teleconferencing. Students can now access information quickly on CD-ROM encyclopedias and the Internet and print data in minutes. The card catalog can also be found on the computer in many school media centers. *Scholastic Network*, *Prodigy*, *CompuServe*, *America On-Line*, and other Internet programs allow children to communicate with people all over the world. Articles from periodicals can be faxed directly to the students. Interlibrary loan allows for books to be shared among libraries in many states. Since students can now locate multiple resources and information more easily, this releases the teacher from being the primary resource person.

BIBLIOGRAPHY

Bibliography

Amento, B. J., et al. (1991). **From Sea to Shining Sea.** Boston: Houghton Mifflin and Company.

Baldwin, A. Y. (1980). *Webbing: A Technique for Developing Instructional Activities for the Gifted.* **Roeper Review,** 3(1), 27-30.

Barth, R. S. (1990). **Improving Schools from Within: Teachers, Parents, and Principals Can Make the Difference.** San Francisco: Jossey-Bess.

Beane, J. A. (1990). **A Middle School Curriculum from Rhetoric to Reality.** Columbus, OH: National Middle School Association.

Burns, D. E. (1985). *Interest Development Centers: Land of Opportunity.* **Gifted Child Today,** (37), 14-15.

Burns, D. E. (1990). **Pathways to Investigative Skills: Instructional Lessons for Guiding Students from Problem Finding to Final Product.** Mansfield Center, CT: Creative Learning Press, Inc.

Bloom, B. S. [Ed.]. (1954). **Taxonomy of Educational Objectives Handbook I: Cognitive Domain.** New York: Longman Publishers.

Cellerino, M. B. & Story, C. M. (1985). *An Energetic Evolution: Meeting the Needs of the Gifted in the Regular Classroom.* **Roeper Review,** 8(2), 105-109.

Connecticut State Department of Education. (1987). **Connecticut's Common Core of Learning.** Hartford, CT: Connecticut State Department of Education.

Davis, G. (1986). **Creativity is Forever.** Dubuque, IA: Kendall-Hunt Publishers, Inc.

DeBono, E. (1986). **CoRT Thinking, CoRT 1.** New York: Pergamon Press.

Eberle, R. F. (1987). **SCAMPER: Games for Imagination Development.** East Aurora, NY: DOK Publishers.

Fogarty, R. (1991). **The Mindful School: How to Integrate the Curriculum.** Palatine, IL: IRI/Skylight Publishing Company.

Isaksen, S. G. & Treffinger, D. J. (1985). **Creative Problem Solving: The Basic Course.** Buffalo, NY: Bearly Limited.

Jacobs, H. H. (1991). *Planning for Curriculum Integration.* **Educational Leadership,** 49(2), 27-28.

Jacobs, H. H. & Borland, J. H. (1986). *The Interdisciplinary Concept Model: Theory and Practice.* **Gifted Child Quarterly,** 30 (4), 159-163.

Kaplan, S. N. (1986). *The Grid: A Model to Construct Differentiated Curriculum for the Gifted.* **Systems and Models for Developing Programs for the Gifted and Talented,** J. S. Renzulli [Ed.], (pp. 180-193). Mansfield Center, CT: Creative Learning Press, Inc.

National Commission on Excellence in Education. (1983). **A Nation at Risk: The Imperative for Education Reform.** Washington, DC: The National Science Foundation.

Osborn, A. F. (1963). **Applied Imagination.** New York: Charles Scribner's Sons.

Reis, S. M. & Cellerino, M. B. (1983). *Guiding Gifted Students Through Independent Study.* **Teaching Exceptional Children,** 15, 136-141.

Renzulli, J. S. (1977). **The Enrichment Triad Model: A Guide for Developing Defensible Programs for the Gifted and Talented.** Mansfield Center, CT: Creative Learning Press, Inc.

Renzulli, J. S. (1982). *What Makes a Problem Real? Stalking the Illusive Meaning of Qualitative Differences in Gifted Education.* **Gifted Child Quarterly,** 26(4), 148-156.

Renzulli, J. S. (1994). **School for Talent Development: A Practical Plan for Total School Improvement.** Mansfield Center, CT: Creative Learning Press, Inc.

Renzulli, J. S. & Reis, S. M. (1985). **The Schoolwide Enrichment Model: A Comprehensive Plan for Educational Excellence.** Mansfield Center, CT: Creative Learning Press, Inc.

Renzulli, J. S., Reis, S.M. & Smith, L. H. (1981). **The Revolving Door Identification Model.** Mansfield Center, CT: Creative Learning Press, Inc.

Renzulli, J. S. & Smith, L. H. (1977). **The Management Plan for Individual and Small Group Investigations of Real Problems.** Mansfield Center, CT: Creative Learning Press, Inc.

Renzulli, J. S. & Smith, L. H. (1978). **The Learning Styles Inventory: A Measure of Student Preference for Instructional Techniques.** Mansfield Center, CT: Creative Learning Press, Inc.

Renzulli, J. S. & Smith, L. H. (1978). *What Makes Giftedness? Re-examining the Definition.* **Phi Delta Kappan,** 60(3), 180-184.

Taylor, C. W. (1986). *Cultivating Simultaneous Student Growth in Both Multiple Creative Talents and Knowledge.* **Systems and Models for Developing Programs for the Gifted and Talented,** J. S. Renzulli [Ed.], (pp. 306-351). Mansfield Center, CT: Creative Learning Press, Inc.

Vars, G. F. (1991). *Integrated Curriculum in Historical Perspective.* **Educational Leadership,** 49(2), 14-15.

Ward, V. (1961). **Basic Concepts in Psychology and Education of the Gifted.** (W. B. Barbe and J. S. Renzulli [Eds.]). New York: Irvington Publishers.

APPENDICES

Appendix A

INTERDISCIPLINARY STUDIES
LESSON PLANNING GUIDES

Appendix A Listing

Interdisciplinary Studies Lesson Planning Guides
Native Americans of the Plains Study

Lesson 1:   Tower Simulation (Cooperative Group Lesson)
Lesson 2:   Introduction to Brainstorming*
Lesson 3:   Introduction to SCAMPER*
Lesson 4:   SCAMPER/Brainstorming
Lesson 5:   Introduction to Webbing*
Lesson 6:   Webbing
Lesson 7:   Outlining
Lesson 8:   Introduction to Decision Making*
Lesson 9:   Decision Making
Lesson 10:   Introduction to Creative Problem Solving*
Lesson 11:   Creative Problem Solving
Lesson 12:   Type I Debriefing or Follow-up Discussion
Lesson 13:   Sequencing/Task Analysis
Lesson 14:   Compare and Contrast
Lesson 15:   Cause and Effect
Lesson 16:   Expository Writing: Descriptive Essay
Lesson 17:   Information Gathering
Lesson 18:   Analysis of Dwellings
Lesson 19:   Oral Presentation Skills
Lesson 20:   Topic/Problem Focusing
Lesson 21:   Modified Management Plan

*General introductory lessons not related to the theme.

Interdisciplinary Studies
Lesson Planning Guide

Interdisciplinary Unit: _____ Lesson Title: _____

Teacher: _____ Grade: _____ Introductory _____ Midway _____ Follow-up _____

Instructional Strategies:

_____ Lecture
_____ Discussion
_____ Cooperative Learning
_____ Peer Tutoring
_____ Learning or Interest Center
_____ Simulation or Role Playing
_____ Learning Games
_____ Guided Independent Study
_____ Other _____

Disciplines Included:

_____ Language Arts
_____ Social Studies
_____ Mathematics
_____ Science
_____ Music
_____ Art
_____ Personal/Social Development
_____ Other _____
_____ Other _____

Instructional Objectives: Include content, process or skills, attitudes and attributes.

Description: Include any previous learning or necessary background material.

Resource Materials: Include chapter and page references to textbooks and/or other sources.

Assessment/Follow-up: List the method(s) you will use to assess mastery of objectives.

Lesson 1

Interdisciplinary Studies
Lesson Planning Guide

Interdisciplinary Unit: _____Native Americans: Plains_____ Lesson Title:__Tower Simulation___
Teacher: __M. Beecher__   Grade: __4__   Introductory __X__   Midway_____   Follow-up _____

Instructional Strategies:

_____	Lecture	
_____	Discussion	
_____	Cooperative Learning	
_____	Peer Tutoring	
_____	Learning or Interest Center	
__X__	Simulation or Role Playing	
_____	Learning Games	
_____	Guided Independent Study	
__X__	Other___Small and Large Groups	

Disciplines Included:

__X__	Language Arts
_____	Social Studies
__X__	Mathematics
_____	Science
_____	Music
__X__	Art
__X__	Personal/Social Development
__X__	Other _Critical Thinking_
__X__	Other _Creative Thinking_

Instructional Objectives: Include content, process or skills, attitudes and attributes.

In small groups students will plan and construct tall, free-standing structures. The students will analyze the effectiveness of their groups in the planning and construction of their towers.

Description: Include any previous learning or necessary background material.

The study of Native Americans of the Plains will require your class to engage in many small group, problem solving activities. This simulation will help you to analyze and assess your students' abilities to work effectively with each other and determine if you need to use other team-building activities prior to commencing the study.

Students will be asked to use Legos to build the tallest free-standing structure possible in a given period of time. Small groups of students will be given 15 minutes to plan how to build the structure. During this time, they will not be allowed to "touch" the materials. Groups will then be given 15 minutes to build the structure. During this time students are not allowed to talk to each other. The materials used for the structure and the time can be adjusted as needed.

Resource Materials: Include chapter and page references to textbooks and/or other sources.

Lego Bricks or any other building materials.

Assessment/Follow-up: List the method(s) you will use to assess mastery of objectives.

A small and large group discussion will be used to evaluate the effectiveness of the simulation. Students will list the pluses, minuses, and interesting* aspects of the process of their small group. They will then share their findings with the whole class.

*DeBono, E. (1986). **CoRT Thinking, CoRT I**. New York: Pergamon Press.

Lesson 2

Interdisciplinary Studies
Lesson Planning Guide

Interdisciplinary Unit: _____All Studies_____ Lesson Title: __Introduction to Brainstorming__

Teacher: __M. Beecher__ Grade: __All__ Introductory __X__ Midway _____ Follow-up _____

Instructional Strategies:

_____	Lecture
__X__	Discussion
__X__	Cooperative Learning
_____	Peer Tutoring
_____	Learning or Interest Center
_____	Simulation or Role Playing
_____	Learning Games
_____	Guided Independent Study
__X__	Other __Large Group__

Disciplines Included:

__X__	Language Arts
_____	Social Studies
_____	Mathematics
_____	Science
_____	Music
_____	Art
__X__	Personal/Social Development
__X__	Other __Creative Thinking__
__X__	Other __Critical Thinking__

Instructional Objectives: Include content, process or skills, attitudes and attributes.

The students will define the four components of creative thinking: fluency, flexibility, originality, and elaboration. The students will learn the rules of brainstorming.

Description: Include any previous learning or necessary background material.

Imagine that you bought a raffle ticket because the 1st prize was a trip to Disney World and the EPCOT Center in Orlando, Florida. However, you did not win the 1st prize. Instead, you won the 3rd prize, which was a lifetime supply (1,250,000) of cottonballs. Lucky you! Now, what are you going to do with all those cottonballs?

Review the creative thinking process:

Fluency:	The production of a large number of ideas, products, or plans.
Flexibility:	The production of ideas or products that show a variety of possibilities or realms of thought.
Originality:	The production of ideas that are unusual and unique.
Elaboration:	The production of ideas that display intensive detail or enrichment.

Define brainstorming as a technique which is used to generate numerous possible ideas and/or solutions for a given problem.

Write the following rules of brainstorming on a chart and discuss them with your class. This chart should be kept in a visible place in the classroom until all students have mastered the rules of brainstorming (Osborne, 1963).

1. Generate as many ideas as you possibly can.
2. Think of unusual, wild ideas.
3. Don't judge contributions of the group.
4. Build upon or modify the ideas of others.

Ask students to think of as many ways as possible to use their lifetime supply of cottonballs. List the ideas on a chalkboard or flip chart. Be certain to have enough space for all ideas.

When students can no longer think of new ideas, divide the class into groups of four. Ask them to look at the list on the board and then generate at least twenty more ideas. Then ask student groups to select the two ideas they like best. Ask groups to share their ideas and add them to the list on the board.

Resource Materials: Include chapter and page references to textbooks and/or other sources.

Components of creative thinking: fluency, flexibility, originality, elaboration and rules of brainstorming written on charts or chalkboard.

Assessment/Follow-up: List the method(s) you will use to assess mastery of objectives.

In small cooperative groups students will be asked to define the following and be prepared to share orally with the class:

1. Four components of creative thinking
2. Rules of brainstorming

Osborne, A. (1963). **Applied Imagination.** New York: Charles Scribner's Sons.

Lesson 3

Interdisciplinary Studies
Lesson Planning Guide

Interdisciplinary Unit: ____All Disciplines____ Lesson Title: __Introduction to SCAMPER__
Teacher: __M. Beecher__ Grade: __All__ Introductory _X_ Midway _____ Follow-up _____

Instructional Strategies:

_____	Lecture
_____	Discussion
__X__	Cooperative Learning
_____	Peer Tutoring
_____	Learning or Interest Center
__X__	Simulation or Role Playing
_____	Learning Games
_____	Guided Independent Study
__X__	Other ____Inductive Lesson____

Disciplines Included:

__X__	Language Arts
_____	Social Studies
_____	Mathematics
_____	Science
_____	Music
_____	Art
__X__	Personal/Social Development
__X__	Other __Creative Thinking__
__X__	Other __Critical Thinking__

Instructional Objectives: Include content, process or skills, attitudes and attributes.

The students will be able to define the meaning of each letter in the SCAMPER acronym and use the SCAMPER technique to enhance their brainstorming.

Description: Include any previous learning or necessary background material.

Share the following scenario with your students: "There has been a severe drought in the mid-western states. In several of the zoos, the ponds that once provided water for the large animals are now dry. In an attempt to save the animals, one zoo decided to install bathtubs and are trying to keep them filled with water. In his eagerness to get to the water, an elephant somehow became stuck in one of the tubs."

Ask students to brainstorm many different ways to get the elephant out of the tub. Record their ideas on the chalkboard or flip chart.

During brainstorming ask students some or all of the following questions but not necessarily in this order:

S -	Substitute	Imagine the elephant stuck in an elevator. How would you get him out?
C -	Combine	What if you motorized the tub and eliminated the bottom?
A -	Adapt	Could you motorize the tub?
M -	Modify	What might happen if you elongated the tub?
	Magnify	What might happen if you enlarged the tub?

Minify	What might happen if the tub was very tiny?
P - Put to Other Uses	Think of the tub as a shelter for the elephant.
	What ideas does this make you think of?
E - Eliminate	Could you cut off the bottom of the tub?
R - Reverse	How could you turn the tub upside down?

It is appropriate to ask these questions when students are finding it difficult to think of more ideas. When SCAMPER is used in this way, it enhances individual and group brainstorming.

Share the meaning of the SCAMPER acronym with your students and explain how you used it to help them generate more ideas. Have SCAMPER acronym written on a chart.

S - SUBSTITUTE	stuck in elevator
C - COMBINE	motorize and eliminate bottom of tub
A - ADAPT	motorize tub
M - MODIFY	elongate tub
MAGNIFY	make the tub larger
MINIFY	make the tub tiny
P - PUT TO OTHER USES	use as shelter
E - ELIMINATE	cut off bottom
R - REVERSE	turn upside down
REARRANGE	put legs on bottom

Resource Materials: Include chapter and page references to textbooks and/or other sources.

SCAMPER acronym on a chart. This chart would be displayed in the room following this lesson and referred to when needed.

Assessment/Follow-up: List the method(s) you will use to assess mastery of objectives.

In small groups students will be asked to explain the meaning of SCAMPER and list the ways its use encourages the generation of more ideas when brainstorming.

Eberle, B. (1987). **SCAMPER: Games for Imagination Development.** East Aurora, NY: DOK Publications.

Lesson 4
Interdisciplinary Studies
Lesson Planning Guide

Interdisciplinary Unit: ___Native Americans: Plains___   Lesson Title: ___SCAMPER/Brainstorming___

Teacher: ___M. Beecher___   Grade: ___4___   Introductory _____   Midway __X__   Follow-up _____

Instructional Strategies:	**Disciplines Included:**
_____ Lecture	__X__ Language Arts
__X__ Discussion	__X__ Social Studies
__X__ Cooperative Learning	_____ Mathematics
_____ Peer Tutoring	_____ Science
_____ Learning or Interest Center	_____ Music
_____ Simulation or Role Playing	_____ Art
_____ Learning Games	__X__ Personal/Social Development
_____ Guided Independent Study	_____ Other _____
__X__ Other ___Brainstorming/SCAMPER___	_____ Other _____

Instructional Objectives: Include content, process or skills, attitudes and attributes.

The student will use the SCAMPER technique to generate ideas for possible leisure activities for a Plains Indian family.

Description: Include any previous learning or necessary background material.

Imagine for a moment that you are a Plains Indian child, and because of the severe winter snowstorms and ten foot high snowdrifts, you and your family have been confined to your teepee for several weeks. The time is passing slowly and you and your brothers and sisters are trying to think of some family fun or entertainment during these long hours.

Review the SCAMPER acronym and explain that students will use the SCAMPER technique to help them think of more ideas when they are brainstorming.

Before you begin, have the class list all items that they might find in a teepee of a Plains Indian family. Using this list, have students brainstorm activities for the snowbound Indian family. During brainstorming encourage students to SCAMPER in order to generate more ideas. Ask the following questions and/or make some of these suggestions:

S - SUBSTITUTE   Pretend that the family is not in a teepee, but a cave.

C - COMBINE   Could you combine some of the items in the teepee and use them in a unique way?

A - ADAPT	What if all the items in the teepee were made of rubber?
M - MODIFY	Change the shape of the teepee.
MAGNIFY	Imagine the teepee the size of a football field.
MINIFY	Picture everything in the teepee fitting into the palm of your hand.
P - PUT TO OTHER USES	Find one item on your list. How could you use it differently? How could you play with it?
E - ELIMINATE	Imagine that one side of the teepee is glass.
R - REVERSE	Picture the teepee upside down.

Resource Materials: Include chapter and page references to textbooks and/or other sources.

SCAMPER chart for easy student reference.

Assessment/Follow-up: List the method(s) you will use to assess mastery of objectives.

The type of responses will indicate if children are using the SCAMPER technique. In pairs, have students analyze and list how SCAMPER helped them generate more ideas.

Eberle, B. (1987). **SCAMPER: Games for Imagination Development.** East Aurora, NY: DOK Publications.

Lesson 5
Interdisciplinary Studies
Lesson Planning Guide

Interdisciplinary Unit: ___Native Americans: Plains___ Lesson Title: ___Introduction to Webbing___

Teacher: ___M. Beecher___ Grade: ___4___ Introductory _____ Midway __X__ Follow-up _____

Instructional Strategies:

_____ Lecture
__X__ Discussion
_____ Cooperative Learning
_____ Peer Tutoring
_____ Learning or Interest Center
_____ Simulation or Role Playing
_____ Learning Games
_____ Guided Independent Study
__X__ Other ___Brainstorming (Webbing)___

Disciplines Included:

_____ Language Arts
_____ Social Studies
_____ Mathematics
_____ Science
_____ Music
_____ Art
_____ Personal/Social Development
__X__ Other ___Creative Thinking___
_____ Other _____

Instructional Objectives: Include content, process or skills, attitudes and attributes.

The students will learn the concept of webbing, which is a technique used to explain a topic and to explore the relationships in that topic.

Description: Include any previous learning or necessary background material.

Ask students to think about all the things that are of interest to them and write these ideas on a piece of paper.

Talk about your own interests and explain that they seem to be in specific categories and have many dimensions. Explain that you can list your interests in different ways, but that you have decided to "web" yours. Define webbing as stated in the objective.

Create your own web on the chalkboard, overhead, or chart as children observe and participate in the process. Have them assist you in categorizing your interests.

Students are then asked to create their own interest web by using and categorizing their list.

(See Sample Interest Web).

Resource Materials: Include chapter and page references to textbooks and/or other sources.

Chalkboard, overhead, or chart.

Assessment/Follow-up: List the method(s) you will use to assess mastery of objectives.

Share your web with your neighbor. What did you like about webbing? What was difficult? How might it be useful to you in the future?

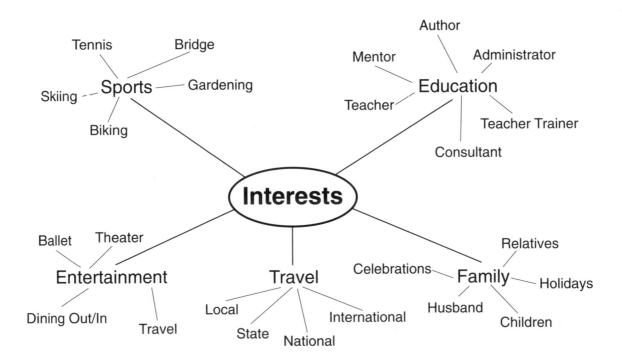

Lesson 6
Interdisciplinary Studies
Lesson Planning Guide

Interdisciplinary Unit: ___Native Americans: Plains___   Lesson Title: ___Webbing___
Teacher: ___M. Beecher___   Grade: ___4___   Introductory __X__   Midway _____   Follow-up _____

Instructional Strategies:

- __X__ Lecture
- __X__ Discussion
- _____ Cooperative Learning
- _____ Peer Tutoring
- _____ Learning or Interest Center
- _____ Simulation or Role Playing
- _____ Learning Games
- _____ Guided Independent Study
- _____ Other _____

Disciplines Included:

- __X__ Language Arts
- __X__ Social Studies
- _____ Mathematics
- _____ Science
- _____ Music
- _____ Art
- _____ Personal/Social Development
- _____ Other _____
- _____ Other _____

Instructional Objectives: Include content, process or skills, attitudes and attributes.

The students will create a content or topical web of the Native Americans of the Plains.

Description: Include any previous learning or necessary background material.

The teacher states, "For the past two weeks we have been exploring the topic of the Native Americans tribes of the Plains. We have already learned a great deal from our different speakers, Interest Development Center, films and filmstrips, textbooks, and many other books that we have in our room. Think for a moment about the many aspects of this culture. Today we are going to create a web of this culture. We will use the same method of webbing that we used to create our interest webs a few weeks ago."

Refer to the web you created when you planned this study. The web the students create with you will not and should not be a duplicate of yours.

Define the purpose of webbing as a technique used to expand a topic and explore relationships inherent in that topic. Review one of the student interest webs.

Place the words "Native Americans of the Plains" in the center of the blackboard and attempt to elicit the major sub-topics of this culture from the children, i.e., religion, art, music, clothing, major battles, leaders, etc. If the children don't give you major topics, you can assist them in finding major categories. For example, if students

mention the Sun Dance before the topic of religion has been introduced, ask them under what sub-topic that might appear in a text or encyclopedia. It is assumed that the children will have been introduced to the concept of major and minor topic areas.

Children should be encouraged to continue expanding the web until they have exhausted all of their ideas. Remember that you can participate too! Assure children that this is a continuous or "growing" web and that they can expand upon it throughout their study.

This web should be created on the chalkboard or poster paper. This will enable you and your class to modify the web during the brainstorming of ideas. The web should be placed in a permanent place in the classroom, such as a bulletin board.

Another method used to create a web includes having students generate a linear list of varied aspects of the Plains culture. Students can then categorize the list and create a web. Many teachers prefer doing it this way. Use whatever method you think will work best for you and your students.

A student-created web is shown on the next page. At this grade level, the student web will initially be less sophisticated and complete than the teacher's web.

Resource Materials: Include chapter and page references to textbooks and/or other sources.

Chalkboard or Large Poster Paper.

Assessment/Follow-up: List the method(s) you will use to assess mastery of objectives.

Look at the web and discuss it with your neighbor. Is there anything you would like to add at this time? Have we included all of the important or major parts of this culture? Students will continue to add to the web as they gather and learn new information about the Native Americans of the Plains.

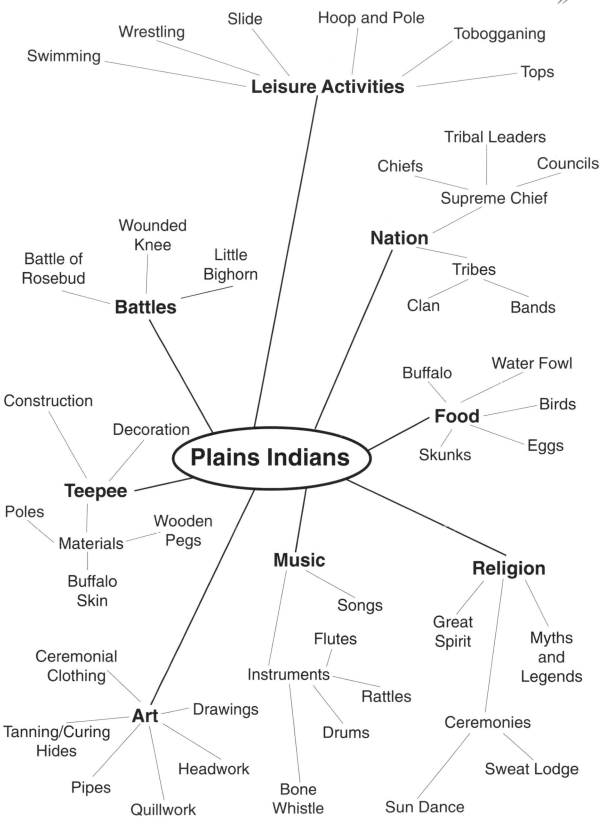

Swimming
Wrestling
Slide
Hoop and Pole
Tobogganing
Tops

Leisure Activities

Tribal Leaders
Chiefs
Councils
Supreme Chief

Nation

Tribes
Clan
Bands

Wounded Knee
Battle of Rosebud
Little Bighorn

Battles

Buffalo
Water Fowl
Birds

Food

Skunks
Eggs

Construction
Decoration

Plains Indians

Teepee
Poles
Materials
Wooden Pegs
Buffalo Skin

Music
Songs
Flutes
Instruments
Rattles
Drums
Bone Whistle

Religion
Great Spirit
Myths and Legends
Ceremonies
Sweat Lodge
Sun Dance

Ceremonial Clothing
Art
Drawings
Tanning/Curing Hides
Pipes
Headwork
Quillwork

Lesson 7
Interdisciplinary Studies
Lesson Planning Guide

Interdisciplinary Unit: ___Native Americans: Plains___ Lesson Title: ___Outlining___

Teacher: ___M. Beecher___ Grade: ___4___ Introductory _____ Midway __X__ Follow-up _____

Instructional Strategies:	**Disciplines Included:**
_____ Lecture	__X__ Language Arts
__X__ Discussion	__X__ Social Studies
__X__ Cooperative Learning	_____ Mathematics
_____ Peer Tutoring	_____ Science
_____ Learning or Interest Center	_____ Music
_____ Simulation or Role Playing	_____ Art
_____ Learning Games	_____ Personal/Social Development
_____ Guided Independent Study	_____ Other _____
__X__ Other ___Large and Small Groups___	_____ Other _____

Instructional Objectives: Include content, process or skills, attitudes and attributes.

The students will use webbing to expand their self-selected independent study topic.

The students will create a formal outline from the content of their web.

Description: Include any previous learning or necessary background material.

The teacher says, "Now that you have decided on your topic and have been reading and gathering information about it, let's use webbing to expand your topic. Begin with your topic as the center of the web. Think of the major sub-topics related to your topic. Finally add as many details as you can." An example of a topic web is shown at the end of this description.

Students will web their topic using the resources in the room when additional information is needed.

Outlining will be defined as a way to organize a topic into major and sub-topic areas. Explain that you can outline easily once you have webbed a topic. Use the teepee web and transform it into an outline on the blackboard. Have students then create their own outline from their web. The following outline is based on the teepee web at the end of this lesson.

THE TEEPEE

I. Materials
    A. Buffalo Skins
    B. Long Poles
    C. Ground Pegs
    D. Wooden Pins

II. Structure
    A. Funnel-Shaped
        1. Broad Base
        2. Pointed Top
    B. Poles
        1. Circled at Top
        2. Twenty-five Feet High

III. Interior
    A. Top Opening
    B. Center Fire Pits
    C. Seats and Beds
    D. Buffalo Robes and Blankets

VI. Teepee Decorations
    A. Paintings
        1. War Exploits
        2. Hunting Expeditions
    B. Drawings
        1. War Exploits
        2. Hunting Expeditions

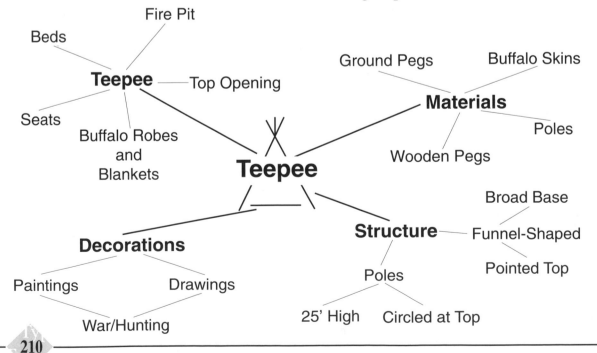

Resource Materials: Include chapter and page references to textbooks and/or other sources.

Chalkboard.

Assessment/Follow-up: List the method(s) you will use to assess mastery of objectives.

Students will review each other's webs and outlines in groups of two and will add or delete information. The teacher will then ask students to respond to the following questions:

- In what ways does webbing assist you in developing an outline?
- How does an outline help you to organize your thinking?
- Which is the best way for YOU to organize your thinking?

Lesson 8

Interdisciplinary Studies
Lesson Planning Guide

Interdisciplinary Unit: ___All Studies___   Lesson Title: _Decision Making—Introduction_
Teacher: _M. Beecher_   Grade: _All_   Introductory _X_   Midway _X_   Follow-up _____

Instructional Strategies:

_X___ Lecture
_X___ Discussion
_____ Cooperative Learning
_____ Peer Tutoring
_____ Learning or Interest Center
_____ Simulation or Role Playing
_____ Learning Games
_____ Guided Independent Study
_X___ Other ___Large and Small Groups___

Disciplines Included:

_X___ Language Arts
_____ Social Studies
_____ Mathematics
_____ Science
_____ Music
_____ Art
_X___ Personal/Social Development
_X___ Other ___Critical Thinking___
_____ Other _____

Instructional Objectives: Include content, process or skills, attitudes and attributes.

The student will be able to define decision making.

The student will determine the steps of decision making through a metacognitive process.

The students will use a decision making process to assist the facilitator in determining which car to buy.

Description: Include any previous learning or necessary background material.

Teacher states, "We often need to make decisions about many things such as what to buy, what to do with our free time, which television shows to watch, etc. Think of a decision you've made or will have to make and write it on the paper I've given you. We will talk about this later in the lesson."

Define decision making for students as a strategy for systematically selecting among alternatives.

Ask students to help you make a decision that you and your family are having difficulty making. Tell them that you want to buy a car and can't decide among the following four-door vehicles: a Honda Accord LXI, an Acura Legend, and a BMW. All of these cars come in your choice of color and have the following features that you would like: power brakes and steering, cruise control, stereo and tape deck, and rear defroster.

Explain that you will use the following chart to help with your decision making and explain how it is used. Then work together to make a decision.

EVALUATION CRITERIA	ALTERNATIVES		
	Honda	Acura	BMW
Style	3	2	3
Spaciousness	2	3	2
Cost	2	2	1
Reliability	3	3	3
Front Wheel Drive	3	1	3
TOTAL	13	11	12

RATING SCALE: 3 - Excellent
                2 - Average
                1 - Poor

Resource Materials: Include chapter and page references to textbooks and/or other sources.

Decision Making Matrix on Overhead Transparency. Overhead Markers.

Assessment/Follow-up: List the method(s) you will use to assess mastery of objectives.

With a partner, write the definition of decision making and analyze the steps of the decision making process. Think about and share a decision you made recently with your partner. How would the steps you have learned and the chart help you with the process?

Lesson 9
Interdisciplinary Studies
Lesson Planning Guide

Interdisciplinary Unit: _____Native Americans: Plains_____   Lesson Title:_____Decision Making_____

Teacher: ___M. Beecher___   Grade: ___4___   Introductory _____   Midway___X___   Follow-up _____

Instructional Strategies:

_____	Lecture
__X__	Discussion
_____	Cooperative Learning
_____	Peer Tutoring
_____	Learning or Interest Center
__X__	Simulation or Role Playing
_____	Learning Games
_____	Guided Independent Study
_____	Other _____

Disciplines Included:

_____	Language Arts
_____	Social Studies
_____	Mathematics
_____	Science
_____	Music
_____	Art
_____	Personal/Social Development
__X__	Other ___Critical Thinking___
_____	Other _____

Instructional Objectives: Include content, process or skills, attitudes and attributes.

The students will use the decision making strategy to determine the topic they wish to research for their independent study.

Description: Include any previous learning or necessary background material.

Teacher states, "As I mentioned earlier you will have an opportunity to select the topic that you would like to study more about during our Plains Indian Unit. You will become the 'expert' in this area and will develop a product of your choice related to this topic. Ultimately, you will teach others in the class what you have learned. You may choose a topic from the web or any other topic. It is most important that you are really interested in what you choose. To assist you with this, we will use our decision making process."

Review the definition of decision making, i.e., a strategy for systematically selecting among alternatives.

Model the process by making a decision together as though you were trying to decide.

Students are asked to select two or three alternatives or topic ideas and use the same procedure for making their decision about their project.

As students are working on their decision making, the teacher will circulate and assist anyone having difficulty. All children should have made a decision at the conclusion of this lesson.

An example done with a group of fifth graders is as follows:

EVALUATION CRITERIA	ALTERNATIVES		
	Teepee	Arts	Clothing
Interest	3	2	2
Reference Books	3	2	3
Time	2	2	2
TOTAL	8	6	7

RATING SCALE: 3 - Excellent
                2 - Average
                1 - Poor

Resource Materials: Include chapter and page references to textbooks and/or other sources.

Decision Making Chart for each student.

Assessment/Follow-up: List the method(s) you will use to assess mastery of objectives.

In your cooperative group, analyze the process you just used to make your decision. Make at least three positive statements about the process. What is one way you could improve the process? Can you think of other ways to improve the process?

Lesson 10

Interdisciplinary Studies
Lesson Planning Guide

Interdisciplinary Unit: _____All Studies_____   Lesson Title: __Introduction to Creative Problem Solving (CPS)__

Teacher: __M. Beecher__   Grade: __4__   Introductory __X__   Midway _____   Follow-up _____

Instructional Strategies:

__X__ Lecture
__X__ Discussion
__X__ Cooperative Learning
_____ Peer Tutoring
_____ Learning or Interest Center
__X__ Simulation or Role Playing
_____ Learning Games
_____ Guided Independent Study
__X__ Other __Problem Solving__

Disciplines Included:

__X__ Language Arts
_____ Social Studies
__X__ Mathematics
__X__ Science
_____ Music
_____ Art
_____ Personal/Social Development
__X__ Other __Creative Thinking__
__X__ Other __Critical Thinking__

Instructional Objectives: Include content, process or skills, attitudes and attributes.

The students will learn the six steps in the Creative Problem Solving process.

The students will solve a problem using the CPS process.

Description: Include any previous learning or necessary background material.

Teacher says, "Many of you seem to be concerned with a predicament we have in our classroom. It is the same situation every year in many classrooms in schools across the country. Let's discuss our "pencil predicament."

Discuss the predicament related to the problem of losing pencils in the classroom.

Introduce the class to the CPS process or strategy.

Define the six steps and explain the process involved in each one.

Suggest to students that they may be able to solve this problem by using CPS.

Mess Finding

Have students present an oral description of the predicament or "mess."

Fact Finding

When students seem to have a clear understanding of the "mess," have them make a list of all facts that are associated with this situation.
For example:

       Pencils are being lost.
       We've lost 40 pencils in one month.
       The pencils are blue #2 with erasers.
       We have a supply of 120 pencils which must last for one school year.
       No one has been seen taking the pencils.
       The people who use our pencils are: teachers, students, and visitors.
       There are approximately 70 students in and out of the room each week.
       Students borrow pencils from the teachers desk as needed.
       Pencils are in a holder on top of the desk.

Problem Finding

Ask students to look at the facts and generate problems that are reflected in these facts. Encourage students to think of as many problems as they can and begin each statement with ...

In what ways might we ...   prevent pencils from disappearing.
                         obtain more pencils.
                         change the procedure for borrowing pencils.

Students must now look at all the problems and decide which problem they would like to address. It may be the one they feel is most critical or important or it may be a combination of several problems. It is important that a group consensus be reached before proceeding.

Idea Finding

The problem is then written on the chalkboard or flip chart and students generate as many solutions to the problem as possible.

Solution Finding

From the ideas generated, students will need to determine their solution by establishing a criteria and evaluating the ideas that are most promising against the criteria.

Since this is the decision making step in CPS, you can use the steps of decision making at this point. It will be necessary for the children to narrow their ideas to the

best four or five. This can be done in many ways, but voting seems to be both time-efficient and democratic. Students decide on the five alternatives and criteria. Student ratings are also recorded. See sample chart below.

EVALUATION CRITERIA	ALTERNATIVES				
	Door Monitor	Collateral (Shoe)	"Lightbulb" * Pencil	Electric Eye	Numbered/ Pencil Holder **
Availability of Materials/Personnel	3	3	3	1	3
Lasting Effect	1	2	3	3	2
Ease of Doing	3	1	3	1	2
Little Time	2	2	2	3	2
Little Cost	3	3	3	1	3
TOTAL	12	11	14	9	12

RATING SCALE: 3 -   Excellent
                 2 -   Average
                 1 -   Poor

  * Use existing pencils and make yellow paper mache light bulbs on top of each pencil.
** Each child would have a number!

Acceptance Finding

Once a solution has been agreed upon, the group needs to decide a plan of action. This plan will include the following specific information about the implementation of the idea. Have students answer the questions who, what, where, when, why, and how.

Note: This lesson may take more than one session, but try to have it be no longer than two periods. Your goal is to have your students get a comprehensive, holistic view of the six steps. This is especially true until students have mastered the strategy.

Resource Materials: Include chapter and page references to textbooks and/or other sources.

Six Steps of CPS written on Overhead Projector or Chalkboard.

Assessment/Follow-up: List the method(s) you will use to assess mastery of objectives.

With a partner, write the six steps of the CPS process and briefly describe what you do at each step.

The entire class will then discuss and review the process.

 # Lesson 11
Interdisciplinary Studies
Lesson Planning Guide

Interdisciplinary Unit: _____Native Americans: Plains_____ Lesson Title: _Creative Problem Solving_____

Teacher: __M. Beecher___ Grade: __4__ Introductory _____ Midway _X_ Follow-up _____

Instructional Strategies:

_____ Lecture
__X___ Discussion
__X___ Cooperative Learning
_____ Peer Tutoring
_____ Learning or Interest Center
__X___ Simulation or Role Playing
_____ Learning Games
_____ Guided Independent Study
__X___ Other ____Problem Solving____

Disciplines Included:

__X___ Language Arts
__X___ Social Studies
__X___ Mathematics
__X___ Science
_____ Music
_____ Art
__X___ Personal/Social Development
__X___ Other __Creative Thinking__
__X___ Other __Critical Thinking__

Instructional Objectives: Include content, process or skill, attitudes and attributes.

The students will use Creative Problem Solving to resolve a young Plains Indian's dilemma.

Description: Include any previous learning or necessary background material.

Teacher says, "I'd like you to close your eyes and visualize yourself as a twelve year old Plains Indian. You are about to participate in your first Sweat Lodge Ceremony. As you know, it is customary for a young man to participate in this ceremony at the beginning of his manhood. As you approach the Sweat Lodge, you notice the frame is made of willow rods bent to form a hemispherical shape. It is covered with skins and seems large enough to accommodate several people. The hole dug near the door is filled with heated stones. After you enter the Lodge the stones are sprinkled with water to generate steam and the doorway is covered with a skin."

"You and the other young men offer prayers during your time in the Sweat Lodge and know this will purify your body. When you leave the lodge, you and the other young men are told to plunge into a cold stream. You hold your breath and dive in. You can't believe the shock your body feels as it hits the cold water. You sure hope you're purified."

"You are now taken by your father and five uncles to a remote spot far from your village and you are left there wearing only moccasins and a breech cloth. You will spend the next three days here by yourself."

"Please open your eyes. Well, that's quite a predicament. Let's use the Creative Problem Solving (CPS) process to see how you will survive this challenge."

Review the six steps of the CPS process. Discuss and clarify the young man's predicament to be certain students have enough content knowledge.

Mess Finding

Have students present an oral description of the predicament.

Fact Finding

Have students brainstorm a list of all the facts that relate to this mess. Facts can be drawn from the scenario, readings, and background information. Facts might include:

> You are a twelve year old Plains Indian and you ...
> > have participated in your first Sweat Lodge Ceremony.
> > have been left by your father and uncles in a Plains area far from your village.
> > are expected to survive <u>by yourself</u> for three days.
> > have been left with no food or water.
> > know there are no other villages nearby.
> > know they will come for you at the end of three days.

Problem Finding

Ask students to look at the facts and find problems in them. Remind them that problems will be worded as statements such as:

> In what ways might I...
> > find water and/or food.
> > stay warm.
> > remain safe from wild animals.
> > meet this challenge and survive for three days.

Students must now look at all of the problems and decide which problem they would like to address. It may be the one they feel is the most critical or important or may be a combination of several of the problems. It is important that a group consensus be reached before proceeding. Students might decide on the following problem statement: In what ways might this young Plains Indian meet this challenge and survive for days?

Idea Finding

The problem is then written on the board or flip chart and students generate as many solutions as possible. Rules of brainstorming will be followed.

Solution Finding

From the ideas generated, students will need to determine their solution by establishing a criteria and evaluating the ideas they feel are the most promising against the criteria. The matrix used in Lesson 10 will be used in this step.

Acceptance Finding

Once a solution has been found, the children need to decide how their plan will be implemented. Just as if they were the young Indian, they must answer the who, what, where, when, why, and how questions.

Resource Materials: Include chapter and page references to textbooks and/or other sources.

Six Steps of CPS written on a chart which is permanently displayed in the classroom.

Assessment/Follow-up: List the method(s) you will use to assess mastery of objectives.

In pairs, students will be asked to review the six steps of CPS and determine any questions they might have. These questions will be addressed with the entire class.

Lesson 12
 **Interdisciplinary Studies**
Lesson Planning Guide

Interdisciplinary Unit: _____ Native Americans: Plains _____ Lesson Title: _Type I Debriefing or_ _Follow-up Discussion_

Teacher: ___ M. Beecher ___ Grade: ___ 4 ___ Introductory __ X __ Midway _____ Follow-up _____

Instructional Strategies:	**Disciplines Included:**
_____ Lecture	__X__ Language Arts
__X__ Discussion	__X__ Social Studies
_____ Cooperative Learning	__X__ Mathematics
_____ Peer Tutoring	__X__ Science
_____ Learning or Interest Center	__X__ Music
_____ Simulation or Role Playing	__X__ Art
_____ Learning Games	_____ Personal/Social Development
_____ Guided Independent Study	_____ Other _____
_____ Other _____	_____ Other _____

Instructional Objectives: Include content, process or skills, attitudes and attributes.

The students will participate in a debriefing or follow-up discussion following a Type I presentation.

Description: Include any previous learning or necessary background material.

A debriefing or follow-up discussion should be conducted after all presentations. Some questions students might be asked include:

1. What are some things you liked best or found most interesting about this presentation, demonstration, film, etc?
2. Did this Type I raise any questions in your mind or leave any questions unanswered? What else might be explored?
3. Did anyone get any good ideas that they might like to follow-up?
4. Where could we find more information about this topic or what resources might be related to this topic? Is there any place we could visit or anyone we could contact to get more information?
5. Of all the Type I's we have had so far, how many of you felt this was the most interesting to you? If so, why?

These questions are only suggestions. Whatever approach works best for you should be used to stimulate thinking and discussion.

Resource Materials: Include chapter and page references to textbooks and/or other sources.

Possible follow-up or debriefing questions.

Assessment/Follow-up: List the method(s) you will use to assess mastery of objectives.

An informal assessment of student participation in this discussion will help to monitor and adjust your questioning. Students lack of involvement may indicate adjustment in questioning is needed or the difficulty level of the presentation is not commensurate with their abilities.

Lesson 13
 **Interdisciplinary Studies
Lesson Planning Guide**

Interdisciplinary Unit: ___Native Americans: Plains___ Lesson Title: ___Construction of a Teepee___

Sequencing/Task Analysis:

Teacher: ___M. Beecher___ Grade: ___4___ Introductory _____ Midway __X__ Follow-up _____

Instructional Strategies:

_____	Lecture
__X__	Discussion
_____	Cooperative Learning
_____	Peer Tutoring
_____	Learning or Interest Center
_____	Simulation or Role Playing
_____	Learning Games
_____	Guided Independent Study
__X__	Other ___Large Group Planning___

Disciplines Included:

__X__	Language Arts
__X__	Social Studies
__X__	Mathematics
_____	Science
_____	Music
__X__	Art
_____	Personal/Social Development
__X__	Other ___Critical Thinking Analysis___
_____	Other _____

Instructional Objectives: Include content, process or skills, attitudes and attributes.

The class will plan how to construct a life-size teepee in the classroom, which will remain for the duration of the study.

Description: Include any previous learning or necessary background material.

The class will discuss their desire to construct a life-size teepee in the classroom. The teacher will explain that in order to do this, they need to plan how they will proceed.

The children will be introduced to the Process/Sequencing Chart and learn how it will help them to determine the steps needed to complete their task.

As a whole group, the teacher (recorder) and the class will complete the Sequence Chart. Both a blank and complete chart are attached.

Resource Materials: Include chapter and page references to textbooks and/or other sources.

Sequence Chart for Overhead Projector.

Assessment/Follow-up: List the method(s) you will use to assess mastery of objectives.

Children will critique the outcome of their efforts and respond to the following questions once the teepee is constructed.

1. Were we successful in building our teepee?
2. Is it sturdy? Will it remain standing for the duration of our study?
3. Should we have done anything differently? If so, what?
4. How could we improve it?

Name:_____Jane Smith_____

Process Chart / Sequencing

Process:
Building a Life-Size Teepee in the Classroom

Step 1:
Small trees are cut down and limbs and leaves cut off to make the poles. They should all be the same length—between five and six feet. (Poles are cut in the young forest which is on school property). The class received permission from the principal and board of education.

Step 2:
Poles are held upright in a circle with a different person holding each pole. Each person leans their pole into the center of the circle.

Step 3:
One person, standing on a chair, ties all of the poles together near the top with rope or twine.

Step 4:
Large rolled brown paper (approximately three feet wide) will then be wrapped over the poles and taped from the inside until all of the poles are covered. A small opening will be left at the top.

Finally:
A semi-circle opening will be cut at the base of the teepee to act as a door. All students will then have an opportunity to draw their picture paintings on the teepee if they choose to do so.

Name:_____

Process Chart / Sequencing

Process:
Step 1:
Step 2:
Step 3:
Step 4:
Finally:

Lesson 14
Interdisciplinary Studies
Lesson Planning Guide

Interdisciplinary Unit: ____Native Americans: Plains____ Lesson Title: _Compare and Contrast_____
Teacher: __M. Beecher__ Grade: __4__ Introductory _____ Midway _X_ Follow-up _____

Instructional Strategies:

_X_	Lecture
_X_	Discussion
_X_	Cooperative Learning
___	Peer Tutoring
___	Learning or Interest Center
___	Simulation or Role Playing
___	Learning Games
___	Guided Independent Study
___	Other _____

Disciplines Included:

_X_	Language Arts
_X_	Social Studies
___	Mathematics
___	Science
___	Music
___	Art
___	Personal/Social Development
_X_	Other __Critical Thinking__
___	Other _____

Instructional Objectives: Include content, process or skills, attitudes and attributes.

Students will work cooperatively in groups of two to compare and contrast four characteristics of three Native American cultures: Northwestern, Plains, and Desert.

Description: Include any previous learning or necessary background material.

Before beginning this lesson, students will have obtained background knowledge of the Plains, Northwestern, and Desert tribes. This information will make it possible for students to successfully complete the activity.

Students will be introduced to Concept Map 1 and shown how it can be used to compare and contrast information about many things. Using the overhead projector, the teacher will fill in the ellipses with words in the attached model and show how one aspect of the culture might be compared, e.g.., the dwellings. Students will also be given the option of using Concept Map 2 and this will again be modeled by the teacher.

Students will then work in pairs using the concept maps of their choice to compare and contrast four characteristics of the three defined tribes.

Resource Materials: Include chapter and page references to textbooks and/or other sources.

1.   Graphic Organizers - Concept Map 1 and Concept Map 2.
2.   Reference Books from the Interest Development Center.

3. Notes from speakers and videos.
4. Overhead Projectors.

Assessment/Follow-up: List the method(s) you will use to assess mastery of objectives.

Students will share their concept maps with another student group and discuss. The teacher will then record group findings on a chart, the overhead, or chalkboard, in order to create a composite of student ideas. Duplicate ideas will not be recorded. In the event that this is too much duplication, the groups will "search" again and share their results.

Concept Maps 1 and 2 can easily be expanded in order to compare and contrast more than four topics or items.

Name: _____

Concept Map 1

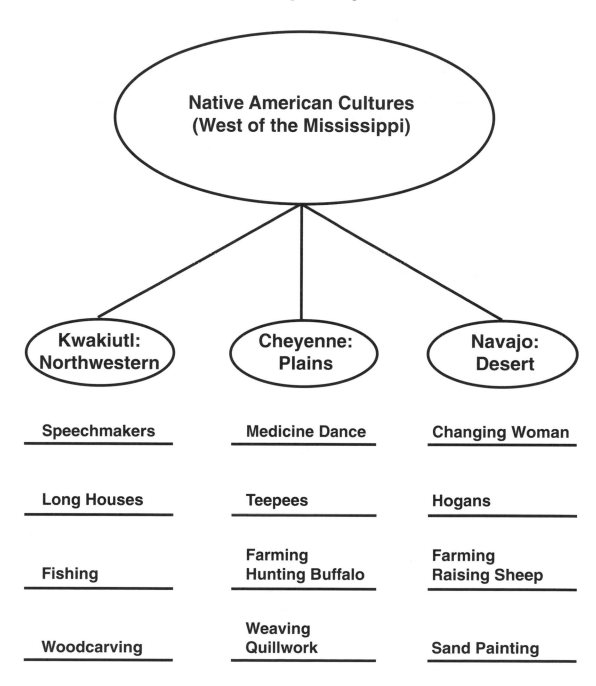

**Native American Cultures
(West of the Mississippi)**

**Kwakiutl:
Northwestern**

**Cheyenne:
Plains**

**Navajo:
Desert**

Speechmakers	Medicine Dance	Changing Woman
Long Houses	Teepees	Hogans
Fishing	Farming
Hunting Buffalo	Farming
Raising Sheep
Woodcarving	Weaving
Quillwork	Sand Painting

Name: _____

Concept Map 1

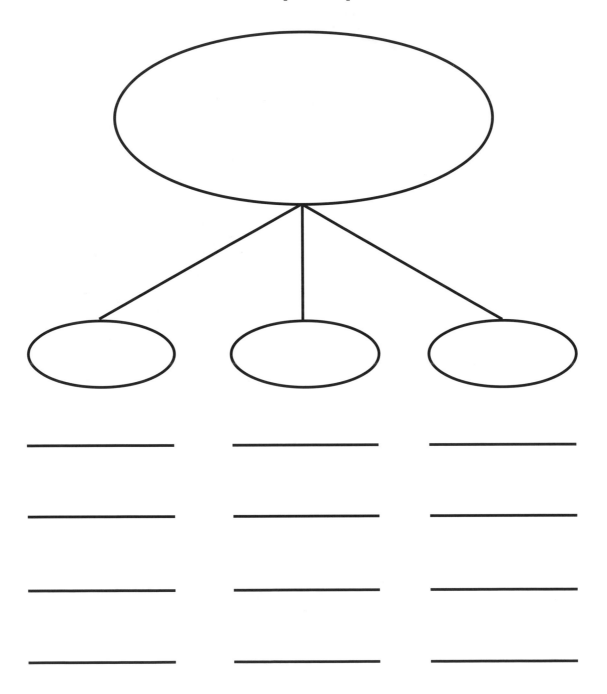

Name:

Concept Map 2

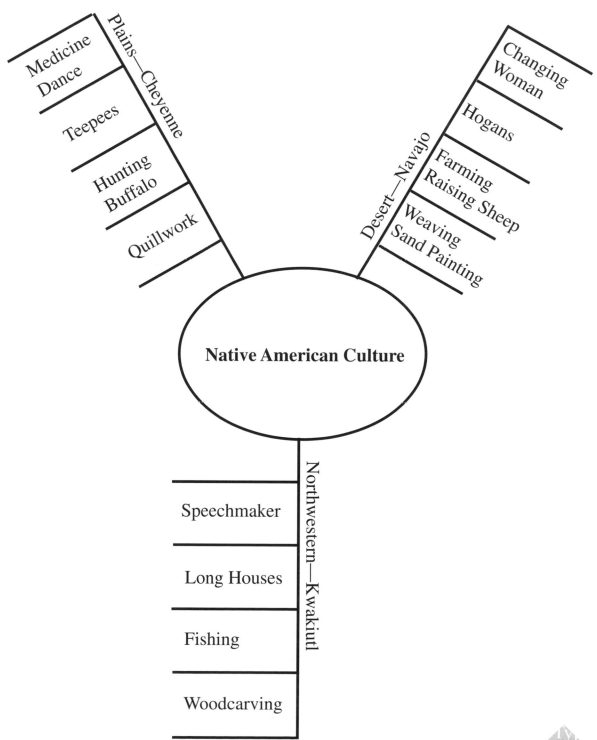

Plains—Cheyenne
- Medicine Dance
- Teepees
- Hunting Buffalo
- Quillwork

Desert—Navajo
- Changing Woman
- Hogans
- Farming Raising Sheep
- Weaving Sand Painting

Native American Culture

Northwestern—Kwakiutl
- Speechmaker
- Long Houses
- Fishing
- Woodcarving

Name: _____

Concept Map 2

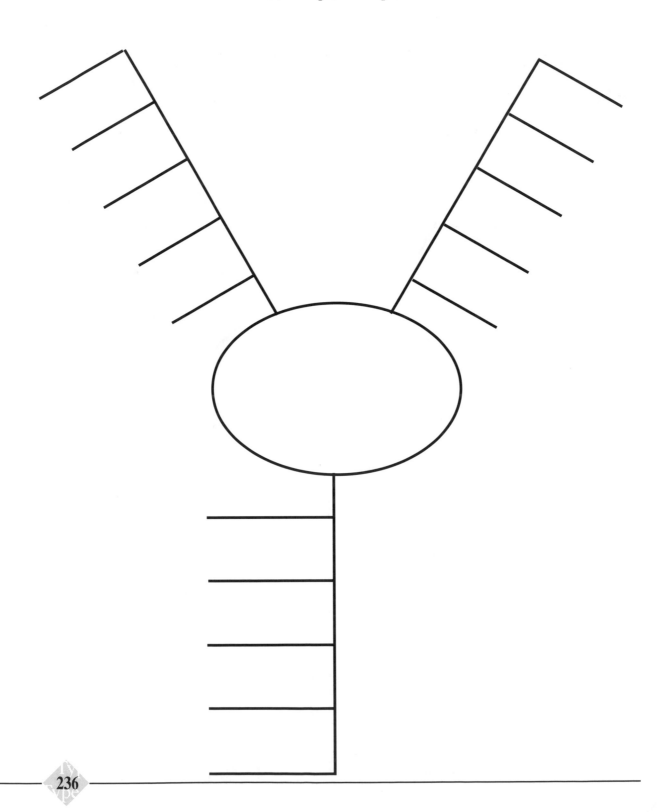

Lesson 15

Interdisciplinary Studies
Lesson Planning Guide

Interdisciplinary Unit: ____Native Americans: Plains____ Lesson Title: ____Cause and Effect____

Teacher: ____M. Beecher____ Grade: ___4___ Introductory _____ Midway _____ Follow-up __X__

Instructional Strategies:

_____	Lecture
__X__	Discussion
__X__	Cooperative Learning
_____	Peer Tutoring
_____	Learning or Interest Center
_____	Simulation or Role Playing
_____	Learning Games
_____	Guided Independent Study
__X__	Other ____Independent/Small Group____

Disciplines Included:

__X__	Language Arts
__X__	Social Studies
__X__	Mathematics
__X__	Science
__X__	Music
__X__	Art
_____	Personal/Social Development
__X__	Other ____Critical Thinking____
__X__	Other ____Analysis and Evaluation____

Instructional Objectives: Include content, process or skills, attitudes and attributes.

The students will analyze the causes and effects of the Native American conflict with the Europeans.

Description: Include any previous learning or necessary background material.

Using the attached graphic organizer, students will work individually and then in small groups to list the causes and effects of the Native American conflict with the Europeans. The small groups will share their work with the entire class and the teacher will create one comprehensive, cause/effect graphic organizer on the overhead projector.

Students will then analyze the causes and effects by justifying why each one is listed and providing background information related to each.

Resource Materials: Include chapter and page references to textbooks and/or other sources.

Cause and Effect Graphic Organizers for individuals and small groups.

Cause and Effect Graphic Organizer for the overhead.

Assessment/Follow-up: List the method(s) you will use to assess mastery of objectives.

Cause and Effect Chart 1 will be successfully completed by the entire class. If they are unable to do so, more information will be gathered and the causes and effects will continue to emerge until the end of the study.

Name:

Cause and Effect Chart - 1

Effects

Warfare:

    Battles, Destruction, Massacres

Reservations Established:

    Loss of Freedom / Native Americans

    Way of Life Changed

Buffalo Close to Extinction

Cattle and Sheep on Plains

Railroads Traverse the Plains

Telegraph Wires

The Plains Become States of the United States of America

The Native American Culture is Changed

The Native American Conflict with the Europeans

Causes

Settlers—White Men

Rifles and Horses

Fire Water

Missionaries

Whispering Wires

Cattle

Iron Horse

Gold Rush

Name: _____

Cause and Effect Chart - 1

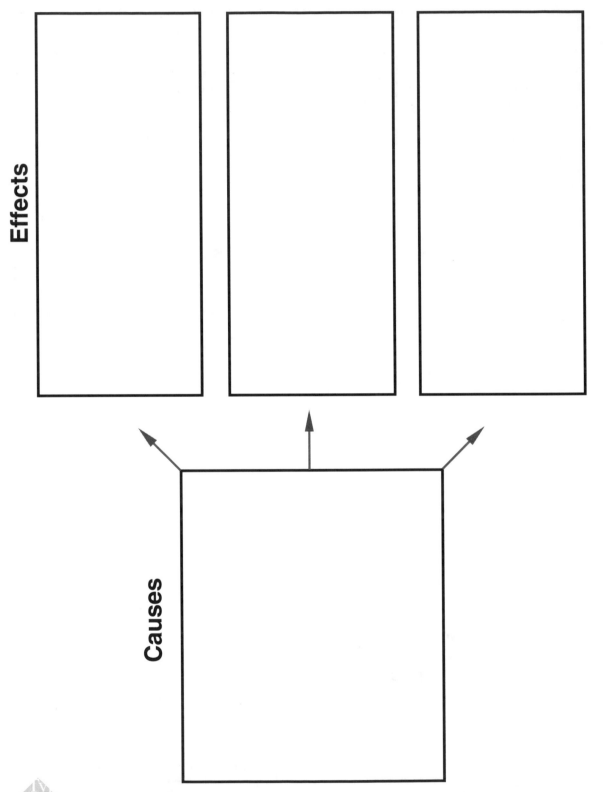

Effects

Causes

Lesson 16
Interdisciplinary Studies
Lesson Planning Guide

Interdisciplinary Unit: _____Native Americans: Plains_____

Lesson Title: Expository Writing: _____Descriptive Essay_____

Teacher: ___M. Beecher___ Grade: ___4___ Introductory _____ Midway ___X___ Follow-up _____

Instructional Strategies:

__X__	Lecture
__X__	Discussion
_____	Cooperative Learning
__X__	Peer Tutoring
_____	Learning or Interest Center
_____	Simulation or Role Playing
_____	Learning Games
_____	Guided Independent Study
__X__	Other ___Individual Writing Activity___

Disciplines Included:

__X__	Language Arts
__X__	Social Studies
__X__	Mathematics
__X__	Science
__X__	Music
__X__	Art
_____	Personal/Social Development
_____	Other _____
_____	Other _____

Instructional Objectives: Include content, process or skills, attitudes and attributes.

Students will write a descriptive essay related to a Native American scene, object, or person using the critical attributes of this writing genre.

Description: Include any previous learning or necessary background material.

Students will be asked to think of a scene, object, or person of interest to them in their study of Native Americans. They will be asked to create an informal web that lists words and phrases describing the scene, object, or person. (It is helpful if students are given enough "think" time for this activity. You might ask them to think about it for homework and have the writing done in class the next day.) Students will then describe their topic orally to a partner.

The teacher will share a descriptive essay he/she has written about a famous person and define the attributes of a descriptive essay for the students. If exemplary student examples of descriptive writing are available, they can be used instead of a teacher-written piece.

A descriptive essay presents a scene, object, person, state, or a combination of them.

Critical Attributes: Indicates a clear purpose to the description.
  Determines why the subject is significant.
  Sticks to one point of view.
  Avoids details that are irrelevant which can detract from the mood.

Creates a dominant mood, for example, humor, sadness, melancholy, inspiration, nostalgia.

Students will be asked to use these attributes to critique the model essay. The essay can be changed based on student input. The web and essay can be enlarged and shown on the overhead projector. Students should have a copy at their desks.

The essays used as models are most effective if they are excellent student models. If these do not exist, you might write an essay of your own to model for your class. These two methods add more meaning to the lesson. However, whatever model you use, the most important aspect of the lesson is to show students an excellent model of this writing genre.

Students will then be asked to write their own descriptive essay. These essays will be shared and holistically scored during subsequent lessons.

Resource Materials: Include chapter and page references to textbooks and/or other sources.

Definition of a Descriptive Essay on a Chart.

Example of a Descriptive Essay and Web for Overhead Projector.

Assessment/Follow-up: List the method(s) you will use to assess mastery of objectives.

Descriptive essays will be holistically scored by both students and the teacher.

Lesson 16 Essay

HARRIET BEECHER STOWE

"So you're the little lady who started the Civil War!" This was what Abraham Lincoln said when he first met Harriet Beecher Stowe, who was the mother of seven children, teacher, and author of **Uncle Tom's Cabin** and other books. Mrs. Beecher Stowe is one of my ancestors and I have always been interested in knowing more about her and her interesting life.

She became famous for writing **Uncle Tom's Cabin.** This book was written and published during a time when slavery was a smoldering issue between the northern and southern states. This book sympathized with the anti-slavery movement and angered a lot of people.

Several members of Harriet's family were also famous. Her father Lyman was a well-known and respected minister of the Congregational Church in Litchfield, Connecticut in the early 1800's. All of her five brothers became ministers. One who became well-known for being a great orator was Henry Ward Beecher.

I once read in our family's book **Saints and Sinners** that on one occasion when Harriet was living in Brunswick, Maine with her husband and seven children, Henry Ward visited them. As they talked, he held seven rubies and emeralds, which he liked to carry in his pockets. Interestingly, he never shared his wealth with his sister and her family, who lived in very modest circumstances.

Harriet was also a teacher. She taught in seminaries in Hartford, Connecticut and Cincinnati, Ohio. These two schools were founded by her sister Catherine Beecher.

If Harriet Beecher Stowe visited our class today, I would have many questions to ask her. I would like to know what prompted her to write a book about slavery. I'd like to know what it was like to be a teacher in the 1800's. I'd question her about my ancestors and carefully record every word she said.

I would share our family's genealogy with her and stories that spanned 180 years. She might be interested in knowing about schools today and the strides our country has made in equalizing the rights of all Americans. I think this little lady who President Lincoln thought had a hand in starting the Civil War would like what she saw today.

Written by: Margaret Beecher

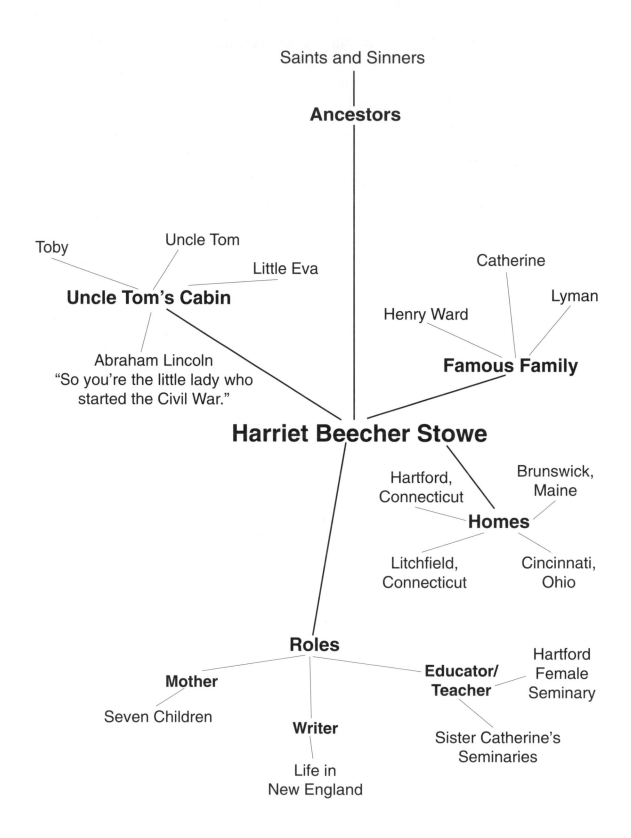

Saints and Sinners

Ancestors

Toby

Uncle Tom

Little Eva

Uncle Tom's Cabin

Abraham Lincoln
"So you're the little lady who started the Civil War."

Catherine

Lyman

Henry Ward

Famous Family

Harriet Beecher Stowe

Hartford, Connecticut

Brunswick, Maine

Homes

Litchfield, Connecticut

Cincinnati, Ohio

Roles

Mother

Seven Children

Writer

Life in New England

Educator/ Teacher

Hartford Female Seminary

Sister Catherine's Seminaries

Lesson 17
Interdisciplinary Studies
Lesson Planning Guide

Interdisciplinary Unit: ___Native Americans: Plains___ Lesson Title: _Information Gathering_

Teacher: ___M. Beecher___ Grade: __4__ Introductory _X_ Midway _X_ Follow-up _____

Instructional Strategies:

- _X_ Lecture
- _X_ Discussion
- _____ Cooperative Learning
- _____ Peer Tutoring
- _____ Learning or Interest Center
- _____ Simulation or Role Playing
- _____ Learning Games
- _X_ Guided Independent Study
- _____ Other _____

Disciplines Included:

- _X_ Language Arts
- _X_ Social Studies
- _X_ Mathematics
- _X_ Science
- _X_ Music
- _X_ Art
- _____ Personal/Social Development
- _____ Other _____
- _____ Other _____

Instructional Objectives: Include content, process or skills, attitudes and attributes.

Students will learn a technique that may assist them in taking notes from lectures, films, filmstrips, videos, etc.

Description: Include any previous learning or necessary background material.

An Information Gathering Chart will be given to each student. The teacher will explain that students can write information they learn from their textbooks, speakers, films, videos, etc. in this chart during the entire study. This will assist them in all discussions, project work, and any tests they might have.

Explain the meaning of each column and give examples of what might be included in each. Read a few pages in the text and discuss what might be added to the chart. Record the information on the chart as they say it. Tell students that they are free to create another chart if they would like to add additional headings.

Resource Materials: Include chapter and page references to textbooks and/or other sources.

Information Gathering Chart and Overhead Projector.

Assessment/Follow-up: List the method(s) you will use to assess mastery of objectives.

All students will assess the usefulness of their charts at the end of the study. The teacher will provide on-going guidance in how the charts can be used effectively.

Lesson 17

Native Americans of the Plains

Information Gathering Chart

Name: Grade: School:

Dwellings	Occupation	Clothing	Family Life Entertainment	Natural Resources	Ceremonies Beliefs & Customs	Art & Music	Tribes	Chiefs	Weapons & Battles	Other

Lesson 18

Interdisciplinary Studies
Lesson Planning Guide

Interdisciplinary Unit: ____Native Americans: Plains____ Lesson Title: ___Analysis of Dwelling_____

Teacher: ___M. Beecher____ Grade: ___4___ Introductory _____ Midway __X__ Follow-up _____

Instructional Strategies:

_____ Lecture
_____ Discussion
__X__ Cooperative Learning
_____ Peer Tutoring
_____ Learning or Interest Center
_____ Simulation or Role Playing
_____ Learning Games
_____ Guided Independent Study
_____ Other _____

Disciplines Included:

__X__ Language Arts
__X__ Social Studies
_____ Mathematics
_____ Science
_____ Music
_____ Art
_____ Personal/Social Development
__X__ Other ___Critical Thinking___
_____ Other _____(Analysis)_____

Instructional Objectives: Include content, process or skills, attitudes and attributes.

Students will analyze three Native American dwellings - hogan, long house, and teepee - by using a Semantic Analysis Chart.

Description: Include any previous learning or necessary background material.

Students will have some background knowledge about Native American dwellings. The Semantic Analysis Chart provides a way for students to determine the similarities and differences of each dwelling based on specific criteria. The chart can be used whenever similar tasks need to be accomplished. Use the overhead projector and list the homes in the first column of the chart. The group then needs to determine the attributes they will use to compare and contrast the dwellings. Once this is done, students will work in groups of four and use the coding system in the chart to analyze each dwelling. Resource books will be available to use as needed by the groups.

Resource Materials: Include chapter and page references to textbooks and/or other sources.

Semantic Analysis Chart: One blank transparency and one chart for each student. Overhead Projector.

Assessment/Follow-up: List the method(s) you will use to assess mastery of objectives.

When groups have completed this task, a chart will be completed with the assistance of the entire group. If group findings are not consistent, each group will need to provide "proof" regarding their data.

Lesson 18

Name: _____

Semantic Analysis Chart

Native American Dwellings

Dwellings	Buffalo Hide	Mud	Log Poles	Rectangular Shape	Cylindrical Shape	One Family	Many Families			
Hogan	-	+	+	-	+	+	-			
Long House	-	*	+	+	-	-	+			
Teepee	+	-	+	-	*	*	*			

Attributes

+ indicates YES
- indicates NO
* indicates Sometimes

Lesson 18

Semantic Analysis Chart

Name: _____

Lesson 19
 **Interdisciplinary Studies Lesson Planning Guide**

Interdisciplinary Unit: _____Native Americans: Plains_____ Lesson Title: _Oral Presentation Skills_____

Teacher: ___M. Beecher___ Grade: ___4___ Introductory _____ Midway __X__ Follow-up _____

Instructional Strategies:

__X__ Lecture
__X__ Discussion
__X__ Cooperative Learning
_____ Peer Tutoring
_____ Learning or Interest Center
_____ Simulation or Role Playing
_____ Learning Games
__X__ Guided Independent Study
_____ Other _____

Disciplines Included:

__X__ Language Arts
__X__ Social Studies
_____ Mathematics
_____ Science
_____ Music
_____ Art
_____ Personal/Social Development
__X__ Other ___Critical Thinking___
_____ Other _____(Evaluation)_____

Instructional Objectives: Include content, process or skills, attitudes and attributes.

The students will establish criteria for making oral presentations by describing an excellent presentation and then listing its critical attributes.

Description: Include any previous learning or necessary background material.

Students will be in the process of completing their projects and aware of the fact that they will be sharing their work with parents at the class Powwow.

In groups of four, students will describe an excellent oral presentation and list its critical attributes. As a whole group, they will establish a checklist which can be used to judge their effectiveness in giving oral presentations.

The criteria are written on a checklist and might include, but not be limited to, the following:

ASSESSMENT CHECKLIST
ORAL PRESENTATION

	Possible Points	Assessment Student	Teacher
1. The speaker can be heard by everyone in the audience.	___	___	___
2. The speaker shows interest and enthusiasm.	___	___	___
3. The rate of speaking is appropriate.	___	___	___
4. The speaker makes eye contact with individuals throughout the audience.	___	___	___
5. The presentation is organized with a beginning, body of information, and conclusion.	___	___	___
6. There is a clear focus to the presentation and the focus is not lost.	___	___	___
7. The main ideas support the focus and there are clear transitions between main ideas.	___	___	___
8. It is clear that the speaker knows his/her subject.	___	___	___
9. Visual aids are well done, can be seen by all, and add to the presentation.	___	___	___
10. The presentation is creative and interesting.	___	___	___
Totals	___	___	___

Resource Materials: Include chapter and page references to textbooks and/or other sources.

Chalkboard, Overhead Projector, or Chart Paper.

Assessment/Follow-up: List the method(s) you will use to assess mastery of objectives.

The entire group can assess whether the criteria they have established are adequate. This is an excellent example of student-developed, performance-based assessment.

Lesson 20
Interdisciplinary Studies
Lesson Planning Guide

Interdisciplinary Unit: ___Native Americans: Plains___ Lesson Title: _Topic/Problem Focusing_
Teacher: ___M. Beecher___ Grade: __4__ Introductory _____ Midway __X__ Follow-up _____

Instructional Strategies:	Disciplines Included:
__X__ Lecture	__X__ Language Arts
__X__ Discussion	__X__ Social Studies
_____ Cooperative Learning	__X__ Mathematics
_____ Peer Tutoring	__X__ Science
_____ Learning or Interest Center	__X__ Music
_____ Simulation or Role Playing	__X__ Art
_____ Learning Games	_____ Personal/Social Development
__X__ Guided Independent Study	_____ Other _____
__X__ Other ___Student Pairs___	_____ Other _____

Instructional Objectives: Include content, process or skills, attitudes and attributes.

Students will learn to use webbing as a technique to focus the topic or problem they have selected for their independent study.

Description: Include any previous learning or necessary background material.

The students have already learned how to create a web. They are now going to web the topic or problem they have selected for their study. If the topic is too broad, they will continue webbing until they have focused the study. The attached example of the "train" and "locomotive" webs and focused problem will be used as a model with students.

Resource Materials: Include chapter and page references to textbooks and/or other sources.

Example of Student Topic Focusing.

Assessment/Follow-up: List the method(s) you will use to assess mastery of objectives.

Students will review their own topic webs and decide if their topics are focused enough. They will work with a partner and also critique each other's webs.

TOPIC/PROBLEM FOCUSING

Step # 1

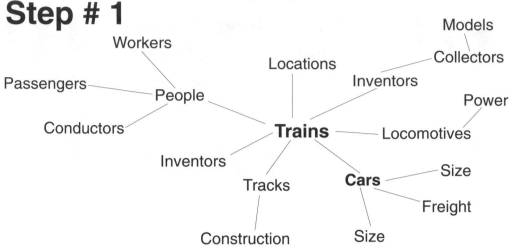

Workers

Passengers — People — Locations

Conductors

Inventors

Models

Collectors

Inventors

Power

Trains — Locomotives

Tracks

Cars — Size

Freight

Construction

Size

Step # 2

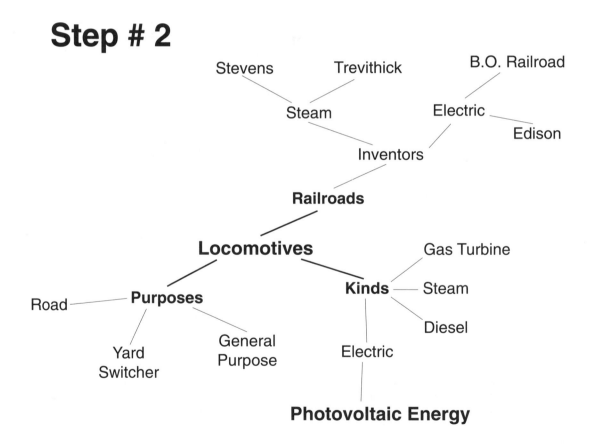

Stevens   Trevithick   B.O. Railroad

Steam   Electric

Edison

Inventors

Railroads

Locomotives

Road — **Purposes**   Gas Turbine

Kinds — Steam

Yard   General   Diesel
Switcher   Purpose

Electric

Photovoltaic Energy

FOCUSING TOPIC/PROBLEM — SPECIFIC AREA OF STUDY

I plan to find out about locomotives and how they are powered and about photovoltaic energy. I will design a locomotive (model) that will be powered by photovoltaic cells.

Lesson 21
 **Interdisciplinary Studies Lesson Planning Guide**

Interdisciplinary Unit: _____Native Americans: Plains_____ Lesson Title: _Modified Management Plan_

Teacher: _M. Beecher_ Grade: _4_ Introductory _____ Midway _X_ Follow-up _____

Instructional Strategies:

- _X_ Lecture
- _X_ Discussion
- _____ Cooperative Learning
- _____ Peer Tutoring
- _____ Learning or Interest Center
- _____ Simulation or Role Playing
- _____ Learning Games
- _X_ Guided Independent Study
- _____ Other _____

Disciplines Included:

- _X_ Language Arts
- _X_ Social Studies
- _X_ Mathematics
- _X_ Science
- _X_ Music
- _X_ Art
- _X_ Personal/Social Development
- _____ Other _____
- _____ Other _____

Instructional Objectives: Include content, process or skills, attitudes and attributes.

The students will learn how to plan their independent or small group studies by using the Modified Management Plan.

Description: Include any previous learning or necessary background material.

At this point in the study, students will have selected the topic they will create using their decision making strategies.

All students will be given a blank Modified Management Plan and the teacher will have a form shown on the overhead projector. Each part of the form will be described as follows.

After filling in their name, grade, teacher, and school, the teacher will inform students about the beginning and estimated ending dates of their studies.

    General Area of Study:
        Students will check all disciplines that will be involved in their study.
    What is the topic of your study?
        The topic of the study decided upon by students will be written here.
        The topic should be based on student interest since this will provide the necessary motivation for the study.

<u>What do you hope to find out?</u>
Now the student must think about exactly what he/she wants to learn about during the study.

<u>List three things to do to get started.</u>
The students must become concrete in their thinking and describe what they plan to do in the beginning of their study.

<u>List the resources.</u>
The students will be told that this list is an on-going account of all the resources used during the study. They will also be given direction and information on how to record each resource (bibliography or works cited).

<u>What form will your final product take?</u>
As a whole group, students will have already brainstormed a long list of possible product ideas for their projects. The project each student plans to complete will be written here. The project should be based on student interest and strength areas.

<u>With whom will you share your product?</u>
The teacher needs to help students brainstorm possible audiences. Students need to know they can have more than one audience and can add others to their plan during the study. Audiences are sometimes found when the study is completed.

The teacher will then show students a completed Modified Management Plan on the overhead projector and explain it clearly to students.

The students will then begin to complete their own plans. This needs to be done on a step-by-step basis. All children will complete the first question as the teacher walks from desk to desk, observes their process, and makes suggestions. Children can give examples of what they have written for a specific question.

The same procedure is repeated for each question on the matrix. The students will not be ready to complete this form independently if this is their first or even second experience with the Modified Management Plan. The teacher becomes the facilitator of this process.

Both plans are attached for your information. Keep in mind that this lesson may require several sessions to complete.

Resource Materials: Include chapter and page references to textbooks and/or other sources.

- Modified Management Plan - on an overhead transparency.
- A Modified Management Plan for each student.
- Overhead Projector.

Assessment/Follow-up: List the method(s) you will use to assess mastery of objectives.

The completed Modified Management Plans will determine the students' mastery of this lesson. The students' abilities to follow their plans also warrants assessment.

MODIFIED MANAGEMENT PLAN

Name: Maria Jones   Grade: 4

Teacher: M. Beecher   School: Smith School

Beginning Date: December 1   Estimated Ending Date: December 14

General Areas of Study (Check all that apply).

   X   Language Arts   ____ Music
   X   Social Studies   X   Art
   ____ Mathematics   ____ Personal/Social Development
   ____ Science   X   Other: Oral Presentation

What is the topic of your study?
 I would like to know more about the myths and legends of the Plains tribes.

_____

_____

_____

_____

_____

What do you hope to find out?
I would like to know why there are so many myths and legends and where they came
from. I would also like to know more about the tribe's storytellers and what role
they played in village life.

_____

_____

_____

List three things you will do to get started.
Find books in the library and begin reading myths.
Call Tamunk and ask him about storytellers and where to find real myths and legends.
Ask him if he knows any storytellers.
Learn how to tell a story.

_____

_____

List the resources that you will use during your study. This might include books, films, records, movies, maps, etc., and any people who might help you.

Resource Persons: _____

_____ The School Librarian: She can help me find information about this topic. _____

_____

_____ Tamunk: He told an interesting legend. I will call him and ask him if he _____

_____ knows how I can find others. _____

Books: _____

_____ Burland, C. (1965). **North American Indian Mythology.** New York: Peter

_____ Bedrick Books. _____

_____

_____ Baylor, B. (1975). **They Put On Masks.** New York: Charles Scribner's _____

_____ Sons. _____

_____

_____

_____

What form will your final product take?

I plan to become a tribal storyteller and tell the class about the myths and legends

of the Plains tribes. I will also write my own myths and legends. _____

_____

_____

_____

With whom will you share your product?

I will share the myths and legends with my class, other classes, and parents when we

have our Powwow. _____

_____

_____

_____

_____

MODIFIED MANAGEMENT PLAN

Name: _____   Grade: _____

Teacher: _____   School: _____

Beginning Date: _____   Estimated Ending Date: _____

General Areas of Study (Check all that apply).

_____ Language Arts   _____ Music
_____ Social Studies   _____ Art
_____ Mathematics   _____ Personal/Social Development
_____ Science   _____ Other: _____

What is the topic of your study?

_____

_____

_____

_____

_____

_____

What do you hope to find out?

_____

_____

_____

_____

_____

_____

List three things you will do to get started.

_____

_____

_____

_____

_____

_____

List the resources that you will use during your study. This might include books, films, records, movies, maps, etc., and any people who might help you.

What form will your final product take?

With whom will you share your product?

Appendix B

STUDENT PRODUCT
ASSESSMENT FORM

Student Product Assessment Form

Joseph S. Renzulli
Sally M. Reis

Rationale Underlying this Assessment Form

The purpose of this form is to guide your judgment in the qualitative assessment of various types of products developed by students in enrichment programs. In using the instrument, three major considerations should always be kept in mind. First, the evaluation of more complex and creative types of products is always a function of human judgment. We do not think in terms of percentiles or standard scores when we evaluate paintings, architectural designs or the usefulness of a labor-saving device. We must consider these products in terms of our own values and certain characteristics that indicate the quality, aesthetics, utility, and function of the overall contribution. In other words, we must trust our own judgment and learn to rely upon our guided subjective opinions when making assessments about complex products.

A second consideration relates to the individual worth of the product as a function of the student's age/grade level and experiential background. For example, a research project that reflects an advanced level investigation and subsequent product by a first grader might not be considered an equally advanced level of involvement on the part of a sixth grader. Similarly, the work of a youngster from a disadvantaged background must be considered in light of the student's overall educational experiences, opportunities and availability of advanced level resource persons, materials and equipment.

The third consideration relates to the most important purpose of any evaluation—student growth and improvement. This assessment instrument should be used to guide students toward excellence, and therefore, we strongly believe that it should be shared and discussed with students *before* the product is started. In other words, we believe the instrument should be reviewed with students during the early planning stages of the product. Students should have the opportunity to know and fully understand on what basis their final products will be assessed.

Instructions for Using the Assessment Form

Although most of the items included in the form relate directly to characteristics of the final product, it will also be helpful if you have access to planning devices that have been used in the development of the product. Such planning devices might include logs, contracts, management plans, proposals, or any other record keeping system. A planning device can help you to determine if pre-stated objectives have been met by comparing statements of objectives from the planning device with the final product. If such a planning device has not been utilized or is unavailable, you may want to request students to complete a form that will provide you with the necessary background information. It is recommended that some type of planning device accompany all products that are submitted for rating. If it can be arranged, you may also want to interview the student who completed the product.

In using the Student Product Assessment Form it will sometimes be necessary for you to do some detective work! For example, in determining the diversity of resources, you may need to examine footnotes, bibliographies or references and materials listed on the planning device. You may also want to have the student complete a self evaluation form relating to the completed product. This form may help to assess task commitment and student interest.

The Student Product Assessment Form can be used in a variety of ways. Individual teachers, resource persons or subject matter specialists can evaluate products independently or collectively as members of a team. When two or more persons evaluate the same product independently, the average rating for each scale item can be calculated and entered on the Summary Form. When used in a research setting or formal evaluation situation, it is recommended that products be independently evaluated by three raters. One of these ratings should be completed by the teacher under whose direction the product was developed. A second form should be completed by a person who has familiarity with the subject matter area of the product.

For example, a high school science teacher might be asked to rate the work of an elementary grade student who has completed a science-related product. The third rater might be someone who is independent of the school system or program in which the work was carried out.

Item Format

At first glance the items on the Assessment Form may seem to be long and complicated, but they are actually quite concise. Each item represents a single characteristic that is designed to focus your attention. The items are divided into the following three related parts:

1. *The Key Concept.* This concept is always present first and is printed in large type. It should serve to focus your attention on the main idea or characteristic being evaluated.

2. *The Item Description.* Following the Key Concept are one or more descriptive statements about how the characteristic might be reflected in the student's product. These statements are listed under the Key Concept.

3. *Examples.* In order to help clarify the meanings of the items, an actual example of students' work is provided. The examples are intended to elaborate upon the meaning of both the Key Concept and the Item Description. The examples are presented following each item description.

Important Note: The last item (No. 9) deals with an Overall Assessment of the product. In this case, we have chosen a somewhat different format and examples have not been provided. When completing the ratings for Item No. 9, you should consider the product as a whole (globally) rather than evaluating its separate components in an analytic fashion.

Some of the items may appear to be unusually long or "detailish" for a rating scale but our purpose here is to improve the clarity and thus inter-rater reliability for the respective items. After you have used the scales a few times, you will probably only need to read the Key Concepts and Item Descriptions in order to refresh your memory about the meaning of an item. Research has shown inter-rater reliability is improved when items are more descriptive and when brief examples are provided in order to help clarify any misunderstanding that may exist on the parts of different raters.

STUDENT PRODUCT ASSESSMENT FORM
SUMMARY SHEET

Name(s) _____ Date _____

District _____ School_____

Teacher _____ Grade _____ Sex _____

Product (Title and/or Brief Description)_____

_____

Number of Weeks Student(s) Worked on Product _____

FACTORS	RATING*	NOT APPLICABLE
1. Early Statement of Purpose	_____	_____
2. Problem Focusing	_____	_____
3. Level of Resources	_____	_____
4. Diversity of Resources	_____	_____
5. Appropriateness of Resources	_____	_____
6. Logic, Sequence, and Transition	_____	_____
7. Action Orientation	_____	_____
8. Audience	_____	_____
9. Overall Assessment	_____	_____
A. Originality of the Idea	_____	_____
B. Achieved Objectives Stated in Plan	_____	
C. Advanced Familiarity with Subject	_____	
D. Quality Beyond Age/Grade Level	_____	
E. Care, Attention to Details, etc.	_____	
F. Time, Effort, Energy	_____	
G. Original Contribution	_____	

Comments:

Person Completing This Form _____

*Rating Scales: Factors 1-8   Factors 9A-9G

  5 - To a great extent   5 = Outstanding
  3 - Somewhat   4 = Above Average
  1 - To a limited extent   3 = Average
                                      2 = Below Average
                                      1 = Poor

Non-Applicable Items

Because of the difficulty of developing a single instrument that will be universally applicable to all types of products, there will occasionally be instances when some of the items do not apply to specific products. For example, in a creative writing project (poem, play, story) either the Level of Resources (No. 3) or Diversity of Resources (No. 4) might not apply if the student is writing directly from his/her own experiences. It should be emphasized however, that the Non-Applicable category should be used very rarely in most rating situations.

How To Rate Student Products

1. Fill out the information requested at the top of the Summary Sheet that accompanies the Student Product Assessment Form. A separate Summary Sheet should be filled out for each product being evaluated.

2. Review the nine items on the Student Product Assessment Form. This review will help give you a "mind set" for the things you will be looking for while you examine each product.

3. Examine the product by first doing a "quick overview" of the entire piece of work. Then do a careful and detailed examination of the product. Check pages or places that you might want to reexamine and jot down brief notes and comments about any strengths, weaknesses or questions that occur as you review the product.

4. Turn to the first item on the Student Product Assessment Form. Read the Key Concept, Item Description and Example. Enter the number that best represents your assessment in the "Rating" column on the Summary Sheet. Enter only whole numbers. In other words, do not enter ratings of 3 1/2 or 2 1/4. On those rare occasions when you feel an item does not apply, please check the NA column on the Summary Sheet. Please note that we have only included an NA response option for Item 9a on the Overall Assessment.

5. Turn to the second item and repeat the above process. If you feel you cannot render a judgment immediately, skip the item and return to it at a later time. Upon completion of the assessment process, you should have entered a number (or a check in the NA column) for all items on the Summary Sheet.

6. Any comments you would like to make about the product can be entered at the bottom of the Summary Sheet.

STUDENT PRODUCT ASSESSMENT FORM

Joseph S. Renzulli
Sally M. Reis

1. EARLY STATEMENT OF PURPOSE
Is the purpose (theme, thesis, research question) readily apparent in the early stages of the student's product? In other words, did the student define the topic or problem in such a manner that a clear understanding about the nature of the product emerges shortly after a review of the material?

> For example, in a research project dealing with skunks of northwestern Connecticut completed by a first grade student, the overall purpose and scope of the product are readily apparent after reading the introductory paragraphs.

5	4	3	2	1	NA
To a great extent		Somewhat		To a limited extent	

2. PROBLEM FOCUSING
Did the student focus or clearly define the topic so that it represents a relatively specific problem within a larger area of study?

> For example, a study of "Drama in Elizabethan England" would be more focused than "A Study of Drama."

5	4	3	2	1	NA
To a great extent		Somewhat		To a limited extent	

3. LEVEL OF RESOURCES
Is there evidence that the student used resource materials or equipment that are more advanced, technical, or complex than materials ordinarily used by students at this age/grade level?

> For example, a sixth grade student utilizes a nearby university library to locate information about the history of clowns in the twelfth through sixteenth century in the major European countries.

5	4	3	2	1	NA
To a great extent		Somewhat		To a limited extent	

4. DIVERSITY OF RESOURCES
    Has the student made an effort to use several different types of resource materials in the development of the product? Has the student used any of the following information sources in addition to the standard use of encyclopedias: textbooks, record/statistic books, biographies, how-to books, periodicals, films and filmstrips, letters, phone calls, personal interviews, surveys or polls, catalogs and/or others?

    > For example, a fourth grade student interested in the weapons and vehicles used in World War II reads several adult-level books on this subject which included biographies, autobiographies, periodicals, and record books. He also conducted oral history interviews with local veterans of World War II, previewed films and film strips about the period and collected letters from elderly citizens sent to them from their sons stationed overseas.

5	4	3	2	1	NA
To a great extent		Somewhat		To a limited extent	

5. APPROPRIATENESS OF RESOURCES
    Did the student select appropriate reference materials, resource persons, or equipment for the topic or area of study?

    > For example, a student who is interested in why so much food is thrown away in the school cafeteria had to contact state officials to learn about state requirements and regulations which govern what must and can be served in public school cafeterias. With the aid of her teacher, she also had to locate resource books on how to design, conduct and analyze a survey.

5	4	3	2	1	NA
To a great extent		Somewhat		To a limited extent	

6. LOGIC, SEQUENCE, AND TRANSITION
    Does the product reflect a logical sequence of steps or events that ordinarily would be followed when carrying out an investigation in this area of study? Are the ideas presented clearly and logically and is there a smooth transition from one idea or subtopic to another?

    > For example, a student decided to investigate whether or not a section of his city needs a new fire station with a salaried staff rather than the present volunteer staff. First the student needed to research different

methods of investigative reporting such as appropriate interview skills. Next the student conducted interviews with both salaried and volunteer fire station staff. He then needed to learn about methods of survey design and reporting in order to analyze local resident opposition or support for the new fire station. After other logical steps in his research were completed, his accumulated findings led him to interviews with the Mayor and the Board of Safety in the city and then to several construction companies that specialized in bids on such buildings. His final product was an editorial in the local newspaper which reflected his research and conclusions.

5	4	3	2	1	NA
To a great extent		Somewhat		To a limited extent	

7. **ACTION ORIENTATION**
    Is it clear that the major goal of this study was for purposes other than merely reporting on or reproducing existing information, ideas, or knowledge? In other words, the student's purpose is clearly directed toward some kind of action (e.g., teaching ways to improve bicycle safety, presenting a lecture on salt pond life); some type of literary or artistic product (e.g., poem, painting, costume design); a scientific device or research study (e.g., building a robot, measuring plant growth as a function of controlled heat, light and moisture); or some type of leadership or managerial endeavor (e.g., editing a newspaper, producing/directing a movie).

    For example, a student decides to study the history of his city. After an extensive investigation, the student realizes that other history books have been written about the city. He finds, instead, that no one has ever isolated specific spots of historical significance in the city which are easily located and accessible. He begins this task and decides to focus his research to produce an original historical walking tour of the city.

5	4	3	2	1	NA
To a great extent		Somewhat		To a limited extent	

8. **AUDIENCE**
    Is an appropriate audience specified or readily apparent in the product or management plan?

    For example, the student who researched the history of his city to produce an original walking tour presents his tour to the city council

and the mayor. They, in turn, adopt it as the official walking tour of the city. It is reproduced in the city newspaper and distributed by the local historical society, library and given out to registered guests in the city's hotels and motels.

5	4	3	2	1	NA
To a great extent		Somewhat		To a limited extent	

9. OVERALL ASSESSMENT
Considering the product as a whole, provide a general rating for each of the following factors and mark the space provided to the right of the item:

SCALE
5 = Outstanding
4 = Above Average
3 = Average
2 = Below Average
1 = Poor

A. Originality of the idea. _____
B. Achieved objectives stated in plan. _____
C. Reflects advanced familiarity (for age) with the subject matter. _____
D. Reflects a level of quality beyond what is normally expected of a student of this age and grade. _____
E. Reflects care, attention to detail, and overall pride on the part of the student. _____
F. Reflects a commitment of time, effort and energy. _____
G. Reflects an original contribution for a youngster of this age/grade level. _____

Appendix C

TYPE II TAXONOMY

Taxonomy of Type II Enrichment Processes

Joseph S. Renzulli

Sally M. Reis

I. Cognitive and Affective Training

A.   Creativity. Developing and Practicing the Use of:

Fluency
Flexibility
Originality
Elaboration
Brainstorming
Forced Relationships
Attribute Listing
Fantasy
Imagery
Association
Comparison
Risk Taking

Modification Techniques:
Adaptation
Magnification
Minification
Substitution
Multiple Uses
Rearrangement
Reversal

B. Creative Problem-Solving and Decision-Making: Developing and Practicing the Use of:

Creative Problem-Solving:

Mess Finding
Fact Finding
Problem Finding
Idea Finding
Solution Finding
Acceptance Finding

Decision Making:

Stating Desired Goals and Conditions Related to a Decision That Needs To Be Made
Stating the Obstacles to Realizing the Goals and Conditions
Identifying the Alternatives Available for Overcoming Each Obstacle
Examining Alternatives in Terms of Resources, Costs, Constraints, and Time
Ranking Alternatives in Terms of Probable Consequences
Choosing the Best Alternative
Evaluating the Actions Resulting From the Decision

C. Critical and Logical Thinking. Developing and Practicing the Use of:

Conditional Reasoning
Ambiguity
Fallacies
Emotive Words
Definition of Terms
Categorical Propositions
Classification
Validity Testing
Reliability Testing
Translation
Interpretation
Extrapolation
Patterning
Sequencing
Flow Charting
Computer Programming

Analogies
Inferences
Inductive Reasoning
Deductive Reasoning
Syllogisms
Probability
Dilemmas
Paradoxes
Analysis of:
    Content
    Elements
    Trends and Patterns
    Relationships
    Organizing Principles
    Propaganda and Bias

D. Affective Thinking.

Understanding Yourself
Understanding Others
Working With Groups
Peer Relationships
Parent Relationships
Values Clarification
Moral Reasoning
Sex Role Stereotypes
Assertiveness Training
Self Reliance

Dealing With Conflict
Coping Behaviors
Analyzing Your Strengths
Planning Your Future
Interpersonal Communication
Developing Self Confidence
Developing a Sense of Humor
Showing an Understanding of Others
Dealing With Fear, Anxiety and Guilt
Dealing With the Unknown

II. Learning How-To-Learn Skills

A. Listening, Observing and Perceiving. Developing and Practicing the Use of:

Following Directions
Noting Specific Details
Understanding Main Points, Themes, and Sequences
Separating Relevant From Irrelevant Information
Paying Attention to Whole-Part Relationships
Scanning For the "Big Picture"
Focusing In On Particulars
Asking for Clarification
Asking Appropriate Questions
Making Inferences
Noting Subtleties
Predicting Outcomes
Evaluating a Speakers Point of View

B.   Notetaking and Outlining. Developing and Practicing the Use of:

Notetaking:

Selecting Key Terms, Concepts, and Ideas
Disregarding Unimportant Information
Noting What Needs To Be Remembered
Recording Words, Dates and Figures That Help You Recall Related Information
Reviewing Notes and Underlining or Highlighting the Most Important Items
Categorizing Notes In a Logical Order
Organizing Notes So That Information From Various Sources Can Be Added
        At a Later Time

Outlining:

Using Outlining Skills to Write Material That Has Unity and Coherence
Selecting and Using a System of Notation Such as Roman Numerals
Deciding Whether To Write Topic Outlines Or Sentence Outlines
Stating Each Topic or Point Clearly
Using Parallel Structure
Remembering That Each Section Must Have At Least Two Parts

C.   Interviewing and Surveying. Developing and Practicing the Use of:

Identifying the Information Being Sought
Deciding On Appropriate Instrument(s)
Identifying Sources of Existing Instruments
Designing Instruments (e.g., Checklists, Rating Scales, Interview Schedules)
Developing Question Wording Skills (e.g., Factual, Attitudinal, Probing, Follow-
        up)
Sequencing Questions
Identifying Representative Samples
Field Testing and Revising Instruments
Developing Rapport With Subjects
Preparing a Data Gathering Matrix and Schedule
Using Follow-up Techniques

D.   Analyzing and Organizing Data. Developing and Practicing the Use of:

Identifying Types and Sources of Data
Identifying and Developing Data Gathering Instruments and Techniques
Developing Data Recording and Coding Techniques
Classifying and Tabulating Data
Preparing Descriptive (Statistical) Summaries of Data (e.g., Percentages, Means, Modes, etc.)
Analyzing Data With Inferential Statistics
Preparing Tables, Graphs and Diagrams
Drawing Conclusions and Making Generalizations
Writing Up and Reporting Results

III. Using Advanced Research Skills and Reference Materials

A.   Preparing for Type III Investigations

Developing Time Management Skills
Developing a Management Plan
Developing Problem Finding and Focusing Skills
Stating Hypotheses and Research Questions
Identifying Variables
Identifying Human and Material Resources
Selecting An Appropriate Format and Reporting Vehicle
Obtaining Feedback and Making Revisions
Identifying Appropriate Outlets and Audiences

B.   Library Skills

Understanding Library Organizational Systems
Using Informational Retrieval Systems
Using Interlibrary Loan Procedures
Understanding the Specialized Types of Information in Reference Books Such
     As:

Bibliographies	Yearbooks	Periodicals
Encyclopedias	Manuals	Histories and Chronicles
Dictionaries and	Reviews	of Particular Fields
Glossaries	Readers Guides	Organizations
Annuals	Abstracts	Concordances
Handbooks	Diaries	Data Tables
Directories and	Books of Quotations,	Digests
Registers	Proverbs, Maxims	Surveys
Indexes	and Familiar Phrases	Almanacs
Atlases	Source Books	Anthologies

Understanding the Specific Types of Information in Non-Book Reference
     Materials Such As:

Art Prints	Globes	Films
Talking Books	Maps	Study Print
Videotapes/Discs	Film Loops	Models
Microfilms	Pictures	Filmstrips With Sound
Filmstrips	Records	Flashcards
Realia	Slides	Audio Tapes
Transparencies	Charts	Data Tapes

C.   Community Resources

Identifying Community Resources Such As:

Private Businesses and Individuals
Governmental and Social Service Agencies
College and University Services and Persons
Clubs, Hobby and Special Interest Groups
Professional Societies and Associations
Senior Citizens Groups
Art and Theater Groups

Service Clubs
Private Individuals
Museums, Galleries, Science Centers, Places of Special Interest or Function

IV. Developing Written, Oral and Visual Communication Skills

A. Visual Communication. Developing Skills in the Preparation of:

Photographic Print Series	Overhead Transparencies
Slide Series	Motion Pictures
Filmstrips	Videotape Recordings
Audio Tape Recordings	Multimedia Images

B. Oral Communication. Developing and Practicing the Use of:

Organizing Material for An Oral Presentation
Vocal Delivery
Appropriate Gestures, Eye Movement, Facial Expression and Body Movement
Acceptance of the Ideas and Feelings of Others
Appropriate Words, Quotations, Anecdotes, Personal Experiences, Illustrative
    Examples, and Relevant Information
Appropriate Use of Audio-Visual Materials and Equipment
Obtaining and Evaluating Feedback

C. Written Communication

Planning the Written Document (e.g., Subject, Audience, Purpose, Thesis, Tone,
    Outline, Title)
Choosing Appropriate and Imaginative Words
Developing Paragraphs With Unity, Coherence and Emphasis
Developing "Technique" (e.g., Metaphor, Comparison, Hyperbole, Personal
    Experience)
Writing Powerful Introductions and Conclusions
Practicing the Four Basic Forms of Writing (Exposition, Argumentation,
    Description and Narration)
Applying the Basic Forms To a Variety of Genre (i.e., Short Stories, Book
    Reviews, Research Papers, etc.)
Developing Technical Skills (e.g., Proofreading, Editing, Revising, Footnoting,
    Preparing Bibliographies, Writing Summaries and Abstracts)

INDEX

Index

F

Facilitator 7, 26, 64, 83, 88, 100, 102, 104, 157, 175, 177
Flexible grouping 121, 172

G

Grouping patterns 149

H

Higher level thinking skills 10, 17, 109
How-to books 95, 104, 106

I

Independent study 13, 24, 48-50, 78, 79, 83, 85, 88, 91, 149, 175
Individualized learning 166, 171
Instructional style 11, 13, 17, 49, 78, 178
Interdisciplinary curriculum 137
Interdisciplinary Planning Matrix 29, 59
Interdisciplinary studies 6, 11, 24, 137, 140, 146, 166
Interdisciplinary Teacher Planning Teams 137
Interest 4-7, 9-11, 13, 18, 24-26, 29, 30, 35, 49, 51, 55, 57, 59, 60, 63, 83, 84, 86-88, 94, 96, 98, 100, 122, 125, 126, 139, 144, 157-160, 162, 165, 166, 171, 173-176, 178
Interest Development Centers 12, 49, 57

K

KWL Chart 43

L

Learning how-to-learn skills 6, 47, 76, 166
Learning styles 9, 11, 13, 26, 49, 78, 79, 80, 122, 149
Learning Styles Inventory 78

M

Management 6, 86, 89, 90, 148, 149, 175, 177
Management Plan 25, 88, 91, 99, 159, 178
Mentor 18, 102-105, 126, 157, 174
Middle school 35, 58, 103, 137, 140, 145-150, 154, 172, 173
Modified Management Plan 91-96, 100, 114
Multi-modal 60, 64
Multimedia 60

O

Ownership 26, 64, 86, 175

P

Performance-based assessment 107, 150, 153, 166
Planning 6, 8, 12, 14, 17, 27, 29, 30, 47, 48, 51, 60, 62, 76, 78, 82, 86-88, 91, 94, 109, 121, 131, 137, 143, 146, 148-150, 153, 163, 172, 175-177
Planning Matrix 29, 30, 43, 47, 48, 59, 60, 65, 76, 78, 96, 102, 104, 107, 109, 121, 123, 126, 140, 143, 146, 150
Portfolio 107
Preliminary planning 12, 35, 42